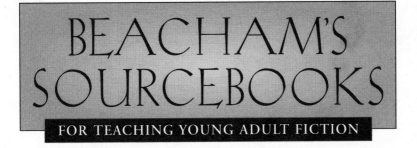

BEACHAM'S SOURCEBOOKS

FOR TEACHING YOUNG ADULT FICTION

Exploring Harry Potter

by Elizabeth D. Schafer

EBURY PRESS

LONDON

PHOTO CREDITS:

Page 187, "The Four Witches Around a Cauldron," by Jacques de Gheyn, Dutch
1565-1629; Credit: Archive Photos
Page 199, "Croatian Magic" painting by Maximilian Vanka; Credit: Archive Photos
Page 203, An engraving of Tom O'Shanter and the witches dancing; Credit:
American Stock/Archive Photos

3 5 7 9 10 8 6 4 2

Copyright © Beacham Publishing Corp. 2000
Beacham's Sourcebooks for Teaching Young Adult Fiction / by Elizabeth D. Schafer

First published in 2000 by Beacham Publishing Corp.
This edition first published in 2000 by Ebury,
Random House, 20 Vauxhall Bridge Road,
London SW1V 2SA
www.randomhouse.co.uk

Random House Australia Pty Limited
20 Alfred Street, Milsons Point, Sydney,
New South Wales 2061, Australia

Random House New Zealand Limited
18 Poland Road, Glenfield, Auckland 10, New Zealand

Random House (Pty) Limited
Endulini, 5A Jubilee Road, Parktown 2193, South Africa

The Random House Group Limited Reg. No. 954009

Papers used by Ebury are natural, recyclable products made from wood grown in
sustainable forests.

Printed and bound by Clays Ltd, St. Ives plc

A CIP catalogue record for this book is available from the British Library

ISBN 0-09-187930-2

Acknowledgments

For my mother Carolyn Henn Schafer, who proves that magic exists every day; my father Robert Louis Schafer, who taught me his Muggle ways; and my grandmother Eunice Bast Henn, who gave me a castle.

In memory of my maternal grandfather, Charles M. Henn, Jr., (1911-1999), raconteur and storyteller extraordinaire, and my paternal grandparents, Pansy Head Schafer (1912-1953) and Marion Louis Schafer (1902-1998), whose stories shaped my life.

With love to Sean Fitzgerald Allen and friendship and gratitude to Harriet Hough, Rieko Okuhara, Sandi Aaron, Carolien van Doorn, Katherine House and Jonathan (future Harry Potter fan), Mary Hammett, Shirley Watkins (my high school English teacher who taught me to read between the lines), William Gill, Jenette and Jason Meneely, Cathy Clark, Anne Ernst, Tracy Churchill, Debbie Smith, Stacey Smith, Karen Van Fossan, Joan Carris, Kit Boling, Marcy Talbert, Audrey Bair, Jane Goldstein, Beth Roberts, Carolyn Nave, John Snow, Marion Sader, Tracy Roberts, Alexandria LaFaye, Hillary Homzie, Marietta Frank, Stella Reinhard, Gail Lambert, Eve Tal, Jeri Watts, Molly Petty, Nancy Deis, Laura Meyers, Elizabeth Eckert, Gina Fromhold, Nancy Moran, Dorothy Pharis, Webb Carlisle, Connie Browning, Bobbie Parkinson, and Donna Stanley; with appreciation for Walton and Deborah Beacham for their vision, Jill Dible for her cover and book design, and Kay Curtis for illustrating the maps. Special thanks to the literary community at Hollins University, the Hogwarts of children's literature, especially Amanda Cockrell (and in fond memory of her mother Marian Cockrell), Richard Dillard, J.D. Stahl, Elizabeth Keyser, Jeanne Larsen, Lisa Rowe Fraustino, Chip Miller, Jill and Bob May, Chip and Anne Sullivan, and Elizabeth Doolittle.

CONTENTS

EDITOR'S INTRODUCTION

To the magic of literature, its creators,
and its passionate readers

We are inaugurating *Beacham's Sourcebooks for Exploring Young Adult Fiction* with the Harry Potter series because Harry has awakened so many readers to the joy of the beautifully written word and the complexities of the ideas they generate. Following soon after is the second volume in the series, C. S. Lewis' *The Chronicles of Narnia.* Our sourcebooks are intended to expand readers' enjoyment and knowledge of the novels by providing insights into the creative process that have made them unique.

Unlike a traditional book of criticism, our sourcebooks do not try to guide a reader through a series of logical arguments that arrive at a conclusion about the merits or meaning of the novel. Rather, they provide background, ideas, questions, and bibliographies that can be used in part or as a whole to encourage critical thinking and to explore the *layers* of meaning in the novels. There are many more projects, discussion questions, and research topics than any one teacher, parent, or reader wants to explore, but the range and depth of these resources provide almost unlimited opportunities to study and admire Harry Potter and his creator.

Sourcebooks are not generally intended to be read cover to cover but to provide answers to questions as a reader becomes more involved in the novel. The extensive index helps locate chapters that may answer your questions about the origins of magic and alchemy; parallels between the novels and mythology, religious symbols and allusions; the mystery of the characters' names; the geography of Hogwarts and Hogsmeade; references to science; and many other ideas.

We have also included websites for internet exploration; an appendix that explains how characters are related to each other by blood, friendship or vendettas, and to history; an interpretative biography of J. K. Rowling; and a long bibliography posted on our website arranged by areas of interest relating to reviews and criticism about the Potter novels, Ms. Rowling, and the intellectual history behind the fiction.

We are presenting the Harry Potter sourcebook in two parts. Sections dealing with analyses and chapter development for teachers are included in this print edition. Sections that will be expanded or need to be continually updated are posted on our website (**www.beachampublishing.com**). The website material is an integral part of the print edition, and the electronic medium will permit us to keep your information current as new Potter novels appear and as critical attention increases.

How Parents Can Use the Sourcebook

There is much more to the Harry Potter stories than most student readers will recognize, and readers who have enjoyed the novels can be easily stimulated to explore related learning ideas. For example, alchemy, which figures prominently in the Potter novels, was an early pseudo-scientific discipline that eventually laid the groundwork for chemistry. A Roman king ordered his alchemists to change ordinary material into gold; in 1388, the real-life Nicholas Flamel is credited with having produced gold using a philosopher's stone; centuries later the Grimm Brothers discovered the fairy tale of Rapunzel, who was forced by a tyrant to spin straw into gold before he would release her to marry the king. Harry's parents had caches of gold whose origin has yet to be revealed. The sourcebook helps you help your children to see Harry's connection across centuries, deep into cultures, and rooted in the universal consciousness of many people.

How Teachers Can Use the Sourcebook

For teachers, we have provided chapter-by-chapter discussion questions (Section III) that develop analytical thinking and vocabulary expansion. These questions can be used to create lesson plans or to construct games that students can play with each other. The timeline is designed to suggest historical research projects that are related to some aspect of Harry's world. There are many, many projects and discussion ideas suggested for teachers, both in this book and on our website, which you can turn into classroom activities or school projects.

How Student Readers Can Use the Sourcebook

Many of the questions are appropriate for students to use as a game to test each other's knowledge of the novels. These questions can be turned into flashcards, a board game, or a quiz show. There are also activities that students can perform without adult supervision. Students with internet access can search our recommended websites for fascinating information and images related to Harry's mystical world.

How Librarians Can Use the Sourcebook

For librarians who are helping students or entire classes locate information related to Harry, such as haunted castles in Scotland, or giving them ideas for research or reports, the sourcebook provides hundreds of suggestions, including websites. The Related Titles chapter discusses other novels students will enjoy based on particular features of the Potter novel.

How Researchers Can Use the Sourcebook

Each of the chapters contains an extensive bibliography and websites related to the chapter topic, which have been posted on the Beacham Publishing website (**www.beachampublishing.com**) along with the extensive General Bibliography. Dr. Schafer's critical analysis in the print edition and the sources posted on the website provide researchers with a gateway for further study.

Ms. Rowling has spoken extensively about her plans for future Potter novels, and stated that the magical number seven will see the conclusion of Harry's education at Hogwarts. As the series continues, visit our website for analyses of newly released novels, or to tell us your ideas about the meaning and achievement of Harry.

WALTON BEACHAM

AUTHOR'S INTRODUCTION

"I had the idea for a boy who had these magical powers but didn't really know what he was."
—J.K. ROWLING

Welcome to Harry's World

Harry Potter has enchanted people from diverse cultures worldwide. Having a timeless, universal quality, Harry represents an archetypal hero who would have been as familiar to ancient Greeks as he is to modern suburbanites. Although British, Harry is not bound to geography, and he appeals equally to readers living in Israeli Kibbutz and New York penthouses.

Harry is like a lot of humans. He is not especially attractive or intelligent, nor is he particularly sure of himself. After enduring years of abuse from his guardians, Harry is tentatively testing his abilities and discovering who he is. He chronically endures bad days and suffers torments from uninformed people. Harry worries about fitting in socially and performing sufficiently well in his studies and sports in order not to fail himself or others. He survives ostracism, belittlement, and exclusion by cruel bullies and snobs.

Speaking to something primal in humans, Harry represents the quest to know oneself and understand the forces of the world he lives in. But he is also realistic, and readers believe he has similar bones, tissues, hormones, marrow, cells, and blood pumping through his system as theirs. Harry is vulnerable to disease, injuries and physical and emotional discomfort, yet he transcends differences of color, ethnicity, religion, politics, and other factors that separate and categorize humans.

Readers recognize Harry as a sort-of-Charlie Brown who actually kicks the football. His compelling adventures reveal the paradoxes of a setting that represent both a sanctuary and a danger zone simultaneously. They satisfy readers by offering a happy ending complete with a vanquished archenemy, restoration of the status quo, and recognition of Harry's prowess.

The Harry Potter series is rich in details. Although the novels are read as entertaining tales of mystery, suspense, and humor or, on a deeper level an exploration of myths, legends, science, and magic, Rowling's vivid creations provide much more than an amusing adventure. Whether readers are seeking momentary vicarious escape to Hogwarts or are interested in analyzing motifs and imagery, the Potter books fulfill varied expectations while providing readers comfort through a recognizable cycle of events.

In each book, Harry is embroiled in some sort of trouble with the Dursley Muggles, escapes from his unbearable situation in their house at the time school resumes, encounters a mystery connected to the sinister Voldemort, undergoes struggles with his peers and whatever form Voldemort or his supporters assume, engages in alarming but gratifying sporting events, advances his wizardry skills as an apprentice studying with Hogwarts masters, gathers more information to battle against his foe (usually with the help of Ron Weasley and Hermione Granger), achieves conflict resolution through a confrontation with Voldemort or one of his allies, humbly accepts congratulations, and returns to the Muggle world to hibernate spiritually until another school term begins. Unlike Peter Pan and Alice in Wonderland, Harry grows up in the process and learns from the lessons presented to him, inside and outside the classroom.

An international phenomenon, Harry Potter has garnered rave reviews and major awards. His story demonstrates that external characteristics and cultures may differ but that people share common struggles, concerns, and triumphs in life. Harry's exploits show that sometimes breaking the rules, within reason, is more beneficial than harmful; that summoning courage despite fear is often necessary; and that making sacrifices is sometimes essential to gain desired goals. Today's Harry Potter readers are our future prime ministers, presidents, parents, teachers, CEOs, artists, writers, or detectives whose young dreams have been shaped in part by Harry's aspirations to do the best he can with his life. Regardless of their age, cultural affiliation, or socioeconomic status, readers will not forget Harry and the lessons he taught them about believing in themselves, being resourceful, and incorporating imagination, a sense of wonder and empathy for humanity in their daily lives to enrich the world.

Purpose and Organization of the Sourcebook

This book is intended to guide readers of the Harry Potter series to appreciate the books' literary qualities more fully. Young readers can apply ideas about the historical, mythological, scientific, and other aspects of Harry Potter's world to supplement their reading experience; teachers can incorporate activities and discussions into lesson plans to broaden students' comprehension of the novels and related literature; parents, guardians, and older siblings can interact with younger readers through questions and creative projects that are provided for each chapter. Numerous internet sites provide on-line fun and research sources.

Discussion of Rowling's imaginary world and the subtle clues she provides, such as the derivation of characters' names, inspire interdisciplinary exploration of the novels. The novels can be applied to history, geography, social studies, mathematics, and science lessons, and suggest related topics, such as history and mythology that share roots from ancient Greece to Scotland. Cross references in subject chapters alert readers to related topics.

Each chapter begins with quotations by Rowling, her characters, or a historical figure who comments on that section's theme. Readers are encouraged to explain how each quotation relates to the story and learn about who made the observation and why. The literary analysis of each book is followed by a brief list of activities for extending the reader's enjoyment of the novels: projects, discussion questions, and developing writing and critical skills. An extensive list of projects and questions is provided in Section III, Teaching Harry. Teachers and adults can also use the ideas for classroom sessions, club meetings, or home activities. The discussion questions are for teachers and adults to pose to students to explore ideas. Both projects and discussion questions can be incorporated into lesson plans according to teachers' objectives, curriculum requirements, classroom resources, and students' maturity level and abilities. The critical skills section alerts adults to the literary qualities of these books while providing ideas for student research projects. A timeline places factual and fictional events in context with Harry Potter topics, Great Britain, and world history. The timeline provides excellent topic ideas for historical research by students.

The sourcebook concludes with a bibliography and two appendices: one that lists and profiles the characters, animals, plants, and objects, and another providing a brief description of the myths and legends cited in Section III: Chapter Development.

Because Rowling refers to the novels by Roman numerals (Book I, II, III), that format will be adopted in this text. One literary device that readers should be aware of is that although the novels seem to be occurring during the present, they actually are past events as chronicled by an omniscient narrator. Told after the fact like a saga or epic poem, Harry's adventures, which occasionally occur in yet another time shift through the telling of events prior to his birth, particularly about his parents' years at Hogwarts, emphasize that often the ordinary is extraordinary and that many people and things are not as they initially seem.

Book IV, *Harry Potter and the Goblet of Fire*, was published on July 8, 2000. At the same time, this sourcebook discussing the first three Harry Potter books was in the final stages of preparation for publication. Book IV elaborates about several characters' backgrounds and explains their motivations for both good and evil. Themes, symbolism, and mythological motifs addressed in this sourcebook are also present in Book IV such as Draco Malfoy's mother being named Narcissa, suggesting her vain and selfish nature. Readers can consult this sourcebook for answers regarding overall qualities of the four-book Harry

Potter series. Specific information about Book IV will be posted at http://www.beachampublishing.com and indepth discussion of *Harry Potter and the Goblet of Fire*, such as its dragon, giant, and leprechaun imagery and historical similarities to the post-World War II Nuremberg trials and Cossack and Ku Klux Klan ambushes of targeted groups, will also be incorporated in a future expanded volume of this sourcebook.

ELIZABETH D. SCHAFER

SECTION I

—

BEGINNINGS

CHAPTER 1

POTTERMANIA

"Can you imagine what that feels like to get out of a car, and think normal book signing, and there's a thousand people outside screaming at you. It is amazing." —J.K. ROWLING

"You don't have to burn books to destroy a culture. Just get people to stop reading them."
—RAY BRADBURY

HARRY'S APPEAL

Reporters have referred to the phenomenal public reaction to the Harry Potter series as "Pottermania" and "Potterism." The books appeal to both male and female readers in different age groups, cultures, geographic areas, and entire countries. The novels have been incorporated into popular culture through use of terms such as "Muggle" and "Quidditch" and by references to characters and plots on television shows and in cartoons. Literary critics, book reviewers, educators, and librarians have speculated why the novels have attracted such a broad and diverse group of fans.

Arthur Levine, Rowling's American publisher, says he likes Harry's humanity and imagination. He emphasizes that people can identify with Harry's initial sense of hopelessness in Book I and then relief when he is rescued by Hagrid and learns that he is special. Most readers feel empowered by vicariously experiencing Harry's adventures in which he gains control over himself and his surroundings. Children consider Harry their friend because he reminds them of themselves. Harry is not perfect, experiences unfair treatment, and has both friends and enemies. Readers admire his resourcefulness in resolving problems. Some readers have admitted to achieving a goal, such as mastering a musical instrument, based on Harry's example of persistence and determination. Others have said they wished they had magical powers because they would be empowered to defend themselves against bullies.

Readers are enchanted by the different elements of fantasy, mystery, suspense, and horror mixed in with the realism of ordinary school events at Hogwarts. They know that the books usually have happy endings and that Harry resolves conflicts with dignity, refusing to cheat on schoolwork or defeating his Quidditch foes with deceitful actions. Harry represents who the readers wish they were. The books' details and Harry's characterization enable readers to feel immersed in the story, almost like a dream some people explain, and fictionally interact with the protagonist.

SALES, PRIZES, AND FAME

The Harry Potter series has achieved unprecedented bestseller status. The books have been included on every major bestseller list in Great Britain and the United States and dominated them for weeks. Rowling's books were the first children's books included on the *New York Times' Bestseller* list since E.B. White's *Charlotte's Web* in 1952. Beginning on November 28, 1999, Rowling's three novels were ranked in the first three positions on the *New York Times' Bestseller* list. When Amazon.com, both in the United States and Great Britain, offered internet customers the opportunity to pre-order Book IV in the spring of 2000, so many orders were placed that the unpublished book achieved bestseller status.

The commercial success of the series has resulted in the American publisher printing extraordinarily large first runs of half a million copies. Several paper mills and printing plants work overtime to meet the publisher's demands. Millions of copies of both hardback and paperback editions have been sold in the United States, and record-breaking sales have occurred in almost every country where the Potter series is sold. Many readers, including children, are choosing to purchase hardcover editions instead of paperbacks because they plan on collecting the series and saving it for the future.

When Book III was released in Great Britain, the publisher asked stores to not sell the book until English schools were closed for the day to prevent truancy. Adults and children paced in anticipation for the appointed time. Reporters compared the frenzy to crowds forming on docks and waiting for ships carrying Charles Dickens' novels. Prior to the release day, a few stores dramatized the upcoming event by displaying Book III in a guarded cage or chaining it in the front window. Some stores hosted parties to celebrate the book's debut, and "Spot Harry" contests involved fans looking for actors dressed like Harry. Another publicity event involved a steam engine designed like the Hogwarts Express being displayed at King's Cross station in recognition of the paperback release of Book II.

Rowling has become famous. Thousands of fans flock to bookstores and stand in line for hours to meet her at book signings and readings. Sometimes Rowling's car has to circle the block until her assistants can clear a way for her to enter the store. Reporters have compared the crowd's reaction to her arrival to that of the Beatles' first America tour. Overwhelmed bookstores have resorted to handing out a specific number of tickets to limit the size of crowds. At a few stores, disgruntled fans have reacted angrily at not being admitted.

Publishers have released variations of the basic Harry Potter book. A boxed set of the first three volumes is available. Large print editions and Braille copies have also been produced. Book club editions are sold through groups with specific interests, such as science fiction and fantasy book clubs or by school distribution. Rosie O'Donnell picked *Harry Potter and the Prisoner of Azkaban* as the inaugural selection of her Rosie's Readers children's book club. Both chain and independent bookstores prominently display the novels, stacking hundreds of copies above shelves and placing recommended books considered similar to the Potter series nearby.

In Great Britain, Germany, and Italy, copies with covers depicting photographs instead of artwork are intended for adult readers. These more mature appearing versions are popular among commuters who felt compelled to conceal the novels behind newspapers. Unabridged audiotapes and CDs of all three books feature the voice of Jim Dale, a Broadway actor whose credits include the movie *Pete's Dragon* (1977).

The novels have been honored with a variety of awards. Even the audio versions have received recognition, including being nominated for a Grammy. British children voted for Rowling as the winner of three consecutive Smarties Gold Awards. She also was selected Author of the Year at the British Book Awards.

HARRY IN TRANSLATION

Harry has enchanted people worldwide, and his magic connects people from different cultures with a common bond. Imagination, humor, and empathy are not confined by geographical borders, skin color, or language. Even though Harry is a British schoolboy, his fears and joys are familiar to most humans regardless of where they live. People understand the universal feelings of shyness and insecurity as well as the concepts of respect and justice. The name Harry Potter is recognizable to native speakers of languages ranging from Arabic to Chinese.

Bloomsbury Publishing has exported books and contracted with foreign publishers, selling 30 million copies globally as of June 2000. The novels have been translated into at least 28 languages for sale in 130 countries, including Australia, Austria, Brazil, Bulgaria, Canada, China, Croatia, the Czech Republic, Denmark, Estonia, Finland, France, Germany, Great Britain, Greece, Holland, Hungary, Iceland, Indonesia, Israel, Italy, Japan, Korea, New Zealand, Norway, Poland, Portugal, Romania, Spain (in Castilian and World Catalan dialects), South Africa, Sweden, Switzerland, and the United States. The series has been included on bestseller lists throughout the world.

Although the Muggle and wizard cultures in which Harry lives are quite different from other cultures, readers nonetheless recognize universal concepts. The exotic details to readers outside Britain enhance the series' fantastical nature. While British readers acknowledge aspects of their own culture and even feel nostalgic or sentimental about boarding schools, foreigners perceive the story as a glimpse through a magical window into another world. They may identify with the humanity of the characters and the universality of the themes, but the specifics of the story are reminiscent of watching a documentary with explanatory subtitles.

17

HARRY'S FANS

Harry Potter exists in yet another sphere separate from Muggles and Hogwarts: in fandom the factual and fictional worlds coexist in the form of fan clubs, small and large, and public events commemorating the series. Bloomsbury Publishing receives thousands of letters from fans, both children and adults, wanting to join the Harry Potter Fan Club. Members receive a certificate, embossed with Hogwarts' crest and motto, that declares the fan is "an honorary pupil of Hogwarts, a personal friend of Harry Potter's, a fierce opponent of the dark side and a thoroughly good egg."

The Unofficial Harry Potter Fan Club hosts a web page where fans can be sorted into one of the Hogwarts Houses. The site offers free Quidditch e-mail accounts and posts fan fiction and art. Interactive games, crafts, and articles are available on this page. The club also offers an on-line version of *The Daily Prophet* written by fans. Fans can read news and rumors and explore the numerous links to other Harry Potter sites. Another indicator of fan reaction to the series is how many people identify themselves with characters' names or a reference from the books as part of their e-mail address. Rowling occasionally schedules chats with fans on Scholastic's web page and answers questions.

While waiting for new novels to be released, fans join groups such as the Harry Potter Withdrawal Club sponsored by Joseph-Beth Booksellers in Cincinnati, Ohio, or other so-called Harry Potter Deprivation Clubs. Bookstores provide fans packets of information about the novels and suggestion lists of similar stories. Fans gather monthly to discuss those books. Young fans can also promote the books for more awards, such as voting for Nickelodeon's Annual Kids' Choice Awards.

MERCHANDISE

Rowling's agent, Christopher Little, receives as many as one hundred inquiries daily from people wanting to use Harry Potter's name to market their goods. Most ideas are rejected because Rowling is protective of her creative property and does not want him to be crudely commercialized. And many readers also say that they prefer to imagine Harry instead of having action figures that depict him. So far, the major merchandising approval has been granted to Mattel and Hasbro to produce Harry Potter toys, broomsticks, board and video games, trading cards, candy, and electronics. Fans hope that Warner Brothers might build a Harry Potter theme park and that a cartoon might be produced.

HARRY IN THE NEWSPAPER AND ON SCREEN

References to Harry in comic strips and on television programs indicate how the series is influencing popular culture. So far, "Family Circus" and "Peanuts" have featured characters praising Harry. Editorial cartoons in the *Cincinnati Enquirer* and the *New Yorker* have commented on the books' popularity and the potential for copycat books to be quickly produced. A *Newsweek* business article described the quick success of a new business as being like Harry Potter.

Harry was mentioned in a "Saturday Night Live" skit. A father read part of a Potter novel to his daughter on the drama "Time of Your Life." In the television show "Once and Again," the Potter novels are twelve-year-old Jessie Sammler's favorite books. The final "Jeopardy" answer during that game show's college championship play was "which title character's school has the motto 'Never Tickle a Sleeping Dragon'?" but none of the contestants knew the question (they suggested "Who is Holden Caulfield?" and "Who is Pete of 'Pete's Dragon'?")

The movie version of Book I is scheduled for release in November or December of 2001. Steve Kloves *(Racing with the Moon,* 1984; *Flesh and Bone, 1993)* wrote the script. As of March 2000, Steven Spielberg decided not to direct the film, and Chris Columbus *(Home Alone,* 1990; *Mrs. Doubtfire,* 1993) was selected as director. Rowling insisted that the movie must be set in Great Britain and star a British actor playing Harry.

HARRY'S DETRACTORS

See Chapter 15, Moral and Social Codes for a discussion of objections to Harry Potter novels by parents identifying themselves as conservative Christians.

THE WHITBREAD PRIZE CONTROVERSY

Although Harry Potter survived banning, for the most part, he was the subject of an intense debate among British critics about his literary merits. In early 2000, the Whitbread Book of the Year rules were changed so that children's books could be considered for the prize. *Harry Potter and the Prisoner of Azkaban* won the children's award and challenged Seamus Heaney's translation of "Beowulf" for the main award. The judges engaged in bitter arguments, with the Heaney supporters attacking the Potter novel as being an inferior book. Newspapers reported how judges blamed the Potter books for encouraging adults to be immature. They said the book could not be considered a classic and that popularity should not be equated with excellence. The Potter promoters stressed that children's literature deserves to be respected and not belittled.

READING FOR RESEARCH

Harris, Cheryl, and Allison Alexander, eds. *Theorizing Fandom: Fans, Subculture, and Identity*. Cresskill, NJ: Hampton Press, 1998. A study of how fans of books and popular culture organize and interact.

Holbrook, David. *Creativity and Popular Culture*. Rutherford, NJ: Fairleigh Dickinson University Press, 1994. Discusses how moral and ethical issues can affect children's creativity.

Jenkins, Henry, ed. *The Children's Culture Reader*. New York: New York University Press, 1998. Information about the role of mass media in children's lives.

Internet Resources

American Library Association's Office for Intellectual Freedom
http://www.ala.org/oif.html

The National Coalition Against Censorship
http://www.ncac.org/

Internet Movie Data Base
http://www.imdb.com

Log on to **www.beachampublishing.com** for many additional projects, discussion questions, writing and research ideas, websites, and bibliography.

CHAPTER 2

INTERPRETATIVE BIOGRAPHY OF J. K. ROWLING

"I have very vivid memories of how it felt to be Harry's age." —J.K. ROWLING

"I wrote something that I knew I would like to read now. But I also wrote something that I knew I would have liked to have read at age 10." —J.K. ROWLING

BOOKS BY ROWLING

Harry Potter and the Philosopher's Stone, Great Britain, 1997;
  published as *Harry Potter and the Sorcerer's Stone,* U.S., 1998
Harry Potter and the Chamber of Secrets, Great Britain, 1998,
  U.S., 1999
Harry Potter and the Prisoner of Azkaban, 1999
Harry Potter and the Goblet of Fire, 2000

ABOUT THE AUTHOR

– Early Life –

Joanne Kathleen Rowling has written fiction since she was a
child and always aspired to be an author. The daughter of
Peter and Anne Rowling, she was born on July 31, 1965, at the
Chipping Sodbury General Hospital in Gloucestershire England.
The Rowling family lived at Yate, near Bristol. Rowling describes
herself as an introverted child who read books, invented stories,
and lived in a fantasy world populated by imaginary friends. Her
parents were avid readers who stocked their house with books, and
Rowling recalls her father reading her *The Wind in the Willows*
when she was sick with measles. She enjoyed telling the stories she
made up to her younger sister Diana. They wanted a rabbit as a
pet but never received one, and Rowling's first lengthy story, entitled "Rabbit," was about a hare who had the measles. Another
story featured Diana falling into a rabbit hole where the rabbits
took care of her. Foreshadowing her first book published twenty
years later, she wrote a tale about seven enchanted diamonds.

The Rowling family moved from Yate to nearby Winterbourne where Rowling and her sister played with neighborhood children, including a family named Potter. Her friends called her Jo, which she liked, but she loathed the pronunciation of her last name because children teased her with jokes about rolling pins and rolling stones. Her father, a manager and engineer for Rolls-Royce, and her mother, a laboratory technician, relocated their family to Tutshill near the Welsh border town of Chepstow situated in the Forest of Dean. Rowling's parents, native Londoners, had dreamed of providing a country home for their daughters who roamed in the fields and explored the Wye River region. Rowling says she was a quiet, freckled, unathletic, bookish girl who wore glasses and earned mostly high grades at Tutshill Primary School. She initially despised Tutshill because her teachers thought she was dumb because she had not been taught fractions at her previous school.

At Wyedean Comprehensive, Rowling enjoyed English classes. She also read books written by Jane Austen (her favorite author), Elizabeth Goudge, Clement Freud, Paul Gallico, Ian Fleming, and Roddy Doyle for pleasure. Her mother gave her a copy of one of her favorite childhood books, Goudge's *The Little White Horse,* when Rowling was eight years old. During lunch, she spun stories for her friends as they ate, featuring them as courageous heroines who tried to perform acts of kindness but often became involved in humorous predicaments. Rowling privately dreamed of writing books and seeing them sold in stores, but she did not confide her hopes for fear people would discourage her, saying she lacked talent. Gaining confidence as she grew older, she became more vocal publicly but was secretive about her writing as a teenager. She was selected Head Girl in her last year at school.

— Early Career —

Rowling earned a French and Classics degree from Exeter University; she credits this education with later helping her invent clever fictional names. Her parents had advised her to focus on languages to become a bilingual secretary, a career that Rowling says she was ill-suited for because she was too disorganized. She preferred writing stories to taking minutes or typing correspondence. During her college studies, she was an auxiliary teacher in Paris to earn credits toward her degree.

For two years she was employed by Amnesty International in London to research human rights issues in Africa before moving to Manchester where her college boyfriend worked. Rowling attained an office position, first at the local university, then at the city's chamber of commerce. In 1980, her mother developed multiple sclerosis. Her mother's death in 1990, as well as a robbery and being fired from her job, resulted in Rowling reevaluating her life. Remembering her teaching assignment in Paris, Rowling considered returning to education as a career and took a class in teaching English as a second language.

— Harry's Beginning —

Throughout her twenties, she continued to write fiction. During the pre-Harry Potter period that she considers to have been her writing apprenticeship, Rowling penned short stories and finished two novels for adult readers, but she did not submit them to publishers because she questioned their literary merit. Rowling was focusing on a novel for adults when the idea about Harry Potter suddenly appeared in her thoughts. While sitting on a stalled train en route from Manchester to London in the summer of 1990, Rowling says "Harry just strolled into my head fully formed." She explains that "It's as mysterious to me as to anyone else." She used the four hour wait to think about him. She realized that he was a pre-adolescent, orphaned boy named Harry Potter who learned that he was a wizard, which explained why unusual things happened in his presence. The book's basic premise would be Harry's search for his identity while he countered evil villains to save good characters and preserve sanctuaries where they would be protected. Rowling decided that Harry's adventures would be addressed in seven books, each novel a part of an ongoing saga that described a year at a wizard school where he was invited to attend.

As soon as the train reached King's Cross station in London, she rushed home to jot down her ideas. During the next five years, Rowling outlined the plots for each book and began writing the first novel. She devised clever names for characters and settings and kept boxes of notes with details about her imaginary world. Through such extensive and exacting planning, Rowling was able to include what seemed to be inconsequential references to characters or events in early stories that actually foreshadow significant participants and occurrences in later books' plots. While writing Harry's initial story, Rowling also drew pictures of her characters for possible illustrations if the book was ever published.

Soon after she had her inspiration about Harry, Rowling moved to Oporto, Portugal, to become an English teacher. She wrote about Harry in the morning before teaching in the afternoon and evening. In 1991 she met a Portuguese television journalist, Jorge Arantes, married him in October 1992, and gave birth to her daughter Jessica in July 1993. She named Jessica for Jessica Mitford, an author and human rights advocate whom Rowling admired. She gave Mitford's book, *Hons and Rebels,* which Rowling had read as a teenager, to Jessica as a christening gift. Rowling had completed the first three chapters about Harry Potter before her work was interrupted when she divorced her husband. In December 1993, she moved to Edinburgh, Scotland, where her sister Diana lived. Intending to leave after Christmas, Rowling remained in Scotland for six months and shared her chapters about Harry with Diana, who encouraged her to continue writing the novel.

Impoverished because she could not locate a job that paid a large enough salary to afford child care for infant Jessica, Rowling qualified for public assistance and decided to work on her wizard novel until she could secure adequate employment. She refers to this time as her "Grim Period." To get out of her bleak flat, she walked around the city, pushing Jessica's stroller until the baby fell asleep, then wrote for several hours in area cafes, particularly a bistro named Nicolson's. She typed the final draft for submission on a manual typewriter. Although she has since bought a word processor, Rowling admits to savoring longhand composition and the feel of paper underneath her fingers as she writes. She credits the creation of the first Potter novel with helping her retain a sense of achievement and recovering her self-esteem and identity during her personal crisis. Rowling originally created the story to entertain herself and did not intentionally pen a children's book. She considered her imaginary world as a personal escape from despair, and she praises the book for providing a challenging project that boosted her morale.

— Finding a Publisher —

In 1996 The Scottish Arts Council gave Rowling an $8,000 grant, which was the largest literary award offered by the group to a children's author. Having completed the novel in 1995, she contacted an agent, Christopher Little, who submitted the book to publishers while she taught French at a local school. Several publishers rejected the novel, saying it was too long and literary, but in 1996 she received an offer of publication and a $3,300 advance from Bloomsbury Publishing. Titled *Harry Potter and the Philosopher's Stone,* the book's publisher insisted that Rowling use her initials "J.K." rather than "Joanne" because he thought boy readers would not believe that a woman would understand a boy hero. By 1997, the American publisher, Scholastic Inc., beat competitors in an auction and offered Rowling an advance of $105,000 to print copies in the U.S. with the title changed to *Harry Potter and the Sorcerer's Stone* to appeal to American readers. This was an enormous advance that enabled her to write full time. She admits to experiencing writer's block when she became

aware of and overwhelmed by the ramifications of this sale. Later, Rowling signed a contract with Warner Brothers for film rights to the Potter stories. Harry Potter action figures and other items were also planned, and Rowling's commercial success was considered an anomaly in the children's book market.

— Harry's Success —

Almost immediately, Harry became a cultural phenomenon. Reviewers praised the book as a unique, imaginative fantasy, and Rowling won the British Book Awards Children's Book of the Year, the Smarties Prize, *Publishers Weekly* Best Book of 1998, *School Library Journal* Best Book of 1998, and the *Parenting* Book of the Year Award 1998. *Harry Potter and the Chamber of Secrets* was the 1999 Children's Book Award winner, for both long novel and overall novel categories, selected solely by children, and Rowling was the first author to win the Smarties Prize in two consecutive years. She was named author of the year at the 2000 British Book Awards. Her books remained at higher positions on lists of bestsellers longer than popular novels written for adults. The Potter novels were the first children's books to claim a spot on the *New York Times'* bestseller list since E.B. White's *Charlotte's Web* in the 1950s. By the fall of 1999, the three Harry Potter novels simultaneously were numbers one, two, and three on the *New York Times'* list, causing that newspaper to contemplate creating a separate children's bestseller roster. The Potter series also achieved the first three spots on the *Wall*

Street Journal's bestseller list and retained prestigious places on *USA Today's* roster. In 2000, the Whitbread award permitted Rowling's book to be considered for the main prize instead of only limiting it to the children's category.

The British press has produced reams of copy about Rowling and Harry Potter. In the U.S., Harry was featured on a *Time* magazine cover, the first cover story ever devoted to a children's author. In addition to newspaper stories and book reviews published globally, Rowling has been interviewed by the British Broadcasting Corporation in Great Britain and by National Public Radio, C-Span, "60 Minutes," "The Today Show," and "The Rosie O'Donnell Show" in the U.S. Harry's success has been portrayed in an editorial cartoon in which American presidential candidates' books are displayed on a table of bestsellers at a bookstore and a customer declares that he plans to vote for Harry Potter.

Accompanied by her daughter, Rowling enjoys traveling on book tours in the United States, France, Spain, and Italy to sign books, promote her work, and lead Harry Potter trivia contests. Journalists have compared the crowds waiting for her arrival to the frenzied fans of the Beatles. Lines begin to form hours before Rowling is scheduled to arrive. Her signature is in such demand that Rowling has to wear a wrist brace to support her hand, signing as many as 2,000 books in one day at Chicago bookstores at the estimated rate of 4.91 seconds per book. Rowling states that she first realized the impact her books had made on children when she visited the U.S. and was greeted by huge crowds with many children in costume pretending to be their favorite Harry Potter character.

Creatively fulfilled, Rowling has ample resources to continue construction of her world of wizards and witches. Sources indicate that she is Great Britain's third richest woman as of the year 2000. Rowling does not like journalists who are fixated on how much money she earns or a Scottish newspaper that named her that country's most eligible female. Amazed by her astounding success, which she declares that she would have never dreamed was possible because most writers of children's books do not earn much money and usually "do it for love," Rowling says she sometimes get "cold chills" when she realizes what she has accomplished. She has bought a house in Edinburgh, where she, Jessica, and their pet rabbit enjoy what she calls a happy, dull existence of housework and full-time writing without having to worry about finances.

— Harry Encouraging Reading Skills —

Rowling encourages children who tell her they have read all of her books to try other children's books she thinks they will enjoy. Her recommendations have resulted in the increased printing of titles such as Dodie Smith's *I Capture the Castle*. Rowling also advises aspiring writers to read voraciously, to learn vocabulary, to appreciate good writing, and to write as much as possible about what they know with the realization that quality work requires time to achieve.

Market analysts claim that Rowling's series has boosted the sale of other children's literature because Harry has stimulated their interest in reading. Since the Potter novels have been on the market, paperback sales of children's books increased by 24 percent totalling $660 million, and hardcover sales expanded by 11 percent totalling $1.6 billion. Books whose sales have significantly increased include C. S. Lewis' "The Chronicles of Narnia" series and Lloyd Alexander's "The Black Cauldron series."

— Objections to Harry Potter and Rowling's Response —

Although most public reaction to her books has been profoundly supportive, some conservative groups malign Rowling and her stories (See Chapter 15, Moral and Social Codes). Parents in several communities have condemned Rowling's books as being too scary, hateful, violent, and evil, with disrespectful characters who ignore authority figures. They claim the stories are dark and malevolent, focusing on death, and they have demanded that boards of education prohibit teachers from reading and discussing Rowling's books in classrooms. The head teacher of St. Mary's Island Church of England banned the novels because his magical powers go against the teachings of the Bible and do not conform with her school's "church ethos." Some more paranoid book banners have incorrectly alleged that Rowling is a witch, attempting to convert children to black magic. An attendant of the Church of Scotland, Rowling resents such false accusations.

Rowling's success has led to scrutiny of her life and thoughts, and she has frequently been asked if she believes in magic and witchcraft, declaring that she does not. She defends her novels, asserting that she cannot lie to children by pretending that evil is not horrible. She stresses that she has the responsibility to show what evil means and she believes that children are perfectly capable of differentiating between fantasy and reality. Rowling insists that her books present moral stories because the protagonists make their own choices based on their character and integrity. She thinks that people are innately good unless they have been damaged through emotional or physical abuse. Rowling argues that her books are beneficial for children because the consequences and victims of evil must be explained and not ignored or treated flippantly. She especially takes offense at adults who trivialize or underestimate children, stating that children are able to understand complicated issues and concepts, jokes, and puns, and that books should not be "dumbed down" to accommodate younger readers.

Rowling admits that if she had magical power she would transform herself into a more organized person, and put a spell on irritating people so that they became small enough to trap under a teacup to silence them temporarily. Instead, she uses words to create magical settings where she is in control. Rowling focuses on the magic in her imaginary world instead of realism. Preferring anonymity to fame, she resembles her hero who humbly and unselfishly tries to better his community while coping with his problems and concerns.

— Rowling's Creative Process —

Writing for her own amusement, Rowling says she developed some of her ideas to pass time while traveling and staying in hotels, filling notebooks with sketches, names, and rules for wizard activities, classes, and spells. She tries to intertwine humor, rich characters, a strong plot, and tension to produce a book that she would want to read. Rowling finds that scary situations appeal to her readers who identify with the characters' reactions. She tries to remain true to her characters' natures and not stereotype them or be didactic, stressing that Harry is not a conformist and often breaks rules during his adventures.

Rowling knows how her characters and plots will evolve and has already written the last chapter of book seven in which Harry will have completed his wizardry apprenticeship and assume adult roles. She bases many of her characters, settings, and plot twists on her childhood memories, remembering how powerless children are and how they create their own society inaccessible to adults. She focuses on her ideas, sense of humor and adventure, and recollections. Unaware of what triggers her imagination, Rowling prefers to indulge her creativity without analyzing its source. She does admit that the character Hermione resembles her when she was a child, although the fictional version is more adept than her creator. Many of Rowling's details were inspired by her personal history or are tributes to family and friends. For instance, her parents met on a train, and Harry entered her consciousness on a train. Rowling enjoys watching basketball and adapted its rules to create the game of Quidditch. Harry's friend Ron is modeled after one of her closest friends, Sean Harris, and the Weasley siblings and parents are all redheads like Rowling. Harry and Rowling share the same birthdate. Disliking chemistry in school, she made Harry's potions teacher Severus Snape aberrantly sadistic. She notes that her mother's death resulted in her writing a more intense, serious scene when Harry peers into the Mirror of Erised and sees his deceased parents.

— Her Personal Life Today —

Although she prefers anonymity and does not consider herself a celebrity, Rowling is sometimes recognized in public and tolerates excited fans posing with her for photographs. Rowling enjoys amusing children and goes shopping with her editors' children. She allows curious children to congregate around her house, joking that she should secure the final chapter in her attic to prevent its contents from being purloined.

Rowling writes when Jessica is attending school so they can spend time together afterwards. Rowling has begun reading her new Harry Potter stories to Jessica, who suggests ideas of what her mother should include in future books. Rowling does not always take Jessica's suggestions, and she good naturedly tells Jessica that she, like all other Harry Potter fans, will have to wait to learn the ending.

Unfazed by her sudden fame, Rowling retains most of her pre-Harry Potter patterns, returning to Nicolson's for coffee and interviews with journalists. Appropriately, she hosts an annual Halloween party to celebrate her favorite holiday and share her literary successes with revelers. She acknowledges that she will probably feel grief when she writes the final Harry Potter book. Passionate about her work and compelled to write, Rowling plans to pursue other literary projects after Harry has completed his final teenage adventure and to continue to serve as a literary mentor through her magical words and worlds.

VOCABULARY

aberrant: deviating from what is normal or expected

Amnesty International: an organization to help mistreated people

anomaly: abnormal, unusual

auxiliary teacher: a teacher in training who assists and learns from other teachers.

avid: enthusiastic

Beatles: a famous British singing group in the 1960s and 1970s

foreshadowing: predicting an event in the future

Head Girl: female student leader chosen by a school's administrators and faculty to serve as a role model because of her academic skills and good behavior.

introverted: a person who is shy or keeps to themselves

multiple sclerosis: a disease of the central nervous system

public assistance: financial aid from the government

purloined: stolen

Rolls-Royce: a very expensive English automobile

sadistic: delight in cruelty

voraciously: insatiable, uncontrollable

READING FOR RESEARCH

Faussett, Charles. *Edinburgh*. London: Cadogan Books, 1999. Historical and geographical discussion of the community that Rowling has made her home and which inspires her fiction.

Nicholson, Louise. *London*. Washington, D.C.: National Geographic Society, 1999. A vividly illustrated book of the metropolis where Rowling sets Diagon Alley. It is the factual home of her publisher and King's Cross station.

Rollyson, Carl. *Biography: An Annotated Bibliography*. Pasadena, CA: Salem Press, 1992. Instructs researchers how to locate and interpret source material to compose biographies, such as Rowling's.

INTERNET RESOURCES

These are sites that provide information about some of the communities where Rowling has lived.

Chipping Sodbury, England
    http://www.chippingsodbury.com
    http://www.walusoft.co.uk/yate/

Chepstow, England
    http://www.chepstow.co.uk

Log on to **www.beachampublishing.com** for many additional projects, discussion questions, writing and research ideas, websites, and bibliography.

SECTION II

READING HARRY

CHAPTER 3

CHARACTERS AND THEMES

*"I love them all, even the horrible ones are really
fun to write about."* —J.K. ROWLING

*"It is our choices, Harry, that show what we really are,
far more than our abilities."* —ALBUS DUMBLEDORE

THE CAST

See Appendix A on page 447 for a full list of the significant characters, animals, plants, and enchanted objects.

Rowling introduces readers to an assortment of characters, ranging from extremes of good to bad, enlightened to dumb, and capable to confused, with most being somewhere in between. Many characters are introduced in Book I, even if their names are merely mentioned once. These characters resurface in later books where they play a more prominent role or are significant to advancing the plot. Others are introduced and banished within one book. Several characters never materialize beyond serving as a cleverly inventive author's name appropriate for a specific textbook or as a pun to alleviate tension. Some characters are recurring and have consequential functions in each book's plot as well as the overall serial development.

Because Harry lives mostly in a fantastical world, characters are not only humans but also creatures, plants, and enchanted objects. Many Muggles remain anonymous and are identified only as a group rather than individually. The elusiveness of Voldemort both in physical and verbal description casts him as an omnipotent force. Characters that seem initially insignificant may ultimately prove to be a pivotal player, or their masquerade may be misinterpreted. Most characters mature as time progresses in each book, although some stagnate or even worsen in their behavior and treatment of others.

The characters who populate Harry's world represent archetypes based on biblical, mythical, legendary, and fairy tale figures (see Chapter 9, Myth, Legends and Fairy Tales; and Chapter 10, Archetypes and Biblical Allusions). Some characters are stereotypical and derivative, but this portrayal is necessary to exaggerate their traits or emphasize a point. Like the novels' settings, characters depict opposing traits with others and even within themselves, often representing an amalgam of good and bad. Themes also are paradoxical. The novels revolve around the fundamental theme of good versus evil in the form of confrontations between Harry and Lord Voldemort. The two characters initially appear to be distinct opposites, but they share several similarities.

HARRY VERSUS VOLDEMORT

Harry, the novels' protagonist, is an orphan whose parents, James and Lily, were murdered by Lord Voldemort when Harry was one year old. Raised by his mother's sister, Petunia Dursley, and her husband, Vernon, Harry was told that his parents died in an automobile accident. Rewriting Harry's history, his guardians conceal the fact that Harry's parents were a powerful wizard and witch because they are afraid of Harry's potential powers and are ashamed of his magical connections. They think he is abnormal, and the omniscient narrator describes him as being "as not normal as it is possible to be." Harry has no clue about who he really is. Like the mythical King

Arthur, he gradually develops an awareness of his potential, and, true to his surname, Potter, he shapes himself metaphorically from a lump of clay into a recognizable and serviceable vessel. Also, his name suggests his initial pauper status because of the term potter's field, which in the Bible is a place for the burial of paupers or unknown persons.

Similarly, Lord Voldemort was also orphaned and raised by foster parents who were Muggles. Both characters are half-bloods, descended from Muggle and wizard ancestors, who learned about their talents as young boys and were invited to attend Hogwarts. Their wands have feathers from the same phoenix. Along with Salazar Slytherin, one of the founding wizards of Hogwarts, they are believed to be the only Parselmouths—wizards who can communicate with snakes—ever to study at Hogwarts. Harry, however, has virtuous qualities that are the antithesis of Lord Voldemort's corrupt traits. He boldly confronts terrifying situations that cause others to hesitate or flee. Harry is not afraid to use Lord Voldemort's name, while other wizards refer to him as You-Know-Who or He-Who-Must-Not-Be-Named. By not verbally summoning Lord Voldemort's name, these wizards hope to prevent him from appearing to menace them. Not speaking the names of dark forces is a common strategy used by good characters to pretend evil villains do not exist. In Cuba today, many people are afraid to speak Fidel Castro's name aloud in fear that the government might take punitive action against them for being so bold, so instead, when with friends they move their fingers across their chin as if stroking a beard to indicate that they are talking about Castro.

Harry's name, however, is frequently said because he is famous in the wizard world; every wizard toddler knows who Harry is. The only Potter to survive Voldemort's attack, Harry is regarded as a miracle. His parents became martyrs for dying while fighting evil, and Harry progresses from anonymity to acclaim because during the attack he usurped some of Voldemort's powers, forcing him into exile. Possibly the most powerful wizard, Harry is almost regarded as royalty, somewhat like his peers, England's Princes William and Harry, the sons of Charles and Diana.

HARRY'S EARLY LIFE

Only a toddler, Harry does not remember Voldemort assaulting him on Halloween 1981, when he is branded by a lighting-bolt-shaped scar on his forehead that signifies he is the chosen child among the wizards. Delivered to his aunt for shelter, Harry grows up as a Muggle oblivious to his abilities, although he wonders why strange things happen to him. Harry is conditioned to abuse and does not expect any alleviation of his miserable existence. On his eleventh birthday, he experiences an awakening symbolic of emerging adolescence. Harry learns that his guardians have hidden his true identity and legacy and that he belongs to another type of society and culture where he is appreciated for who he is.

His rescue from the restrictive Dursley home by characters who are surrogate parents signals Harry's emergence from his decade-old cocoon spun with intolerance. Welcomed at Hogwarts, his parents' alma mater, Harry finds his true home, physically, emotionally, intellectually, and spiritually. He is transformed from an ordinary boy who discovers that he is special, a universal human desire, into an extraordinary defender of goodness. As an apprentice wizard, Harry undergoes training and rites of passage, much like a tradesman, to master the craft of magic. Despite his genetic legacy, Harry is not an extraordinary student and sometimes feels like an outsider because of his past and inexperience with magic.

Like his creator, Harry has a summer birthday which marks his transition, or rebirth, from paralysis in the Muggle world to new life in the wizard realm. Each book develops Harry's character, adding new details for readers to incorporate into his biography. In Book II, Rowling reveals that Harry was born in late July 1980, which is symbolic. That summer witnessed international crises, including the boycotted Olympic Games in Moscow in protest of the Soviet invasion of Afghanistan, the failed rescue mission to liberate American hostages held by Iran, and race riots in Miami. The volcanic eruption of Mount St. Helens, more powerful than 500 atomic bombs, stunned the world. Harry's birth represents the possibility of a peaceful savior emerging during a time of chaos to restore order. Harry becomes an icon for wizards who invest their hopes in him for salvation from Voldemort. Considered a hero because of his historic defiance against Voldemort, Harry assumes the burden of protecting good wizards and witches in order to fulfill his destiny.

HARRY THE HERO

Harry is an archetypal hero. He suffers a tragedy while young, and his spiritual scar, much like his lightning bolt scar, remains with him throughout his quest to avenge his parents' murder. Like most heroes, Harry expresses reluctance to begin his journey, questioning whether he is capable of the tasks required of him. He is motivated by his personal need for fulfillment and the encouragement of a mentor. In Harry's case, Hagrid is his first guide who reveals details of Harry's history; Dumbledore and Lupin assume this role at different times. As with most heroes, Harry attracts friends because he is loyal, kind, and courageous and continues these relationships despite the others' flaws and limitations. Harry survives challenges, dangers, and obstacles, and faces overwhelming enemies. He is a small, naive child bravely opposing much larger and more experienced foes. At times, like many heroes, Harry is tempted by evil but refuses to cooperate.

The quest may seem doomed and impossible, but the hero prevails. Like most heroes, Harry learns that respect must be earned and that sacrifices are often necessary to achieve success. Such offerings can be material objects or the act of suffering pain, as Harry experiences during his battles with Voldemort. The hero must fight alone and exceed his limitations. Many heros realize how to use a tool in their possession, whether it is a weapon or a way to think, such as Harry's enhanced reasoning skills evident in the Shrieking Shack. Only through the acquisition of knowledge can the hero complete his trials. His innate goodness empowered by his enlightenment defeats all that is wicked.

A final confrontation between good and evil results in the archetypal hero's victorious return home, and this should be Harry's ultimate fate. During this process, the hero matures and acquires unique wisdom, powers, and rewards to complete his metamorphosis. The archetypal hero, as represented by Harry, symbolizes the virtues most readers respect. The hero secures a fictional, ideal world that enables readers to vicariously escape the realities of their own lives.

HARRY'S HEROIC TRANSFORMATION

Harry is appealing because of his authentic human characteristics. Although he is often bold and brave, Harry also experiences self-doubt and is afraid, asking for help when he is terrified and feels powerless. He is often untidy and suffers queasiness and stomachaches when he experiences emotional turmoil. Harry represents the contradictions of adolescence. He is primarily selfless, sharing his meager scraps of food with Hedwig when they are imprisoned at the Dursleys', but can be self-absorbed when focusing on solving a mystery related to his parents. Despite being surrounded by friends and classmates, he often is isolated. Harry is mostly wise but sometimes vulnerable and innocent. Respectful to authority figures, he occasionally breaks rules.

These traits in addition to his divergent environments and similarities to Voldemort suggest that Harry is split into two personalities which direct his actions. Aware of his dual personality, he worries that he was able to repulse Voldemort's attack because he possesses evil powers rather than through natural goodness.

But Harry's positive characteristics outweigh any negatives. His humility, loyalty, determination, and perseverance cause both his friends and readers to care about his fate as he fights for his survival against enemies, all of them adult so far, who wish him dead before he attains his full powers. Harry represents the power of faith and friendship to make anything possible. He learns that he can resist oppressors and fight back if he trusts his instincts and dutifully pursues honor, retaining his integrity. Harry is honest and has a clear perception of right from wrong.

A mythical figure, Harry commences a quest in search of his identity and to reach maturity while simultaneously subduing villains, which he considers to be his responsibility and mission in life. Although he is an average student, Harry exhibits great skill at certain activities such as Quidditch. He symbolically is chosen as his team's Seeker, meaning his job is to locate the Golden Snitch, an elusive ball darting around the players. Harry is considered the player most agile and swift to pursue this small globe. Being Seeker implies that he has superb vision, both physically and metaphorically, to see the reality of situations. Capture of the Snitch usually guarantees a team sufficient points to claim victory. Two larger balls known as Bludgers chase and pummel the Seekers. In Book II, Harry is knocked off his broom by a charmed Bludger, breaking his right arm which Professor Lockhart accidentally makes disappear, rendering Harry temporarily powerless until the school nurse can regrow his bones, symbolic of a strengthening of his character. The game of Quidditch mimics Harry's pursuit and capture of villains. Harry's sports achievements can also be considered moral triumphs over the less savory Hogwarts students.

Harry's life is divided into the periods before and after he learned about his parents' murder and discovers his unique powers. Sacrifice and the fragility of human relationships are pervasive themes in the novels. Harry loses his parents and identity as a small child. He knows he survived only because his mother sacrificed her life in exchange for his, and he feels obligated to be worthy of her sacrifice. The only contact he has with his parents is by looking in the Mirror of Erised or at the photo album which Hagrid gave him, but those images are flat, illusional representations of James and Lily Potter. Harry endures emotional and physical abuse from his guardians who callously disregard him—not even remembering his birthday—to show they wish that he did not exist. Because Harry has no parents to share affection with, he invests his emotions in friendships that include adults who are his mentors but not parent substitutes. James and Lily Potter remain substantial characters in their son's life even though he cannot remember them. Harry is constantly reminded of their tragic demise and he vows to seek vengeance.

Despite his soul-draining experiences with the Dursleys, Harry is trustingly naive and believes in the inherent goodness of people. His innocence, optimism, and hopefulness in a hostile climate reinforce the portrayal of him as a sympathetic protagonist. Harry, though, is truly human, and Rowling does not sugarcoat his characterization. He can be irritable or empathetic, tired or energetic, and clueless or proficient. His moods range from extremes between misery and joy. At times, Harry seems too noble, ignoring being insulted and exploited by others, and at other moments, he is obsessed with defeating evil wizards who threaten him, his friends, and his community.

Harry immerses himself into his new role as a wizard, preparing for his future, and discovers his abilities and limitations through various tests inside and outside the classroom. Having been isolated by the Dursleys, he is eager to form deep friendships and realizes that everyone has the potential for magic even if they are unreceptive to it. Harry also learns that all people have the capacity for evil and that he must distinguish between reality and falsehoods. Ironically, Harry is an enigma who keeps secrets from others and himself. He gradually recognizes truths about his abilities. The theme that goodness is often an unconscious response while malevolence is a deliberate action is always evident. Harry is appealing because he represents someone entirely powerless becoming empowered beyond most people's expectations.

Harry gains autonomy from the adults in his family and can control his future through the choices he makes, an enviable situation to many young readers. His donning of the Invisibility Cloak in Book I symbolizes Harry's new identity, maturity, and healthy self-esteem. Harry's example stresses the message that individuals should believe in themselves and persevere despite obstacles. Even though Harry is perceived as the most likely suspect behind the malicious activities at Hogwarts when the Chamber of Secrets is reopened, he doggedly pursues his adversary to prove that sometimes the most obvious conclusions are incorrect. Struggling against cruelties, both physical and emotional, Harry relies on his abilities and trusts his friends as he experiences themes of betrayal and loyalty, love and loss. Readers care about Harry as if he were a friend or a brother. He serves as a fantasy mentor who demonstrates that anything is possible because of determination and work.

HARRY, RON AND HERMIONE:
THE WIZARDLY TRIO

Harry is the wizard world's savior. He is assisted by disciples, his two closest friends, Ron Weasley and Hermione (Her-my-oh-nee) Granger, much like King Arthur's knights or Robin Hood's Merry Men assisted them. At first glance, Harry and his friends appear unremarkable. None of them are unusually attractive, and they seem stereotypical of most children their age. Their similarities bind them, and their differences strengthen their unity. Harry, Ron, and Hermione are all skinny children. Their coloring contrasts: Harry's hair is black, Ron's red, and Hermione's brown. While Harry has green eyes (and wears round-lens eyeglasses), Ron has blue irises and Hermione brown. Harry and Hermione are only children. Both of Hermione's parents are Muggles (they are dentists), and Harry is descended from both wizards and Muggles. Only Ron has pure wizard blood. (see Chapter 9, Mythology, for an interesting but unsubstantiated fan insight about Ron's name)

Ron is a mediocre student, and Harry is average, excelling in some classes while struggling with others. Hermione is an overachiever and aces all of her courses. Harry has access to his parents' abundantly-filled bank vault, while Ron endures his family's poverty. Interestingly, Harry does not reimburse the Weasleys when they host him at their house nor does he offer to share his wealth. Hermione's parents seem to be comfortably middle class. Harry is the only member of the trio to have been abused; both the Weasley and Granger families are nurturing. All three children express concern about people's well-being, and they cope with moral dilemmas which sometimes result from their reactions and behaviors to circumstances they encounter. On the verge of puberty, they are about to undergo significant life changes.

The wizardly trio is connected by their friendship, faith, and sense of wonder with each other, and their teamwork is essential to vanquish foes. They are all members of the Gryffindor House at Hogwarts, which is considered to consist of the most reliable and moral students. Ron is Harry's best friend, confidante, and source of advice about wizard protocol. He shares characteristics with Harry, such as bravery and loyalty, but Ron is not as strong, sensible, or courageous as Harry. He is embarrassed by his secondhand clothing and is anxious for Harry to approve of his room and belongings. He encourages Harry to be impulsive, and they share detention and demerits for their misdeeds. Ron has six siblings, five brothers and one sister, and is the youngest boy. None of his family members exhibit any traits of a weasel that might be assumed of someone with the name Weasley. Ron's father, Arthur, is fascinated with Muggles, especially their technology which baffles him. For the Ministry of Magic, he is in charge of making and enforcing rules regarding wizards owning Muggle-manufactured items.

Ron's mother Molly cherishes her children and Harry, and she serves as an Earth Mother figure guiding him in his transition from mere mortal to eminent wizard. Ron plays chess with his grandfather's set, but no additional information is provided for readers to know this man's possible significance to the series. All of the Weasley children attend Hogwarts or have graduated from the school and begun magical careers. Ron's twin brothers, Fred and George, provide comic relief through their pranks and distorted sense of humor. They daringly help Harry escape from the Dursleys' home by driving the flying car and resisting Harry's guardians' efforts to restrain him, just as in their role as Quidditch team Beaters who are responsible for thwarting attacks. Percy, the eldest Weasley at Hogwarts, is a school leader called a "prefect," and acts as if he is perfect, demanding that Ron, Harry, and Hermione conform to his rigid standards of conduct. Ginny, Ron's younger sister, is one year behind him at Hogwarts and adores Harry. Her immaturity and infatuation enable Voldemort to invade the school.

Hermione defies detractors who suggest that Muggle-born students are incapable of being wizards and witches. She is the epitome of intellectual resilience and studies even during vacations. Her genius allows her to resolve problems creatively and resourcefully, using books and her lessons. Hermione's parents remain on the edges of the wizard's world like most Muggles. Unlike the Dursleys, they are supportive of their daughter's magical gifts and encourage Hermione to study at Hogwarts; they even accompany her on trips to buy school supplies in Diagon Alley shops.

Hermione is symbolic of a woman warrior, like Joan of Arc who fights for causes she believes in regardless of reality; the name Hermione resembles the word heroine. It also can represent harmony and hormone, both alluding to her feminine tendencies to be sisterly and motherly to her friends. Her sense of right and wrong is more acute than the other characters', and Hermione is sometimes considered shrill and annoying by even her best friends because of her lecturing and disapproving tone. Her inconsistent behavior reveals her insecurities about belonging at Hogwarts, especially after messages declare that all Muggle-born students will be exterminated.

Unfortunately, this portrayal of Hermione also perpetuates stereotypical images of females being moody, fickle, and unreliable. Hermione attempts to disguise her discomfort by focusing on her studies and earning top grades, and her talents prove beneficial to Harry and Ron. She justifies breaking rules only to prevent crimes. Disappointingly, however, after Hermione brainstormed the idea and assertively initiated brewing the Polyjuice Potion, secured ingredients, and puzzled out part of the mystery's solution in Book II, she is first transformed into a cat, preventing her from participating in the deceptive adventure in the Slytherin common room, then petrified, like Sleeping Beauty, which almost seems to be punishment for her pursuing risks. While she is out of commission, Harry and Ron use her information to solve the mystery and defeat the intruder. Hermione only becomes conscious after the action has concluded and she praises the boys when they tell her about their deeds. Harry seems to be Hermione's prince, awakening her with his bravery.

THE DURSLEYS

Harry's friends are the opposite of his first cousin, Dudley Dursley. Whereas Harry's friends are thin and usually neatly groomed, Dudley is an obese slob. A bully, he savors tormenting Harry, and his parents tolerate, and even encourage, his sadistic taunts. Only through threats of using magic does Harry have any control over Dudley's abuse, and the Dursleys forbid him to use magic and his imagination in the house. Hogwarts also imposes a sanction that students are to refrain from performing magic during summer holidays, further isolating Harry from what gives him the most comfort.

Dudley's parents, Vernon and Petunia Dursley are repulsive, ignorant, arrogant, narcissistic, greedy, mean-spirited, humorless people who seem to have no souls. Yet they appear to have some knowledge of wizards, and one wonders if the Dursleys as children could have repressed their contacts with magic in denial of characteristics they despise in themselves. Perhaps, they too are magical, a secret they try to hide through their spitefulness and dullness, which might be revealed in future books. Their indulgent behaviors and smug attitudes symbolize their overwhelming nature. They seem content with their ordinariness. The Dursleys are exaggerated opposites of the Potters. Interestingly, Rowling introduces readers to Harry through the Dursleys' distorted distaste of the Potters in the first chapter of Book I. Their misinterpretations alert readers of the opposing characteristics of the Potters and Dursleys that advance the plot and provide a framework for other divergent relationships.

As reluctant guardians, they expect Harry to labor in their

home and yard, somewhat like Cinderella, yet they stingily resent feeding and sheltering him. The Dursleys psychologically devour Harry and do not appreciate his uniqueness, confining him to his room when important business guests arrive. This couple, the Masons, who are builders and have a stone-like rigidity, foreshadow the petrification Harry opposes in Book II. The name Dudley suggests the words "dud" and "deadly." Although Vernon Dursley earns a decent wage working for a drill manufacturer, he deprives Harry of many basic needs while indulging Dudley with two rooms, one to sleep in and one for his toys, as well as a new television when Dudley destroys his. Dudley's every whim and caprice are fulfilled. The Dursleys loathe Harry and misunderstand him. Rowling's descriptions of these disagreeable, repugnant characters (as well as at least one rather benign classmate) unfortunately perpetuate stereotyped characteristics associated with being fat, such as stupidity and laziness. Interestingly, the two primary families in Harry's life, the Weasleys and the Dursleys, both have surnames ending in "-ley," which suggests some parallels between them.

HARRY'S TEACHERS AND THE SIGNIFICANCE OF THEIR NAMES

Hogwarts' professors and staff are perhaps the most stereotypical characters in the novels, perhaps to aid readers' comprehension of their roles. Faculty members are referred to by the title "professor" to exemplify the formal manners expected from Hogwarts' students. Teachers' names are frequently anagrams or word plays based on related academic specialties, personality flaws, or some other descriptive phrasing. Hogwarts' four founding wizards and house namesakes, Godric Gryffindor (god-like), Helga Hufflepuff (huff and puff), Rowena Ravenclaw (ravenous, predator), and Salazar Slytherin (sly, slither), establish the tone for future pupils and professors who mold Hogwarts within those four parameters ranging in extremities of good and evil.

When Hogwarts was created a millennium ago, the founders built the castle far away from Muggles because of persecution against magical people. Afraid of Muggles, Slytherin planned for Hogwarts to educate only full-blooded wizards, prohibiting those with mixed parentage from being admitted. Arguing with Gryffindor, Slytherin secretly built and sealed a chamber so that only his heirs could use its powers to exterminate students who were not descended from esteemed wizard families. Slytherin's prejudices against wizards who interacted with Muggles were the catalyst for turmoil centuries later. Voldemort belonged to the house named for Slytherin, and the two characters often seem to be one person because of their philosophies and behavior.

The wise and benevolent headmaster, Albus Dumbledore, is reminiscent of Merlin from the King Arthur legends, with his long beard and eyeglasses. Extremely powerful, he is the only wizard that Voldemort fears besides Harry, and, like Harry, is not afraid to say Voldemort's name. Harry believes Dumbledore is the most powerful wizard, and Dumbledore may represent what the elderly Harry will be like. The word "Dumbledore" sounds like a contortion of "bumblebee," and the headmaster displays the helpful, cooperative traits of those communal dwellers. He also acts bumbling sometimes, and the words "dumb, stumble, fumble," and "bore" can also be derived from his name, suggesting his traits according to different points of view.

Professor Minerva McGonagall seems prim and proper, her hair tightly pulled into a bun atop her head. Minerva is the name of the Roman goddess of wisdom and war, and Professor McGonagall is one of the wisest people Harry knows. Her Scottish last name hints that she is both bold and bitter.

As the transfiguration professor, McGonagall teaches her students to shape items into different forms. She could be Hermione's double because their personalities are so similar. Also a symbolic fairy godmother, McGonagall is the faculty advisor for Gryffindor House and treats all of her students fairly without favoritism or derision, unlike Severus Snape, the potions master and the mentor for the Slytherin House. His name appropriately describes a man who is severe (as well as one who swerves or severs himself from distasteful situations), who serves others when it advances his interests, who severs allegiances, and who snipes at students he dislikes or fears, such as Harry, whom he resents for his fame. He is embittered against the Potters because of an incident when he was a student at Hogwarts and James Potter saved his life.

Three Defense Against the Dark Arts teachers have taught at Hogwarts since Harry enrolled. Professor Quirrell, whose name suggest his quarrelsome behavior, deceives everyone with his seemingly nervous behavior characterized by his stutter. He introduces Harry to Voldemort, forcing the fledgling wizard's first confrontation with his archenemy since he was an infant. After Quirrell is exposed, Gilderoy Lockhart, a handsome, pompous, vain man, feigns to be a master of evil creatures but is more adept at producing publicity. His name suggests that he is a like a gilded locket, something pretty to look at but that does not hold much substance. He credits himself with other people's acts of bravery and manufactures scenarios to sell books (with cover photographs of Lockhart winking and smiling), yet, when confronted with the opportunity to become a true hero, Lockhart breaks down and loses his mind.

Remus Lupin is more successful as the third Defense Against the Dark Arts professor. Lupin, like Harry, arrives at Hogwarts without fine clothes and drained of energy. He stoically endures taunts from Draco Malfoy and he does not misuse his power to punish or belittle Draco in class. Lupin nurtures and encourages his pupils and refuses to react to Snape's attacks on his character. The names Remus and Lupin suggest his wolf-like tendencies because of the Roman child Remus, who was suckled by wolves. "Lupin" is the Latin name for wolves. The fictional character Uncle Remus (by Joel Chandler Harris) knows how to outsmart all of the creatures in his world, just as Lupin manages to control Grindylows and Kappas. Lupin knew Harry's father and generously tells Harry information that no one else has divulged. He devotes time, almost like a father figure or uncle, to teach Harry how to summon his inner resources to protect himself from his fears.

Rubeus Hagrid is the buffoonish Hogwarts' gamekeeper who speaks with a Scottish brogue. He is a gentle almost-giant man who harbors a secret about his past and why he was expelled from Hogwarts during his third year as a student. His first name suggests that he is a rube or has traits of a rebus puzzle, and his last name hints of his haggardly traits. He delivered infant Harry to the Dursleys after Voldemort's attack and returned to rescue the boy by telling him he is a wizard, welcoming him to Hogwarts, and introducing him to the wizard world. Hagrid watches over Harry and comforts and gives him advice when asked. He resembles jovial Friar Tuck of Robin Hood's Merry Men. Hairy like the creatures he adores, Hagrid's main flaw is that he minimizes the potential harm of the monsters he harbors.

In contrast, Argus Filch, the school's caretaker, is hostile toward the students, suspecting them of purposefully making his job difficult. He is appropriately named for the mythic Greek watchman named Argus who was covered with eyes. His last name indicates his capacity to steal students' time by assigning them detention chores. Filch's cat and spy, Mrs. Norris, is the first victim of the heir of Slytherin.

Sibyll Trelawney's first name indicates that she is a fortuneteller, although not a consistent prophet. She picks favorite students and skeptically dismisses others. Trelawney dramatically forecasts Harry's fate, then later makes an accurate prediction while in a trance but does not believe her own words.

The librarian Madam Pince pounces on demanding students and is stingy about loaning books. Her surname rhymes with pence which might be used to pay library fines. Madam Pomfrey nurses students back to health with flair, and Professor Sprout, advisor for Hufflepuff, teaches herbology and always has dirty fingernails from her work in the school's greenhouses. The history of magic professor, a ghost named Mr. Binns, lulls his students with his lectures but has immense knowledge about Hogwarts' past even if he cannot recall present students' names. Professor Armando Dippet was headmaster when Tom Riddle was a student, and Professor Sinistra teaches astronomy, but their characters are not yet further developed.

HARRY'S PEERS

Harry attends school with classmates who range from almost obsessively adoring to revoltingly hateful. Students are snobby and inclusive, and fill roles as rivals and teammates. The variety of students offers balance to the Hogwarts community. Perhaps the most sinister student is Draco Malfoy, Harry's nemesis, who has a sharp, bloodless face like a vampire with icy grey eyes. His name suggests the ancient Athenian lawyer, Draco, and his Draconian, or harsh law code he inflicted on citizens. Also, Draco is Latin for "dragon" and "serpent" (used interchangeably); the dictionary definition of "dragon" cites the Latin word as the origin of the English term "dragon." There are East Indian and Asian lizards that resemble dragons who belong to the genus Draco.

Malfoy hints of malfeasance. Malfoy is descended from an old, wealthy wizard family, and lives in an elaborate mansion when he is not at Hogwarts. His sidekicks, Crabb and Goyle (suggesting someone who is crabby and grotesque like a gargoyle), assist Malfoy to commit his hateful deeds. They are all Slytherins, and while Malfoy exhibits intelligence, albeit evilly used, Crabb and Goyle are dim-witted, blunderers with more brawn than brains that are easily duped by the trinity of Harry, Ron, and Hermione. Malfoy's brash tactics indicate his feelings of insecurity, and he is so self-consumed with ridding Hogwarts of Muggles and ridiculing the Weasleys and Harry (whom he calls Scarhead) that he fails to listen to other students and is deceived when Harry and Ron transform into Crabb and Goyle to question Malfoy about Slytherin's heir.

Other significant characters include Colin Creevey, the son of a milkman, who, like Harry, learns he's a wizard when he receives a letter from Hogwarts. Oliver Wood is the Gryffindor Quidditch team's gung-ho captain, whose surname sources say is derived from the word "wad," which means crazed or mad. His surname could also indicate the wooden broomsticks that his team flies.

Neville Longbottom is like a fool or jester because he is accident-prone and forgetful. Seemingly loyal to his housemates, Longbottom risks detention and points to help them and even fights for their honor. His carelessness sometimes exposes them at risk. In each book he seems more capable and sure of himself. Lee Jordan, the exuberant Quidditch announcer, is true to the meaning of his surname by acting as a crusader for Gryffindor. Millicent Bulstrode, a haggish Slytherin, is Hermione's archrival. The Slytherin Marcus Flint, who repeats a year, provides an example of what happens to students who perform poorly. Lavender Brown and Parvati Patil are the only students Professor Trelawney thinks have psychic promise. Harry, Ron, and Neville share their turret room with Seamus Finnigan, who has an Irish accent and is the son of a witch and Muggle, and with Dean Thomas, a tall black boy who is an ardent soccer fan. He, the Patil twins, and Cho Chang, Harry's possible future love interest, provide ethnic diversity at Hogwarts. Other students are important to compare Harry's and his immediate friends' strengths and weaknesses as they cope within the Hogwarts community.

The students are either pure-blooded wizards, mudbloods, or squibs, who are wizards that lack magical skills. The word "squib" is a synonym for ridicule and also indicates a scab, or temporary worker who replaces striking employees, or a military recruit who represents the lowest and the most despised rank in the military hierarchy. Many Hogwarts students knew that they were wizards from birth and prepared to attend Hogwarts like previous generations. Mudbloods, however, mostly learn of their powers when they receive their invitation. The bigotry directed against mudbloods is blatant racism which further divides the student body and foments rifts between friends and peers, muddying allegiances. When Malfoy calls Hermione a mudblood, she logically argues that talent supersedes money and ancestry, and level-headed professors remind students that if magical people had not married Muggles, wizards would be extinct. Such hostile situations incite dilemmas.

Harry not only wants to excel as an individual, but he also wants to be accepted as part of a group, which he finds at Gryffindor House. Hogwarts' houses prepare students for more serious life and professional issues as they indulge in rivalries in classrooms and on the Quidditch field. That sport readies Harry physically, intellectually, and emotionally to pursue Voldemort. The house guarantees him sanctuary from bullies and ardent hero-worshippers. Harry feels obliged to earn points so that the house will win overall honors in excellence and defeat their enemies, and he realizes he must be accountable for his actions because his house will be fined points for his misbehavior.

ADULT WIZARDS

Hogwarts' adult alumni contribute to the mood and plot. Draco's father, Lucius Malfoy, suggesting a possible relationship to the devil Lucifer, is a manipulative member of the school's board of governors. One of Voldemort's agents, Malfoy maligns Harry and Dumbledore and tries to cause chaos. He greedily hoards contraband in his home for future profitable resale and deems Harry and his parents as "meddlesome fools." His hateful treatment of his house-elf Dobby and elitist machinations and abuse of power explain why his son is so mean.

Tom Riddle communicates with the former Hogwarts student through his diary. Tom's mother died when he was born and his father had abandoned them before she gave birth to Tom (Tom later killed his father). He grew up in a Muggle orphanage, so he is not exactly an orphan like Harry. Riddle, true to his name, creates more questions than answers, and plays the role of the Riddler to Harry's heroic Batman. His manipulation of Ginny symbolizes his unconscionable callousness to achieve his ultimate goals (somewhat like Vernon Dursley grabbing onto Harry as he flees in Book II even though

he despises the child but gains pleasure from controlling him).
The Minister of Magic, Cornelius Fudge, whose name prompts
the phrase "here comes the judge," is more concerned about
appeasing Hogwarts' governors than assuring justice is secured,
often fudging his duties.

The prime villain, Lord Voldemort, also a Hogwarts alumnus
from the 1940s whose name is French for "flight of death" and
also suggests that he is a bold murderer, knew of Harry's parents, who attended Hogwarts in the 1970s. His obsession with
killing the Potters in his malevolent quest to seize power of the
world by murdering his opposition, primarily virtuous wizards
including the Prewetts, McKinnons, and Bones, results in his
banishment with his evil followers during the years Harry lived
with the Dursleys. Somehow, possibly yet to be fully explained
in future stories, Harry repulsed Voldemort's attack and
stripped him of his powers. Good wizards and witches, afraid of
Voldemort's vengeance, refuse to use his name. Occasionally,
wizards report possible sightings of Voldemort, but his physical
condition and present ambitions are unknown. Voldemort
resurfaces annually and so far has been defeated before retreat-
ing to recuperate during the summer lull.

Voldemort is like Satan, Hitler, or any other demonic
archetypal character who seeks the destruction of people to
achieve more power. As Harry's archenemy, Voldemort per-
petually pursues methods to isolate and punish Harry for surviving his initial assault. And, like a fairy tale, good usually
prevails victoriously so that the righteous wizards protected
by Harry, seeking redemption for not saving his parents, live
happily ever after. Because Lily Potter's maiden name has not

been revealed nor James Potter's parentage divulged, perhaps someone close to Harry at Hogwarts, a teacher or student or colleague or even a villain such as Voldemort, is a cousin who will be pivotal to future plot developments. Harry might even be a family surname because many people have that last name in Great Britain.

Sirius Black is the most significant adult wizard in Harry's life. His name indicates that he is someone to consider seriously and that he has a dark side. Astronomically, Sirius also refers to the dog star, emphasizing his importance to Harry's destiny. Having been James Potter's best friend, Black is Harry's godfather. Falsely accused and imprisoned for Peter Pettigrew's crime, Black seeks redemption which Harry eventually provides. Black symbolizes the themes of forgiveness and second chances. He also represents how happiness often seems unobtainable for Harry. On the other hand, Peter Pettigrew emphasizes the theme of betrayal. His dual nature as a rat whether in human or animal form and cowardice contrast starkly with Black's boldness and ingenuity either as man or dog. Pettigrew's missing finger symbolizes his inability to make his point effectively.

The supporting cast of wizard store clerks and the Knight Bus driver and conductor are crucial for telling Harry information about his past and the present. While many of these characters are named and described, others remain on the periphery of the Muggle world. They are noticeable because of their mismatched clothing and inappropriate actions in public. Unlike Muggles who strive to conform to societal expectations, wizards thrive on being individuals.

MAGICAL ANIMALS AND CREATURES

Amazing creatures also live in the wizard realm. Some enchanted beings are helpful, serving as messengers and companions, while others are malicious, causing disruptions and wounding humans. Each house is represented by a symbolic beast such as a brave lion for Gryffindor and a sneaky snake for Slytherin. Hedwig, the owl named for a medieval saint, shadows Harry, delivering his mail. Owls symbolize wisdom, and although Hedwig does not speak, her actions often inspire Harry to realize what he should do. She also comforts him, and Harry nurtures her, forming a bond that provides him emotional security. Fawkes, Dumbledore's pet phoenix, appropriately named for Guy Fawkes of the historic British gunpowder plot, symbolizes the cycle of rebirth at Hogwarts as new students matriculate. Both birds demonstrate unadulterated loyalty based on kindred love.

Because his family cannot afford an owl for him, Ron has a worn-out rat named Scabbers that reflects Ron's hand-me-down existence. Scabbers' slothful existence and damaged body provide clues about his previous activities and future intentions. He proves to be a rat in more ways than one. Mrs. Norris, Filch's cat, is considered by the students to be an unfair informant, alerting Filch to their whereabouts and possible misdemeanors. Hermione's cat Crookshanks (perhaps named in tribute of fairy tale illustrator George Cruikshanks) is also unsavory but proves to be more loyal than contrary. Readers are left unsure after Book III whether Crookshanks is truly a feline or perhaps an Animagus, the ambiguous human-animals. Dogs also are symbolic in the Potter novels.

Harry could be considered an underdog and a runt. He bypasses the absurdly named Fluffy, the watchdog, on his first adventure, and fears the canine Grim in Book III. Aunt Marge's favorite bulldog, Ripper, loathes Harry and symbolizes the Dursleys' brutish nature. Fang, although somewhat cowardly, helps Harry.

The centaurs are mostly aloof except for Firenze (the name of a medieval city in Italy), whose name suggests that he is a Renaissance man-beast. While the other centaurs are more animalistic and feel no accountability toward Harry, Firenze's human qualities makes him intuitive, empathetic, and concerned about Harry's well being. Buckbeak, the Hippogriff (suggesting a kindredness with the Gryffindors), is another half-horse creature who lacks the centaurs' intellectual reasoning and proves to be a helpful, obedient beast despite the Malfoys' accusations that he is dangerous. An amalgam of dutiful horse and cunning eagle, Buckbeak does not tolerate insults and is able to take revenge against Draco that is forbidden for Harry to enact. The dragon Norbert is Harry's alter ego, acting toward his foster parent like Harry wishes he could act toward the Dursleys, literally biting the hand that feeds him. Norbert is sent to safety in a crate much like toddler Harry was exiled in a bundle of blankets.

Dobby, a house elf who is Lucius Malfoy's indentured servant, tries to warn Harry, whom he idolizes, of the plan Malfoy is plotting to rid Hogwarts of mudbloods. Dobby could be malevolent but he is most harmful to himself, physically punishing himself for talking to Harry and betraying his master. Dobby perhaps best symbolizes the duality of the wizard world's inhabitants. Although he is enmeshed in evil, Dobby tries to be good and is confused about his behavior.

HARRY POTTER

The students test their wizardry skills in class on a variety of supernatural creatures such as pixies, which prepares them for confrontations under less structured circumstances. Aragog, the elephant-sized spider, promises to protect Hagrid but instinctively attacks all other humans to feed his family. The Brazilian boa constrictor that Harry frees from the zoo, gratefully alerts Harry to his ability to communicate with snakes. The basilisk, the king of serpents, however, is purely evil and represents temptation to sacrifice goodness and become wholly evil. Capable of living for centuries, the snake has a gaze that is deadly, symbolizing the blindness of racism. There are also lizards commonly known as basilisks from the genus Basilicus belonging to the iguana family. Other magical creatures in the Potter novels include goblins, vampires, and trolls which function as guards or attackers according to each situation.

GHOSTS, PLANTS, AND PERSONIFIED PROPS

The Hogwarts' ghosts annoy and assist Harry. They are parallel images of the school's students and professors. Peeves, the poltergeist, seeks out students to startle and taunt with embarrassing rhymes, the way Draco Malfoy does in life. Nearly Headless Nick, Harry's dormitory's residential ghost, is friendly like many of Harry's peers although he has ulterior motives, hoping Harry's support can help him secure membership in an elite ghost club. Moaning Myrtle, whose hysterics draw Hermione into the out-of-order bathroom, is narcissistic like Lockhart. The Boggarts represent peoples' worries and can be deflected with humor or happiness sometimes displayed as a Patronus, a wispy protector and supporter produced from love and joy that forms a screen

69

between a victim and his or her tormentor. Although Harry's parents do not appear as ghosts in the stories, his memories of them are the basis of the Patronuses he conjures against the Dementors. These guards, reminiscent of the Grim Reaper, Death, are tall, hooded monsters that might physically be part ghost and demon but actually are the materialized anxiety of their victims. Eager to suck out peoples' souls, the Dementors, as their name implies, seem demented and wreak havoc. They upset Harry's equilibrium and symbolize the horrors and deficiencies of his childhood.

In addition to ghostly apparitions, enchanted artifacts interact with students. Wands choose their soulmates. The materials in each wand indicate wizard's and witch's traits: Hagrid's oaken wand symbolizes his sturdiness. The enchanted Stone in Book I tempts people with infinite life and riches, but is a burden somewhat like Sisyphus' rock. Items such as the Sorting Hat decide what house is appropriate for each student. The Sorting Hat stresses the theme that first impressions are lasting. The hat intuited Harry's dual nature by saying he could be a Gryffindor or Slytherin, presenting him with a dilemma. The barrier at King's Cross station which conveys wizards from one world to another symbolizes cultural barriers. The Invisibility Cloak magically conceals people not only from the world but from themselves. Howlers chastise and shame students publicly. The Marauder's Map offers escape from reality but also delivers Harry to face his worst fears. Figures in portraits, people in moving photos, and the fantastical candies are also vibrant characters that interact with Harry and guide or mislead him. Books scream and bleed, and the monster textbook requires stroking to tame it for use.

Harry's broomstick that he rides in Quidditch games parallels his ability to rise above restraints in his daily life. The position of Seeker symbolizes the quickest player who has the agility to maneuver to catch the Golden Snitch regardless of the game's chaos, and is symbolic of facing and coping with life's problems. This dangerous, violently competitive sport, played in mid air, signifies the limbo Harry and the other student wizards live in, trying to master their art in order to be recognized as mature sorcerers. Plants such as the Whomping Willow, Death Snare, Mandrakes, and trees in the Forbidden Forest serve different purposes. They protect or heal but also wound and entrap people. All of these believable, often personified, items, creatures, and plants provide the fantastical elements and motifs that balance the realism of a boy's difficult life in the human world.

VOCABULARY

anonymity: unknown
enigma: mystery
malevolent: evil
protagonist: the main character who is usually on a search for something
sadistic: cruel
vicariously: learning by someone else's experiences

Log on to **www.beachampublishing.com** for many additional projects, discussion questions, writing and research ideas, websites, and bibliography.

CHAPTER 4

SETTING

"[Hogwarts is] A huge, rambling, quite scary-looking castle, with a jumble of towers and battlements. Like the Weasley's house, it isn't a building that Muggles could build, because it is supported by magic."
—J.K. ROWLING

LANDSCAPE AND DISTANCE

Rowling's imaginative settings help readers visualize the places where Harry Potter lives, learns, and plays. The creative landscapes expand as Harry matures in each book and discovers new locations during his adventures. Starting from the Dursleys' confining home, Harry moves to spaces where he gradually gains more freedom. In each book, readers not only are introduced to additional settings, but they also acquire more information about already familiar buildings and sites. The growth of Harry's world symbolizes his increasing awareness of his environment. Every year Harry's quest against Voldemort requires that he resourcefully maneuver in an unknown setting, usually within or adjacent to Hogwarts. The knowledge that he gains during this confrontation in a hostile place strengthens him.

Rowling has created a fictional world that borders on realism; places and people are arranged into two categories, mortal and magic, that are opposites of each other. The novel's setting is crucial in order for Harry's fantastic magical world to be believable to readers. Harry lives in two distinctive environments, the magical realm of Hogwarts, the prestigious wizard boarding school, and the pedestrian Muggle community, where his guardians reside. He moves between the divergent settings, preferring Hogwarts which he regards as a sanctuary even though the school seems overwhelmingly sinister as compared to the complacent domesticity of the Dursleys' home on Privet Drive in the fictional town of Little Whinging, Surrey.

By being transferred from the dreary desolation and limitations of the mortal setting to the delightful intrigues and abundance in the wizard world, Harry undergoes a metamorphosis of personality and self-confidence represented by the shifts between contrasting environments. The Dursley home serves as an incubator for Harry's childhood during which his magic was mostly dormant. Forbidding imagination, the Dursley home is stagnant and barren while Hogwarts vibrates with creativity and productivity. Harry lives at Hogwarts from September through June, including the Christmas holidays, and suffers the non-wizard world for only two summer months. His movement from the non-magical world to Hogwarts is the catalyst for Harry's pursuit of self discovery and self reliance through the rigors he undergoes. Engaged in a symbiotic relationship, the school saves Harry as he preserves the school from potential termination in each adventure.

WELCOME TO HOGWARTS

Hogwarts operates in a traditional medieval castle known to be at least one thousand years old when the school was established by four prominent wizards. The school is situated atop a steep cliff overlooking a lake and forest and surrounded by mountains. Providing a seven-year curriculum of classes to prepare wizards to practice magic responsibly, Hogwarts is a community unto itself, operating on basic rules understood by students and faculty. Often obscured by fog, Hogwarts might seem perplexing and illusionary to uninformed outsiders, but insiders comprehend fully the logic guiding the code of expected conduct, rites, and learning which models that of many modern British boarding schools (see Chapter 5, School Life).

Hogwarts appears to be a parallel universe to the non-magical Muggle world, paradoxically exhibiting similarities and differences. Both worlds provide Harry a form of shelter, although the quality varies: at the Dursleys' he sleeps in a cupboard (closet) or is locked in a sparse upstairs room, while at Hogwarts he shares an elaborately furnished tower turret with four boys; he has his own four-poster canopy bed. Harry is annoyed by arrogant, dismissive people at both places but he is also appreciated by some of his peers and professors at Hogwarts, which balances out the derision he encounters there. Most importantly, the Hogwarts setting embraces imaginative thought, actions, and creatures. Centaurs and such kindred beings are commonplace. Nothing is considered too bizarre or impossible at Hogwarts where the school has power to control its premises and selected personnel are in charge of certain areas, such as the gates.

Hogwarts is located several hours of travel north from the Muggle world. Rowling says the school is in northern Scotland which is the setting of Celtic lore and legendary figures, such as William Wallace known as Braveheart whose physique and daring somewhat resembles Hagrid, the school's gamekeeper. Hogwarts is like an island, separated by enchanted forests and bodies of water as well as treacherous terrain and extreme climatic conditions (snow coats the school in winter and raindrops are as large as bullets). Students are transported to Hogwarts by a special train. More experienced wizards can use their powers to travel between places or rely on Floo powder, a magical dust that transports wizards via heating ducts such as chimneys and fireplaces. Owls (the owlery is on top of the

West Tower) deliver mail to Hogwarts, and the school and wizards require no external support systems or services. Like the Garden of Eden, Camelot, and Brigadoon, Hogwarts prospers in its unique and isolated setting.

Harry's initial impressions of Hogwarts reveal many details about the school. When the first-year students arrive by train from the Muggle world at a station that readers later learn is in Hogsmeade, they follow a path down a steep hill. Harry sees Hogwarts for the first time when he walks around a curve in the path. A large lake is positioned as a barrier between the path and the mountain where Hogwarts is located. Harry is bedazzled by the castle's towers. He crosses the lake in boats with his classmates, pushing through an ivy-concealed tunnel into the cliff to reach a pebbly harbor. Only by undergoing this process can Harry be initiated into the castle's environment. He passes through the castle's shadow to reach the stone steps and oaken door which represent Hogwarts' sense of mystery and power. Harry is admitted into the torch-filled Entrance Hall. By Book III, a more mature Harry enters Hogwarts through its intricate gates decorated with winged boars.

LIFE AT HOGWARTS

Hogwarts' motto "Drago Dormiens Nunquam Titillandus" (translated to mean "Never Tickle a Sleeping Dragon") symbolizes the cautionary elements always present at the school. Tradition is also represented through this slogan and the school's crest. The student population at Hogwarts is sorted into four houses, each named for one of the founding wizards.

These houses act as pri-
mary settings for many
plot developments. First-
term students are designated
to houses according to
their character and aspirations as determined by an
enchanted hat. Certain areas of
the school serve as living quarters for each of the houses and
represent the nature of its members, such as a dungeon for the
low, devious residents of Slytherin House and turrets for the
noble, uplifted members of Gryffindor House, Harry's home.
So far, the Hufflepuff and Ravenclaw rooms have not been
described. Not only do the houses indicate characters' virtues
and motives to readers, but they also provoke conflict between
competitive rivals in sports and scholarship. The brave
Gryffindors represent good, while the Slytherins symbolize the
potential of evil because of former members such as Lord
Voldemort. The struggles between the houses on the Quidditch
field and in the classroom and campus emphasize the overall
theme of good vanquishing evil.

Because Hogwarts is a boarding school, characters can move
around the premises at night to investigate suspicious places,
such as the forbidden third floor on the right side, and seek
answers to questions. The darkness not only allows nocturnal
evil forces to thrive, but also gives the students mobility to
counter them. A lot of the crucial plot action happens at night,
symbolizing the duality of darkness being composed of both
good and evil. Despite occasionally harboring extreme horrors,

the school also insures the students a certain degree of security which they crave amidst the uncertainties they face.

HOGWARTS' ROOMS AND ARCHITECTURE

The professors' offices perpetuate the medieval imagery and reflect the personalities of the characters. Sinister professors have dank, cold dungeon rooms filled with grotesque objects, while benevolent teachers' offices are located in the castle's upper levels and are reached by spiral staircases. These rooms have windows revealing marvelous views and seem to be more hospitable than ominous. The staff room is a central location for all professors to gather. The different chair styles symbolize the variety of personalities who gather at that location. Harry and his classmates sometimes acquire knowledge or power through their visits to the faculty lounge. The infirmary is also a recurrent setting for characters to make plans, confessions, and apologies. Injuries and healing are integral to the advancement of each book's plot.

Appropriately, the chambers in Books I and II are located deep beneath the school where few wizards venture. The Chamber of Secrets resembles an Egyptian tomb with intertwining snake pillars and a giant wizard statue that may conceal riches or dangers or both and entices intruders to risk their lives to determine its contents. Supposedly, only Slytherin's heir has the capability to open this chamber, and Harry's brief interlude in the chamber significantly alters his life as well as the future of the Hogwarts and wizard communities.

Although Harry's adventures occur in the 1990s, Hogwarts

has an antiquated, old-fashioned atmosphere almost absent of technology, especially as compared to the Dursleys' house. Torches and candles light rooms, and hearths provide heat. Wands also illuminate dark areas as needed. Students write with quills (made of peacock and eagle feathers) and ink, not computers. They conduct research in the musty library (with a forbidden section of Dark Magic books) instead of surfing the internet. Bells ring to signal the start of classes, and these are probably metallic chimes operated manually. An hourglass keeps track of house points won or lost by students. Description of such obsolete practices and decor at Hogwarts is inconsistent. The plumbing seems more modern, consisting of pumps, valves, and toilets, not rudimentary privies or chamberpots that would normally be part of an ancient castle. The lack of technology emphasizes the theme that magic can supply wizards with necessary items as well as comforts to fulfill any imaginable desire at any moment. Muggles, on the other hand, must helplessly depend on technology, which is often unreliable, to sustain their elaborate lifestyles.

A stone fortress which symbolizes strength, Hogwarts' interior spaces reinforce the medieval tone. The school's halls are maze-like, and portraits, suits of armor, and busts of famous wizards line the walls; pictures magically show their subjects moving, sleeping, and interacting with wizards. Many of these objects conceal doors or passages, and students learn passwords to manipulate these objects. Similarly, students follow tunnels to dungeons or staircases or turrets, mastering the ruses and snares of Hogwarts that represent the message that knowledge is power. They metaphorically rise above earthly concerns when they ascend through the trapdoor to the Divination classroom. Likewise, when they descend through a trapdoor, their problems intensify.

Poltergeists and ghosts roam the halls, playing pranks on students or reporting their misbehavior to school authorities. The school's most sinister sites, particularly the Chamber of Secrets but also Moaning Myrtle's bathroom and Snape's office, are in contrast to Hogwarts' safe places such as Dumbledore's quarters and the Great Hall, site of meals, the sorting ceremony, banquets, and group assemblies. The Great Hall's ceiling reflects outside conditions, sometimes illuminating stars on a velvety black background or stormy gray clouds boiling across the sky. Thousands of candles float above tables and the golden stage. The Gryffindor common room is also a refuge, but, like the Great Hall where dueling club battles occur, it is also the site of horrific occurrences, emphasizing the duality of Hogwarts and the simultaneous presence of loyalty and betrayal. No matter their house allegiances, students all share access to Hogwarts' mysteries through their elite connection to the school and participation in its traditions as they are prepared for supernatural careers.

ON HOGWARTS' GROUNDS

The areas surrounding Hogwarts contain buildings and spaces that are vital for plot development. The Quidditch field is a crucial site where the young wizards demonstrate their skills and are permitted to be combative with their foes. Played in an arena somewhat like a soccer field, the wizard sport resembles basketball with higher goalposts because the players ride broomsticks flying high above the grassy field. A total of six goalposts line the field. The nearby changing rooms are where students are transformed into elite players by donning special cloaks and reflecting on their captain's instructions. Harry feels happiest when he is flying above the Quidditch field with his teammates, while his friends and professors cheer for him in the stands (see Chapter 7, Sports).

Hagrid's cottage, which is a rustic one-room cabin, is within walking distance of Hogwarts. He has a vegetable garden in which he grows extremely large produce proportional to his size, such as giant pumpkins used to decorate Hogwarts at Halloween. Harry feels at home when he is in Hagrid's house and often goes there to seek comfort. This cabin is next to the Forbidden Forest, which Harry and his classmates are warned not to enter. The forest is home to both peaceful and aggressive beasts. In each novel so far, the forest has served as a transition setting in which Harry takes risks and is rewarded with clues that contribute to the resolution of his quests. He also meets creatures that assist or hinder his plans. The forest sometimes harbors Harry, especially if he observes rules about remaining on the path, while at other times it poses threats to his life when he strays into uncharted areas. Hagrid's hut shelters Harry and his friends, while the adjacent Forbidden Forest protects the school like a woody moat or threatens the tranquility at Hogwarts because of its dangerous human and animal residents. This close proximity to hazardous beasts symbolizes the wizards' vulnerability to losing their powers to each other, and to the threat of disbelief in their magical power and Muggle attacks.

The paddock where the students learn to ride Hippogriffs is near Hagrid's hut and the forest. A flat area nearby is used for first-year students' flying lessons. The owlery houses birds while they rest between trips, and the greenhouses protect plants necessary for potions and spells. These places are useful to Harry at different times in his adventures or serve as potential traps where enemies might lurk.

NEAR HOGWARTS

— Hogsmeade —

Hogsmeade, a wizard hamlet, adjacent to Hogwarts, provides an outlet for students to shop and temporarily escape from campus tensions and conflicts. Site of the platform where students arrive and depart on the Hogwarts Express, Hogsmeade includes businesses where all third-year and above students can visit.

Especially popular stores include Dervish and Banges, Zonko's Joke Shop, the post office filled with hundreds of "colour-coded" owls, and the Three Broomsticks where people drink warm Butterbeer. All types of people and creatures, including ogres, visit Hogsmeade and interact hospitably because magic and the unknown are respected. Significant incidents in Hogsmeade affect Hogwarts. For example, at the Hog's Head pub, a stranger tricked Hagrid to accept a dragon egg in exchange for revealing the secret of how to disarm Fluffy, the dog guarding the magical Stone.

— The Shrieking Shack —

The Shrieking Shack is considered the most haunted house in Great Britain. Like the shack on the island in the sea where Harry first met Hagrid, this building is also the setting of dramatic changes in the characters' lives. Located on a hill overlooking Hogsmeade, the Shrieking Shack is isolated from daily routines. Its windows are covered with boards, and the gardens are full of weeds. Villagers repeat legends about loud screams being heard at the shack. Most people are afraid to go near the building. Harry and Ron curiously approach the shack where they pull a prank on Draco, Crabbe, and Goyle. This incident foreshadows the showdown Harry, Ron, and Hermione have with Sirius Black, Peter Pettigrew, Remus Lupin, and Severus Snape. The enclosed space where they have their confrontation resembles the chambers of Book I and II, and the broken contents inspire fear of the monster that has had access to the shack. The drag marks in the dust and rickety staircase heighten tension as Harry and Hermione head toward the upstairs bedroom to find Ron and stumble into Sirius Black's trap. Ironically, the bedroom reminds them of their dormitory at Hogwarts. This sense of familiarity and normality fortifies them to speak and act boldly.

— The Tunnels —

The subterranean settings outside Hogwarts are reminiscent of the chambers that hold forbidden secrets. The two tunnels Harry uses to travel between Hogwarts and Hogsmeade are narrow and twisting, like his confused thoughts. He feels cold and damp when he is moving through the earthen paths, and sometimes he must bend over to protect his head, suggesting his feelings of fear and his flexibility to resolve them. Harry slides into the tunnel and climbs up stairs to a trapdoor at Honeydukes, somewhat like his descent into the chambers and ascension to Divination class. He chooses to use his wand to light up the path instead of submissively stumbling in the dark. The tunnel between the Whomping Willow and the Shrieking Shack represents both danger and comfort to Harry. Harry and Hermione cautiously follow Ron and the black dog through that tunnel, where Ron disappears. Harry feels close to his father when he learns that James often used the tunnel as a student. While in the tunnel, Sirius Black offers Harry a home, symbolizing Black's redemption and Harry's rebirth as a wiser wizard.

LONDON SETTINGS

Rowling's wizard world is not entirely remote from daily realities, both emotional and physical. The train station, King's Cross, is a familiar London landmark that has a barrier between platforms 9 and 10 and which serves as the fictional portal to platform 9 and three-quarters that transports wizards to the Hogwarts Express, much like the wardrobe conveys C.S. Lewis' characters to Narnia. Departing every September 1, the train is the sole conduit for students to reach Hogwarts and is the place where Harry is first exposed to magic among his peers. Mixing real locations with fantasy settings causes readers to wonder if they should look behind a picture in a pub or step on the correct stone or confidently approach a wall to move into Harry's world. Harry can visit Diagon Alley, the shopping district that resembles a medieval market, where he buys magical school supplies, by walking through a pub on the street resembling Charing Cross Road and tapping a brick.

Diagon Alley features such interestingly and appropriately named stores such as the Leaky Cauldron, the tavern where wizards enter Diagon Alley and which shelters Harry when he flees from the Dursleys, and Flourish and Blotts, the bookstore where Hogwarts students buy their textbooks. Florean Fortescue's Ice-Cream Parlour, Quality Quidditch Supplies, the Magical Menagerie, Eeylops Owl Emporium, and Ollivanders, the wand shop, all contribute to the imagery of Rowling's books in addition to serving as the source of future plot twists. Pivotal events occur at Diagon Alley such as Harry meeting Professors Quirrell and Lockhart, and Arthur Weasley and Lucius Malfoy fighting about who is qualified to practice magic.

The spectacular wizard bank, Gringotts, perhaps based on the word "gringo" which is a derisive term referring to outsiders, is located on Diagon Alley and has vaults hundreds of miles beneath London's streets (like the real silver vaults beneath modern London) full of wizard gold protected by enchantments. Harry's goblin-escorted journey to his family's vault symbolizes his immersion into the wizard world which cleanses him of Muggle residue that might inhibit his imagination. The bank and adjacent alley serve as a central point that all wizards frequent to share news or gossip.

Knockturn Alley is perpendicular to Diagon Alley and is home to stores that trade in dark magic, such as Borgin and Burkes where Harry arrives in Book II because of misdirected Floo powder. As a result, he observes a malicious exchange between the storekeeper and one of Harry's rival's fathers which reinforces his opinions about good and evil wizards. During his visit to this alley, Harry breaks his glasses and is covered with soot, hinting of his own potential for darkness, and Hagrid symbolically carries him into the sunlight to rescue him from harm.

HARRY'S TWO WORLDS

Perhaps most significant are the contrasts between the novels' settings. Harry's childhood home is cold, sterile, and depressing, while the Weasley home is warm, happy, and harmonious. The Dursleys' house reflects their financial security, in contrast to the Weasleys' dilapidated abode that represents their devotion to family. Named the Burrow, which symbolizes its nurturing nature, the Weasleys' home near the fictional village of Ottery St. Catchpole is reminiscent of the beavers' home in C.S. Lewis' novel, *The Lion, the Witch, and the Wardrobe* (1950). Standing several stories high with crooked staircases and a ghoul in the attic, the Burrow seems like a ramshackle version of Hogwarts. The yard is full of junk, and the garden grows weeds and is inhabited by frogs in a pond and grumpy gnomes whose burrowing could potentially alert Muggles that the home belongs to wizards.

Several chimneys sprout from the red roof like mushrooms, and Harry recognizes that the house's structure must be bolstered by magic for support. Mirrors in the house talk to him, explosions frequently occur, and fireplaces are transportation devices as well as hearths. Compared to the physical superiority and emotional deficiencies of the Dursleys' abode, the Burrow represents all that Harry craves, especially because everyone who resides there wants him to stay and enjoy life, unlike the punitive and exclusive Dursleys.

Muggle settings emphasize the magical nature of Hogwarts and serve as transition points between Harry's two worlds. Vernon Dursley's ninth-floor office at Grunnings seems sterile and mundane. Vernon's chair faces away from the window, symbolizing his refusal to look at his world. The Dursley home operates much like the factory where Vernon works, with routine overshadowing anything unusual and unexpected. Petunia Dursley tends her garden and spies on the neighbors. Dudley Dursley eats all day and torments Harry. The neighborhood's street lamps, brick walls, and hedges are always neat and clean. Harry's cupboard beneath the stairs, however, is crowded, dank, and spider-filled like a prison cell. The reptile house at the zoo resembles Harry's room at the Dursleys' and, by unintentionally releasing the snake, Harry is unconsciously expressing his desire for freedom from confinement. His brief contact with wizards and magical creatures in the Muggle world, both before and after he meets Hagrid, reinforces Harry's movement toward his destiny and acceptance of his true identity.

UNUSUAL AND UNSEEN SETTINGS

Other significant but somewhat strange settings include the flying car which is personified when it uses its lights to express its anger and snorts with its exhaust pipes. The car exhibits a dual nature of being a helper by rescuing Harry twice and transporting him to school, but it is also a fickle friend who abandons him during a crisis. The car's toffee-filled glove compartment and warm interior lose their appeal as the boys become thirsty, overheated, and the car whines from exhaustion. The flying car symbolically lifts the boys above their earthly problems but intensifies their supernatural woes.

Several of the books' settings are only mentioned and are not well described because the action that occurred there was seemingly insignificant (although future books may elaborate on the settings' purposes) or happened before Harry began school at Hogwarts. When the Dursleys leave town, Harry goes to Mrs. Figg's house two streets away where he endures her cats and smelly cabbage. Readers know that Aunt Marge has a house and kennels because of the Dursleys' conversations. She also sends a postcard from the Isle of Wight, but it is unclear whether her travels may be important to later story developments. Harry escapes the horrors of Stonewall High and St. Brutus' Secure Center for Incurably Criminal Boys, and his pre-Hogwarts school is mentioned solely to demonstrate his magical abilities of jumping on the roof to evade bullies.

Harry's first home, the Potter's house in Godric's Hollow north of Bristol, is referred to in Book I as being completely destroyed by Voldemort's attack. Hermione says that Hogwarts is the best wizard school, alluding to other wizard schools at various locations globally. The Ministry of Magic is in London, but readers are not given a specific location. Wizards live throughout Great Britain in Kent, Yorkshire, Dundee, and other regions. Ron's brothers Bill and Charlie work in Egypt and Romania, suggesting that wizards are dispersed in the world's many cultures and communities. Harry's classmates live mostly in Great Britain. Some, like Draco Malfoy, are said to live in magnificent mansions, while others such as Neville Longbottom come from more humble homes like Ron's.

Azkaban Prison is described through comments made by visitors and Black. The prison is located on a small island in the sea, reminding readers of Harry's escape from the shack in Book I. Black says he traveled north to Hogwarts when he swam to the shore. Rowling does not specify whether the prison might be located on Scotland's east or west coast. The street where Peter Pettigrew massacred the Muggles is not named. The countryside that the Knight Bus travels through is vaguely referred to as parts of Wales and England. The unknown hideouts of Voldemort and Black inspire readers' imaginations to envision caves, forests, and even normal houses which conceal their secret occupants.

Log on to **www.beachampublishing.com** for many additional projects, discussion questions, writing and research ideas, websites, and bibliography.

CHAPTER 5

SCHOOL LIFE

"The object of education is to prepare the young to educate themselves throughout their lives."
—ROBERT MAYNARD HUTCHINS

"An education isn't how much you have committed to memory, or even how much you know. It's being able to differentiate between what you know and what you don't."—ANATOLE FRANCE

SCHOOL DAYS

School is the focus of the Harry Potter series. Without Hogwarts, Harry Potter would probably be attending Stonewall High, the comprehensive school in his Muggle neighborhood, and his magical talents would remain untapped. In contrast to Harry's unpleasant experiences at his primary school, Hogwarts liberates him. He and his classmates are immersed into a routine of classes and school and house activities. They seem oblivious to news and events occurring in the external, Muggle world. Hogwarts is almost like a bomb shelter or bunker, shielding the students from any form of external contamination and danger.

The Hogwarts term is scheduled from September 1 to June 30 when the students return home for two months vacation after undergoing rigorous examinations. Beginning students are sorted into houses in September (somewhat like a fraternal society initiation) and are bonded with older students through communal singing of the school ballad at the opening feast. The exact cost of tuition, if any is charged, is not mentioned, nor has Rowling described a graduation ceremony for students completing the seventh year. A final feast in June recognizes achievements attained by individuals and houses.

The Hogwarts' houses are the nucleus for student life. Every house has specific traditions, ghosts, mentors, and foes. Members gather in the house common rooms to write in diaries, play games, and struggle with homework. Each house has approximately seventy members with ten students entering each year. Half of these students are boys and half are girls.

Harry shares his dormitory turret with four boys, and, even though Rowling has not described Hermione's dormitory, it probably resembles Harry's and Ron's room. Approximately 280 students study at Hogwarts, and the faculty is composed of ten to twenty professors and an unknown number of staff working in the kitchens and on the grounds.

HOGWARTS HOUSE MEMBERSHIP AS REVEALED IN BOOKS 1-3 AND THEIR CHARACTERISTICS ACCORDING TO THE SORTING HAT

GRYFFINDOR (*brave and daring*)

Albus Dumbledore

The Potters (James, Lily, and Harry)

The Weasleys (Ron, Percy, Fred, George, Ginny, Molly, Bill, Charlie, and Arthur)

Minerva McGonagall

Hermione Granger

Katie Bell

Lavender Brown

Colin Creevey

Seamus Finnigan

Angelina Johnson

Lee Jordan

Neville Longbottom

Parvati Patil

Alicia Spinnet

Dean Thomas
Oliver Wood
Sir Nicholas de Mimsy-Porpington
possibly: Remus Lupin, Sirius Black, Peter Pettigrew

SLYTHERIN (*cunning and sly*)

Lord Voldemort
The Malfoys (Lucius and Draco)
Severus Snape
Bletchley
Bole
Millicent Bulstrode
Vincent Crabbe
Derrick
Marcus Flint
Gregory Goyle
Terence Higgs
Montague
Pansy Parkinson
Adrian Pucey
Warrington
Blaise Zabini
The Bloody Baron

HUFFLEPUFF (*loyal and hardworking*)

Hannah Abbott
Susan Bones

Cedric Diggory
Justin Finch-Fletchley
Ernie Macmillan
The Fat Friar

RAVENCLAW (*wise and witty, mascot is an eagle*)

Terry Boot
Mandy Brocklehurst
Cho Chang
Penelope Clearwater
Davies
Padma Patil
Lisa Turpin

MAKING THE GRADE

Resembling an aristocratic British boarding school (with the exception of being coeducational), Hogwarts shelters students who attend there. The wizard school values the students because they have magical abilities, as noted by Hogwarts' magical quill at the time of their birth, that need to be developed. They are not accepted because of their family's wealth and prestige. Although some students, such as Draco Malfoy, feel entitled by their financial fortune and illustrious pedigree, most of the student body admire each other's aptitude and character. Hogwarts students realize they need to study diligently to pass class examinations and achieve recognition for their wizardry in order to advance professionally. In addition to developing self-discipline with their individual work, the students also learn to cooperate through teamwork.

Hogwarts students are expected to respect specific standards whether the rules are written or implied; occasionally the rules are contrary to standards in the Muggle community. Obedience, more than conformity, is the primary goal of these directives. Although the students at Hogwarts are stressed by schoolwork and worries concerning losing Quidditch matches and house points and being assigned detention, they do not usually retaliate through the use of magical violence directed against their peers or enemies. Some students, particularly the Weasley twins, enjoy playing pranks and practical jokes.

THE CURRICULUM

The teachers at Hogwarts range from good instructors (McGonagall) to ineffective instructors (Lockhart) to those with traits somewhere in between (Snape). Hogwarts could be considered a charm school, not only teaching students how to cast spells but also insisting they master etiquette, such as using titles when addressing professors. The Hogwarts classes are quite different than what Harry's first cousin, Dudley Dursley, probably studies at his exclusive school named Smeltings. Harry and his classmates learn how to mix potions, defend themselves against evil beings, and nurture magical plants.

Literature and mathematics, standard Muggle courses, are

not part of the Hogwarts curriculum while ancient languages and alchemy are core subjects. However, there are many parallels to the Muggle world: British boarding school students are required to wear uniforms and formal robes resembling Harry's wizard garb; they study in sometimes rustic classrooms; observe precise protocol to greet teachers and schoolmates in public; purchase specific items required by the school at specialty shops that have served previous generations of alumni; and are frequently conveyed by a chartered school train or bus to campus and their dormitory rooms.

While Muggle pupils master calculus, Hermione struggles with arithmancy which involves the use of numerals for divination as developed by the ancient Greeks. Ironically, Hermione has difficulty with her divination class in which Professor Trelawney relies on tea leaves and crystal balls. With study and practice, Hermione, however, seems to master arithmancy techniques. While the examination of abstract information flusters her, Hermione can deal with concrete facts such as totaling the values of letters in a name to make a prediction.

Like other English schoolchildren, the Hogwarts students worry about passing examinations to move up to a higher grade. At age eleven, English students move from primary to secondary school status, much like Hogwarts receives first-year students when they are eleven years old. The pre-Hogwarts educational experiences of students, especially for those who know they are wizards or witches, is not described. When English children complete the fifth year of secondary school, they take tests that determine if they are permitted to continue their education at higher levels and prepare for university admissions examinations. College degrees are designated by each student's level of performance. The Ordinary Wizarding Levels examination (O.W.L.s) and other tests at Hogwarts' resemble those their Muggle counterparts complete.

First year students study a core curriculum of Astronomy, Charms, Defense against the Dark Arts, Herbology, History of Magic, Potions, and Transfiguration with an introductory flying class. Second years study all of these classes except Flying. Planning course schedules is important, and during their second year, students carefully choose required courses and electives crucial for future careers. Classes meet once or several times weekly, and students usually have Friday afternoons free. In some courses, pupils are paired with students from another house, such as Gryffindors and Slytherins, taking what is known as Double Potions. The courses help students prepare for O.W.L.s (Ordinary Wizarding Levels) and N.E.W.T.s (Nastily Exhausting Wizarding Tests), the ultimate test at Hogwarts. These tests are vital for professional consideration at the Ministry of Magic and other employers.

PREPARING FOR SCHOOL

Every August, Hogwarts students flock to Diagon Alley's stores, selling both new and secondhand merchandise, to purchase their school supplies. They withdraw wizard gold from Gringotts bank, are measured for robes and wands, and windowshop for fast broomsticks and expensive trinkets. In Book I, Harry receives a list of required items. Hogwarts students wear normal Muggle attire such as t-shirts, jeans, and sneakers, as a wardrobe foundation. For daily activities, these garments are concealed by black robes which resemble academic gowns worn at graduation ceremonies or legal attire worn by judges. Vividly colored robes representing House colors, such as scarlet for Gryffindor, are donned as uniforms during Quidditch matches. Professors wear robes of varying designs and hues that reflect their personalities and interests. To protect them from the frigid winter climate at Hogwarts, students own thick black cloaks. According to Book IV, fourth-year students and above occasionally wear dress robes in varied colors such as emerald and maroon that are embellished with lace and other decorative trim. Female pupils don pastel party robes for formal dances. Sweaters and socks are given as holiday gifts.

Students also buy hats that are pointed like the traditional image of what witches wear in movies and artwork. Fashion accessories include gloves made from rugged materials such as the hides of supernatural creatures. Students wear watches and jewelry to accentuate their magical clothing, and some children, like Harry, wear eyeglasses. Depending on their year of study, students buy appropriate books and tools for their classes and pack their trunks with both necessary supplies and comforting items including toys, scrapbooks, and posters. Their bookbags resemble the backpacks carried by Muggle children but are filled with magical inks and quills in addition to wands and parchment scrolls. Pupils select enchanted pets and messenger owls at specialty stores, or family and friends give animals to children. These pets serve as both companions and helpers.

BETWEEN CLASSES

The Hogwarts hallways and houses are the setting for crucial character interactions that advance plots. Although prefects monitor students' behavior in the corridors, forbidding the use of magic and insisting on orderly, quiet conduct, many pupils use the castle's passages to harass their classmates and engage in practical jokes. Draco Malfoy often taunts Harry when they are walking between rooms in Hogwarts. Students group together to gawk at Harry or giggle at another student's misfortunes or embarassment. They also use the hallways for impromptu pep rallies to cheer their favorite Quidditch players and attempt to lower the morale of sports and academic foes. Harry is cornered in the hallway by the dwarf delivering Ginny's Valentine. Humiliated, Harry tries to escape to the sanctuary of his house and turret dormitory room but is good-naturedly teased by his housemates.

Students either live in turrets that are connected to their house tower or dwell in rooms that branch off of their house dungeon. In these dormitories, they decorate their living space with personal mementoes from home, such as photographs of their family. Trunks are placed next to beds, and furniture stores wardrobes and supplies. Rugs cover cold stone floors. Cats and rats live with their owners in the dormitories, and owls roost in the owlery located in the West Tower. Each house's common room has comfortable chairs and tables for students to study, talk, or play games. Fireplaces provide warmth on chilly nights as well as to soothe frayed nerves when classes become too intense or friendships and rivalries too antagonistic.

Older students often serve as mentors to first-, second-, and third-year pupils as they adjust to the rigors of Hogwarts. Whether advising what classes to take or revealing secret passages, these mentors transfer school traditions while guiding novice wizards and witches. House members support each other through private conversations in the dormitories or public displays of approval at feasts and ceremonies in the Great Hall or victory celebrations on the Quidditch field. At night, wakeful and often agitated students such as Harry, roam the Hogwarts halls to seek answers to mysteries or explore rooms to satisfy their adventurous natures.

Closets and bathrooms conceal students as they undergo physical transformations and also enable them to eavesdrop and learn more about suspicious people and the motives for their mysterious actions. Risking punishment for breaking rules, including ignoring nightly curfews, students perform detention duties when they are caught. Such distasteful tasks, however, sometimes serendipitously provide clues that initiate confrontations and enable resolution of conflicts. When conditions are less chaotic, students find their favorite places on campus to visit and learn, such as the library and greenhouses. Social activities, including Halloween, Christmas, and Easter parties, complement classroom studies to accentuate each student's character development and maturation so they can thrive in the adult wizard world.

OUTSIDE OF CLASS

Students spend mornings and early afternoons in lessons, and bells summon students to and from classes. Late afternoons and evenings are when Quidditch practices are scheduled, and students can visit with each other or do research in the library. After the evening meal, students are expected to remain in their house and are discouraged from roaming the corridors with the threat of detention. Teachers help students plan class schedules to prepare for future careers. Harry and his classmates tend to spend a lot of time healing in the infirmary from magical mishaps. In their dorms, students keep trunks with their belongings (with name tags as directed), including cloaks, wands, and games. Many students have pets that live in the dormitories, and daily pet care is required to nurture those animals. This responsibility helps students gain self accountability.

Hogwarts students bring money to school or budget spending based on the contents of their Gringotts bank account. Wizard money is spent primarily at Hogsmeade on edible treats and holiday gifts for parents and friends. Care packages and letters from home are sent to students. Unlike other teenagers, no mention is made if any of the Hogwarts students work after school at Hogsmeade or on campus. Book IV reveals that house elves perform the kitchen duties and assist with other housekeeping chores around the castle. The school does not seem to have a newspaper or yearbook. With all of the torches for illumination, Rowling has not indicated whether the students would form a fire fighting brigade if necessary. Nor does she explain who launders their robes and clothing. Hogwarts also does not seem to host traditional school competitions such as spelling bees and science fairs.

READING FOR RESEARCH

Chrystie, Frances. *Pets: A Comprehensive Handbook for Kids*. 4th ed. Topeka, KS: Econo-Clad Books, 1999. Valuable reference that explains how to care for all types of pets.

Quigly, Isabel. *The Heirs of Tom Brown: The English School Story London*. Chatto & Windus, 1982. Analyzes fiction depicting British educational experiences and how these stories are similar or differ from literary precedents.

Richards, Jeffrey. *Happiest Days: The Public Schools in English Fiction*. Manchester: Manchester University Press, 1988. Examines how teachers and students are portrayed in children's literature.

INTERNET RESOURCES

United Kingdom Schools
http://dir.yahoo.com/Regional/Countries/United_Kingdom
/Education/Primary_and _Secondary/Schools/

British Broadcasting Corporation Education Guide
http://www.bbc.co.uk/education/webguide

About.com Pet Sites
  http://dogs.about.com
  http://cats.about.com
  http://birds.about.com
  http://exoticpets.about.com

Log on to **www.beachampublishing.com** for many additional projects, discussion questions, writing and research ideas, websites, and bibliography.

CHAPTER 6

FOOD

"I will eat almost anything except tripe."
—J.K. ROWLING

*"I am the President of the United States. I do not have
to eat broccoli if I don't want to."*
— FORMER PRESIDENT GEORGE BUSH

NOURISHING THOUGHTS

Food is abundant in the pages of the Harry Potter series. The characters enjoy eating meals to celebrate birthdays, special occasions, and sports victories. While the Dursleys deprive Harry of basic nutritional needs for a boy his age, they hypocritically overindulge themselves. Although Petunia Dursley is described as thin, her husband and son heartily consume meats and sweets. They are caricatured and stereotyped as obese and swinish with "piggy" eyes and multiple chins. At the zoo, Dudley and his friends devour ice cream sundaes and candy, and Harry gets Dudley's rejected portions. The Dursleys invest in a television for the kitchen so that Dudley does not have to walk from another room for food while watching shows.

Food is often present during antagonistic moments for Harry at the Dursley home, as emphasized by his confrontation with Aunt Marge at dinner. Harry is ordered to fry bacon for Dudley, and Dobby ruins a rich dessert prepared for company. Compared to the Dursleys' metaphorical starvation of Harry, both physical and emotional, Hogwarts nourishes him physically and spiritually. When Hagrid rescues Harry, he offers him sausage and cake to ease his hunger for food and freedom. Hagrid insults Dudley by referring to his excess fat as resembling pudding, and magically giving him a pig's tail to symbolize his greed for food.

The plates at Hogwarts magically fill with an assortment of delicacies, many of which Harry has never seen before even on the Dursleys' table. On the Hogwarts Express, he purchases assorted candies, and Honeydukes at Hogsmeade sells magical sweets both appealing and revolting. Chocolate is considered a remedy for physical reactions to the Dementors.

The annual Christmas feast features cakes and puddings with surprises hidden in them (symbolizing good fortune). Quidditch victories are celebrated through the consumption of food and candy. The post-examination feast promises plenty of appetizers, main courses, and treats. Students bond together while sipping warm mugs of butterbeer. Professor Dumbledore prefers sherbet lemons (Americanized as lemon drops) for which Rowling also admits a fondness. Fudge and treats are given as gifts. The only food which seems unappealing is the rotting fare offered at the Deathday Party and some of the more macabre candies.

At Hogwarts, food is seemingly abundant without any administrative or student concerns about the prices or preparation of meals. Although specific information about culinary staff is not noted, kitchens are mentioned in the text to provide clues about locations of corridors and classrooms.

The Hogwarts meals could truly be described as comfort food. Students never worry about not having access to food, and most menus meet their exact individual appetites. The Hogwarts' diners do not seem concerned with good nutrition. They do not count calories or obsess about their weight. Quidditch players strive to eat well before matches in the hopes of having plentiful energy and strength, much like athletes consume carbohydrates and proteins before marathons and ballgames. Cholesterol and fat grams are not measured. The faculty and students do not address ethical questions about vegetarianism and eating meat.

The fantastical foods and plants at Hogwarts are similar to bioengineered agriculture. Scientists have genetically altered plants and animals to resist diseases and kill harmful insects without chemical vaccines and pesticides. For example, corn stalks grow taller and produce more ears of corn. Cows make more milk. Genetically engineered potatoes meet the production demands of fast food restaurants to make billions of french fries. Environmentalists question how biotechnology might hurt the land and atmosphere, and biotechnology has become a major issue in international politics and diplomacy. Many farmers have begun to farm organically with minimal use of chemicals and to plant heirloom seeds which are like those used by people centuries ago, somewhat like vegetables grown in gardens at Hogwarts (see Chapter 12, Science).

READING FOR RESEARCH

Mladen, Davidovic. *Traditional Food from Scotland: The Edinburgh Book of Plain Cookery Recipes.* New York: Hippocrene Books, 1996. Contains recipes native to the Hogwarts and Hogsmeade setting.

Rockwell, Lizzy. *Good Enough to Eat: A Kid's Guide to Food and Nutrition.* New York: Harpercollins, 1999. Essential information about the role of nutrition.

Trager, James. *The Food Chronology: A Food Lover's Compendium of Events and Anecdotes, from Prehistory to the Present.* New York: Henry Holt, 1995. Tells about the history of food in society and customs related to eating.

Vezza, Diane Simone. *Passport on a Plate: A Round-the-World*

Cookbook for Children. Illustrated by Susan Greenstein. New York: Simon & Schuster, 1997. Recipes representing foods favored by diverse cultures.

INTERNET SOURCES

The Food Museum
http://www.foodmuseum.com/hughes/main.htm

Simply Food Chocolate Site
http://www.simplyfood.co.uk/chocolate

Tufts University Nutrition Navigator
http://www.navigator.tufts.edu/kids.html

Log on to **www.beachampublishing.com** for many additional projects, discussion questions, writing and research ideas, websites, and bibliography.

CHAPTER 7

SPORTS

"I wanted a sport for wizards, and I'd always wanted to see a game where there was more than one ball in play at the same time. The idea just amused me. The Muggle sport it most resembles is basketball, which is probably the sport I enjoy watching most."
—J.K. ROWLING

THE SPORTING LIFE

The students, both Muggles and wizards, engage in a variety of informal games and competitions. Boys bully and fistfight each other. Girls and boys play games of chess to test their intellectual abilities and symbolize in miniature the power struggles fought by good against evil. Spontaneous snowball fights relieve tension, especially when students aim snowballs at professors, like the Weasley twins did with Quirrell. Games of gobstones, resembling marbles, and other amusements help students relax. Attempts to form a dueling club at Hogwarts were thwarted by rivalries between professors and students, although unofficial bouts occur when insults are exchanged and challenges issued.

The magical game of Quidditch, an aerial sport resembling an amalgam of soccer, basketball, field hockey, lacrosse, dodgeball, rugby, cricket, and polo, is organized and regulated. In some ways it is characteristic of extreme sports that test individuals' physical and mental limits. Quidditch dominates Hogwarts sporting events. Each house has a team, and students enjoy cheering for friends at matches. This team sport has its historical origins in the game of soccer which was first played at English boarding schools, the inspiration for Hogwarts, in the early nineteenth century. By the late 1800s, soccer had spread throughout Great Britain with community teams playing in matches. Associations formed to develop a system to schedule games and award honors to deserving competitors.

Sporting competitions have been popular among humans since ancient times (the Olympic games were started by the ancient Greeks). Sports represented battle. In the Middle Ages, people played Shinty, using a stick to hit a ball, somewhat like a land version of Quidditch. The Aztecs in Mexico played olla-malitzli in which they tossed balls through rings placed high above the field like Quidditch. Tournaments between jousting knights, reminiscent of the racing broomsticks, were prominent during the Middle Ages. As warfare erupted across Europe, an emphasis on military training ended all sporting activity pursued merely for fun. During this time, however, soldiers and prisoners of war participated in some athletic activity to relieve the stresses of combat. As the revolutionary period of the 1700s subsided, interest in sports was revived.

MOUNT YOUR BROOMS

The Quidditch field is a crucial site where the young wizards demonstrate their skills and are permitted to be combative with their foes. Played in an arena somewhat like a soccer field, the wizard sport resembles basketball with goalposts fifty feet high because the players ride broomsticks. Each side has seven players: two Beaters who use clubs to chase the two balls called Bludgers that try to knock players off of their brooms; three Chasers who try to throw the large red ball called the Quaffle through one of the three designated goalposts for their team (a total of six goalposts line the field); a Keeper who guards the goalposts; and the Seeker who chases the elusive Golden Snitch whose capture ends the game and decides the winner. All of these positions and balls' purposes are indicative of personality types and situations the wizards might encounter in life.

Harry excels as a Seeker. He uses his athletic talents to prove that he is capable of more than battling Voldemort. A mediocre student, Harry's prowess on a broomstick balances his average academic performances. Most of his classmates consider him a fabulous player, and professors remark that he reminds them of his father when James Potter played Quidditch at Hogwarts. Because of Harry, Gryffindor House wins its first victories and school cups in seven years, making Harry an instant House hero.

Harry obsesses about playing Quidditch, training and conditioning even when he has greater concerns such as dealing with the fugitive Sirius Black lurking around Hogwarts. Quidditch offers Harry, his teammates, and opposing players many benefits. The players gain self-esteem and self-confidence as they master the sport and are praised for their competence. Because agility and speed are crucial, the players develop endurance, strength, and fitness.

The Gryffindor female players at Hogwarts play the position of Chaser and are often the first people to put the ball in play and score. The Ravenclaw female player, Cho Chang, is also a Seeker like Harry. The only team that does not seem to let girls play, or encourage their playing, are the Slytherins, who even focus their attacks on the Gryffindor female players. The professional (or World Cup level) Quidditch teams such as Ron Weasley's favorite, the Chudley Cannons, include women players.

TEAM SPIRIT

Quidditch players bond together and secure an identity as a cohesive team, as well as appreciating each player's contribution to the group effort. Matches usually provide a form of physical and emotional release from the stresses and monotony of school, or whatever threat Harry is facing.

The game of Quidditch prepares Harry's mind and body for future confrontations with Voldemort and other foes. He copes with deceitful opponents on the field and learns to outsmart and outmaneuver distractions such as the Dementors. Harry endures injuries, losses, and insults as he searches for the Snitch. He learns to follow the game rules even when others ignore them. Harry thinks it is unfair when Draco Malfoy's father furnishes the entire Slytherin squad with swift state-of-the-art broomsticks. The issue of talent versus wealth to accentuate sports performances is hotly debated among the opposing teams.

ON THE SIDELINES

Quidditch matches involve the entire school. Professors serve as referees, while both students and faculty are spectators carrying colorful banners with flashing messages to support their teams. Lee Jordan, as announcer, praises the Gryffindors and chides the Slytherins until Professor McGonagall stops him. Hermione tries to disarm Snape whom she thinks is casting a spell on Harry during a match, and Neville assertively defends himself to Draco Malfoy in a fight underneath the stands. All of the behaviors mimic social relationships and interactions both within the castle and the Muggle world. The action on and off the field heightens suspense by intensifying hostilities, reinforcing loyalties, and moving the plot to another level.

READING FOR RESEARCH

Hutchinson, Roger. *Empire Games: The British Invention of Twentieth-Century Sport.* Edinburgh and London: Mainstream Publishing, 1996. Tells how soccer was introduced in Scottish schools.

Levinson, David, and Karen Christensen, eds. *The Encyclopedia of World Sport: From Ancient Times to the Present.* New York and Oxford: Oxford University Press, 1999. Covers approximately 200 sports, describing their history.

Radnedge, Keir, ed. *The Complete Encyclopedia of Soccer: The Bible of World Soccer.* Hertfordshire: Carlton, Watford, 1999. Provides information about major competitions, players, and statistics.

INTERNET SOURCES

Rugby.com Site
http://www.rugby.com

Soccer
http://www.aron.clara.co.uk

About.com sites for Games and Sport Memorabilia
  http://boardgames.about.com
  http://cardgames.about.com
  http://chess.about.com
  http://sportscards.about.com
  http://worldsoccer.about.com
  the sports page on this site has many other links

Log on to **www.beachampublishing.com** for many additional projects, discussion questions, writing and research ideas, websites, and bibliography.

CHAPTER 8

GEOGRAPHY

"In my imagination, Hogwarts is set in the north of Scotland." —J.K. ROWLING

"We look to Scotland for all our ideas of civilisation." —VOLTAIRE

INTRODUCTION

Even though Harry has transcended boundaries and time periods beyond anyone's expectations, few stories could be more British than Harry's. He is, though much different, the perfect English schoolboy, dedicated to honorably serving his society; he attends the quintessential English boarding school that is as exclusive as Etons; and he is rooted in a geography that has defined the role of the British Isles throughout history. The protective isolation of Britain, and particularly Scotland, has insulated Britain from the rest of tumultuous Europe and provided incubation for developing a culture rich in lore and steeped in tradition. Without its unique geography, Britain would have evolved much differently, and it is useful for serious Potterites to recognize this influence on Harry and his creator.

GEOGRAPHICAL OVERVIEW OF THE BRITISH ISLES

Rowling not only transports her readers to a fantastical, fictional setting, but she also introduces them to real places. Harry was born in England and grew up near London in Little Whinging, a fictional town set in the factual county of Surrey. He attends wizard school in northern Scotland. Both countries geographically are part of The United Kingdom, which includes the countries of England, Wales, Scotland, and Northern Ireland. Neither the Isle of Man nor the Channel Islands are considered part of the United Kingdom because the British Crown, not the British government, has sole jurisdiction over them.

Great Britain and adjacent Ireland are large islands that are part of an archipelago (a group of islands spread across a body of water) known as the British Isles. Located in the Atlantic Ocean, the British Isles are isolated from Europe by the English Channel, the Strait of Dover, and the North Sea. In addition to Great Britain (from the Latin word Britannia as used by Roman invaders), approximately five thousand islands and islets (tiny islands) are in the British Isles. That geographic region has an intriguing history (see Chapter 11, History), vast natural resources, and diverse demographics. In 325 B.C., Pytheas, a Greek navigator, was the first person to explore and document the features of Great Britain's coast. Geographers are interested not only in the physical description of regions but also in learning about the cultural, economic, political, and linguistic characteristics associated with areas. Maps, graphs, and charts document geographical attributes. An awareness of the geographical facts about Great Britain will enhance understanding of the Harry Potter series.

ENGLAND

Derived from the Latin word "Anglia," England comprises the southern half of Great Britain. Containing 130,439 square kilometers (50,363 square miles), England forms 57 percent of Great Britain's landmass. England has been ruled by a monarchy and governed by a hereditary and elected parliament. That country has politically dominated the British Isles throughout history in addition to establishing colonies around the world when imperialism thrived from the eighteenth through the early twentieth centuries.

The English coast fosters the fishing and shipping industries because of its naturally occurring harbors. The abundance of inlets enable seamen to access the ocean and rivers that cross England, their mouths forming estuaries that ocean tides keep filled with sufficient water to create ports to anchor vessels. Inland, western and northern England are mountainous. In central and eastern England, rolling plains form the topography. To the west of central England, the Midlands is home to the Black Country so named because it is industrialized. In the east, the Fens is a marshy area drained of moisture. Moors are located in Cornwall and Devon south of the Bristol Channel. The white chalk hills often shown in movies about England or described in literature are in Devon.

Native animals include deer, rabbits, badgers, and foxes. Birds such as sparrows, crows, and pigeons live in England. Only four species of reptiles can be found in Great Britain. A small percentage of the land is farmed, and woods cover approximately four percent of the country.

The Dursleys travel to London to shop for school clothes and to have Dudley's pig tail surgically removed. Harry and Hagrid go to London to gather school supplies in Diagon Alley, and Harry boards the Hogwarts Express from King's Cross, a real train station in London. The capital of both England and Great Britain, London is located in the southeastern part of the country. The Thames estuary is between London to the west and the North Sea to the east. References to the "City of London" mean the part that was first settled in the first century A.D. by the Romans who built Fort Londinium. London is England's main port and largest city, with almost seven million people.

London is home to a diverse population representing varying professional, social, and cultural interests. People travel by the Underground or "Tube," which is the English subway. Prominent architecture includes the Tower of London, the London Bridge, Big Ben, and Buckingham Palace, and there are numerous museums, cathedrals, art galleries, schools, parks, and theaters. The city has been shaped by historic figures and events like World Wars I and II German bombing raids and the Great Fire of 1666.

SCOTLAND

While London and England represent the more sophisticated and aristocratic side of Great Britain, Scotland symbolizes its mystical and wild nature. Situated on the island's upper third, Scotland's borders meet the Atlantic Ocean and the North Sea to the north and east. In the South, the natural Solway Firth and man-made Hadrian Wall mark the boundary with England. The Irish Sea is to the west, and the North Channel runs between Scotland and Ireland. Scotland has 787 islands, many in the Hebrides (or Western Isles), the Orkney Islands, and the Shetland Islands. Scotland's total area is 78,772 square kilometers (30,414 square miles).

Like England, Scotland has a rough coastline. The inlets, which have deep valleys beneath the surface, are called sea lochs and firths, the Firth of Clyde being one of the most prominent inlets. The country is divided into the Highlands, Central Lowlands, and Southern Uplands. The Highlands, where Hogwarts is probably located, has several mountain chains stretching from the northeast to the southwest. Fewer people live in this region, and the landscape is covered by lochs, thickets, ravines, and valleys.

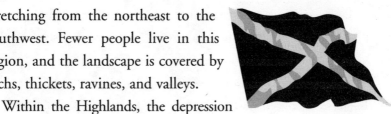

Within the Highlands, the depression known as the Great Glen or Glen More, from Moray Firth to Loch Linnhe, separates two areas. In the north, are weathered peaks, standing as high as 915 meters (3,000 feet). To the south, Scotland's primary mountains, Grampian, includes Ben Nevis, the highest point in Great Britain at 1,343 meters (4,406 feet). The Great Glen has three glacier-carved, land-locked lakes, including the infamous Loch Ness, Great Britain's largest freshwater lake and the alleged home of a monster. The country's population is concentrated in the Central Lowlands, which is hilly and contains the rivers Clyde, Forth, and Tay. The Southern Uplands has a plateau and small mountains composed of sedimentary rock, including the Cheviot Hills adjacent to England.

Native animals include deer (the red deer thriving in the Highlands), rabbits, otters, and wildcats. Golden eagles nest in Scotland and hunt for trout, herring, and salmon. Coal and zinc deposits provide raw materials, and most soil is unsuitable for agriculture. Sheep and cattle graze in rocky fields, and farmers grow wheat, potatoes, oats, and turnips. Natural gas, coal, and petroleum are leading Scottish exports.

Ethnically, Scottish people are descended from groups that settled Scotland or invaded the area, including the Romans, Scandinavians, Celts, and Picts. Within Scotland, people are referred to as Highlanders or Lowlanders, with the first group perceiving themselves as representing Celtic tradition and feeling allegiances to traditional clans, while the latter group are associated more with Teutonic (German) ancestry.

The governmental center is located at Edinburgh which, with approximately 500,000 residents, is second in size to Glasgow, which has a population approaching 700,000. A major port, Glasgow is home to shipbuilding and related industries. Dundee is also another major urban center. Edinburgh retains historic characteristics, including a castle, courtyards, and winding streets. The state church is the Church of Scotland. Scottish people are devout Catholics, Episcopalians, and other Protestant denominations with few Jews living in that country. Some residents of the Highlands and islands speak a Scottish Gaelic dialect. People in the lowlands speak Scots, resembling a mixture of English, French, and Gaelic. Most schools are managed by local educational authorities, and children transfer from elementary to secondary status at age twelve.

Scottish festivals include the New Year's holiday of Hogmanay, which sounds like a Hogwarts-appropriate celebration. Other holidays involve feasting on delicious foods like spice-and-fruit-filled hot cross buns. Informal bouts of handball and football, sometimes referred to as Ba' Games, are played on holidays. Other Scottish traditions are reminiscent of life at Hogwarts. Shortly after midnight on January 1, some Scots participate in "first footing," which involves visiting friends, much like Harry moves around the castle at night. The first of April brings Hunt the Gowk, in which people pull pranks of sending friends on silly errands. On April 2, Preentail Day involves people attaching paper tails to individuals' backs, somewhat like Hagrid giving Dudley a pig tail. In the fall, All Hallows Day, All Souls Day, and Guy Fawkes events all resemble activities or characters at Hogwarts.

Highland Games, in Scotland as well as other geographical locations, feature athletic and dancing competitions. Although clans are no longer powerful military and political forces, many Scottish people retain allegiances to their family groups. The sports of golf and curling were created in Scotland, and bagpipes are a national symbol. Medieval castles are scattered throughout Scotland.

WALES, IRELAND, EUROPE, AND POINTS BEYOND

References to areas outside of Great Britain are made in the Potter novels. The Weasley brothers are employed in Europe and Africa. Charlie Weasley works in Romania, studying dragons. Transylvania, a region in that country, is often associated with vampires, evil, and dark magic. Bill Weasley is employed at the African Gringotts bank in Egypt, an African country sometimes identified with magic and wizardry. The Knight Bus travels through Wales. Several of Harry's classmates, such as Seamus Finnigan, probably are from Ireland because of their names and accents.

Hermione Granger and her parents vacation in France, and the Weasleys spend their prize money on a trip to Egypt to visit Bill. Some Quidditch referees are cursed to exile in the Sahara Desert. The boa constrictor at the zoo escaped and planned to go to its homeland of Brazil. The Dursleys want to buy a second home in Majorca, a Spanish resort island where Aunt Petunia's friend Yvonne visited. Aunt Marge sends the Dursleys a postcard from

 the Isle of Wight, a vacation spot in the English Channel. Magical creatures come from both remote and familiar parts of the world such as Germany's Black Forest. Azkaban is in the North Sea. Sirius Black and Buckbeak are hiding out probably in a warm place according to Rowling. And Voldemort is rumored to be somewhere in Central Europe.

The Knight Bus could have easily popped into Wales, which is located west of England. Anglesey Island is part of Wales, and the total area of the country is 20,768 square kilometers (8,019 square miles). Divided into counties, Wales' topography resembles that of England, with lakes, rivers, bays, marshes, valleys, and mountains. Polecats and pine martens live in Wales but not England. The climate, industry, and population ethnicity are similar to England's. Approximately three million people live in Wales, mostly in mining communities. The capital at Cardiff is Wales' main harbor. An outcropping known as King Arthur's Stone is on Gower Peninsula in West Glamorgan.

Irish students would be within a day's travel to Hogwarts. Ireland consists of two political divisions: Northern Ireland and the Republic of Ireland. Lowlands, plains, and mountains describe Irish topography, and rivers such as the Shannon are formed by connected lakes. Peat bogs and estuaries also exist. Most indigenous animals are extinct except for rodents and birds. No snakes are native to Ireland. The island is divided by contrasting religious beliefs. The Republic of Ireland has a Catholic majority of its citizens. Northern Ireland is primarily Protestant, and political strife, often resulting in deadly violence, has occurred for centuries between Protestants and Catholics.

READING FOR RESEARCH

Brockliss, Laurence, and David Eastwood, eds. *A Union of Multiple Identities: The British Isles, c1750-c1850.* Manchester: Manchester University Press, 1997. Describes national characteristics of England, Scotland, Wales, and Ireland and how those countries formed a group identity.

Johnson, Sylvia A. *Mapping the World.* New York: Atheneum Books, 1999. Brief history of cartography for children.

Turnock, David. *The Making of the Scottish Rural Landscape.* Aldershot, Hants, England: Scolar Press, 1995. Geographical study of how humans have used land in Scotland.

INTERNET RESOURCES

United Kingdom for Visitors
  http://gouk.about.com/

Gateway to Scotland
  http://www.geo.ed.ac.uk/home/scotland/scotland.html

Scottish Culture
  http://scottishculture.about.com

Log on to **www.beachampublishing.com** for many additional projects, discussion questions, writing and research ideas, websites, and bibliography.

CHAPTER 9

MYTHOLOGY, LEGENDS, AND FAIRY TALES

"A mythology doesn't come from the head; a mythology comes from the heart." —JOSEPH CAMPBELL

"Nurture your minds with great thoughts. To believe in the heroic makes heroes." —BENJAMIN DISRAELI

Introduction

Literary critics look for myths, legends, archetypes, and symbols because they know that these are the devices that subconsciously influence readers. In good literature, plot provides a structure through which subconscious influences can operate. Plot can evoke deep emotions in readers, but it cannot achieve a profound impact without tapping into our mythic subconscious. Harry's forehead has been branded with a lightening bolt, the primal symbol of fear produced by the most ferocious of gods, Zeus. Harry had been marked as an outsider who must fulfill some quest to explain his mark. Marking people for death is an ancient rite, and whether readers recognize it through Passover, the holocaust, The Scarlet Letter, *or branding cattle, the pain and power of the mark itself, and the consequences it foreshadows becomes a fearsome symbol. That Harry's mark is a lightening bolt hurtled his way by warring deities makes him an even more persuasive victim/hero entangled in a destiny he cannot escape. As Rowling superimposes layer upon layer of myths and their symbols, she creates a depth of instinctual response that turns readers inward to ask themselves questions far more important than the next twist in the plot.*

FANTASY FRAMEWORK

Giants and trolls, heroes and villains, spells and charms alert readers to the fantastical elements of the novels. These characters, objects, and expressions have their roots in mythology, legends, and fairy tales. Myths are stories that reflect cultural beliefs and traditions through symbolism; they also convey meanings that help people comprehend their environments. Connecting diverse groups who share universal concerns, myths offer explanations for such fundamental questions as how the universe was created or why death occurs. Myths can be presented orally or as art, games, dances, or rites such as ceremonies designed to improve the fertility of agricultural fields.

Myths—such as how ancient people believed the world was created— are usually set in a time separate from and preceding known human history and usually include supernatural elements. Such phenomenal factors provide clues about primitive religious practices of ancient people (see Chapter 10, Archetypes and Biblical Allusions). Scholars have interpreted the meaning, purpose, and application of myths differently based on their personal philosophies and intellectual and socioeconomic trends of the era in which they live. Many researchers have focused on how myths conflict with the logic of reason and history. Others examine the psychological and spiritual functions of mythology. Mythologists are interested in documenting the origins of tales and comparing adaptations as well as exploring the values and beliefs communicated in the stories and how they inspire creativity and imagination through retelling the original story.

Similarly, legends—such as Robin Hood— chronicle stories about heroes and villains who seem to be historically true but whose facts are not easily verifiable, causing listeners and readers to be unsure about their authenticity. Unlike legends, fairy tales are obviously fictional and their origins are unknown. The stories often are designed purposely to be misleading so that readers will be surprised by the plot's outcome. Fairy tales contain elements of truth and popular opinion. Related fictional forms include folklore, which is orally transmitted, and fables which are stories, often narrated by an animal, to emphasize a moral lesson or warn of danger. Like fairy tales, fables sometimes are intentionally deceiving to stress the dangers of evil. Tall tales exaggerate situations to emphasize the stories' objectives.

The study of mythology and its associated variations is complex. Literary scholars study how myth and legend are incorporated into fiction. Thousands of mythological characters, places, objects, situations, and motifs could be compared to similar components of the Potter series. The information in this chapter is intended to provide readers with basic ideas about recognizing such parallels and initiating further analysis and understanding of the mythological and legendary aspects of the Potter novels. Mythology is a vast subject and related to several other topics concerning the Potter series (see Chapter 3, Characters; Chapter 4, Setting; Chapter 10, Archetypes and Biblical Allusions; Chapter 11, History; and Chapter 14, Literary Qualities; and Appendix B).

PATTERNS AND MOTIFS

The fundamental Harry Potter plot is universal, appealing to humanity's mythic core and collective imagination. Characters, places, and events have their origins in fairy tales and fables that reiterate cosmic messages and cautionary tales. Harry is a powerful child hero, even stronger than Dumbledore, who outlasts a seemingly unconquerable villain (for discussion of the hero archetype, see Chapter 12, Archetypes and Biblical Allusions). Most myths have a similar structure of a protagonist like Harry who undergoes a quest, fights evil, and restores order from chaos.

The mythical hero might be uncertain of victory against monsters that initially appear animalistic but usually are proven to be controlled by a human. In Books I, II, and III, Harry faces animal foes—Fluffy, the basilisk, and the Grim—who are facades for a human opponent—Professor Quirrell, Tom Riddle, and Sirius Black. In the latter case, when Harry realizes that Black is actually an ally, Scabbers is exposed in his human form. The hero often suffers an injury or illness during his quest, and Harry's stomach is always queasy or he has an unquenchable thirst, which suggests that he must endure chronic sickness until he has defeated Voldemort. Sometimes the hero visits the underworld, such as Harry's descent to the chambers.

Mythologist Joseph Campbell asserted that in addition to subduing the seemingly impossible, a mythical hero must share aspects of the readers' cultures. Harry's innocence, vulnerability, and determination are traits recognizable to people throughout the world. Campbell believed that the mythical hero must become integrated as part of a group and realize his or her role in that society. Harry accepts his position as Hogwarts' crusader against evil and Gryffindor's Seeker of victory. He also meets Campbell's fourth criteria of acquiring self knowledge and maturing during his ordeals. By doing so, readers identify with Harry's experiences and recognize parallels in their lives. Such personal association is strengthened through the recognition of

motifs which are symbols or ideas that reinforce overall meanings and themes in the series. Recurring motifs in the Potter
novels include invisibility, identity, impostors, and invasion.
Other mythical symbols and themes include storms, magical
animals that guide mortals, a search for parents and self, hidden
messages, repressed memories, and reversals of fortunes.

THE MYTHOLOGY GAME: CAN YOU FIND WHERE HARRY CAME FROM?

The following list contains a brief description of characters
and elements from classical (Greek and Roman) and Norse
(Scandinavian)mythology, the legends about King Arthur, and
fairy tales collected by the Brothers Grimm. These are but a few
of the hundreds of mythical allusions in the Harry Potter novels. See if you can recognize any parallels in the Potter novels to
these characters and situations before you read the analysis that
follows this list. Make your own list of any additional mythical
characters you think relate to the novels.

— Classical Mythology —

Achilles: The bravest of Greek warriors, his mother plunged
him into the River Styx (see below), which made him invincible
except for his heel where she held him. Knowing that he would
perish in the Trojan War, she disguised him as a woman and sent
him into hiding. Through trickery, the commander of the Greek
army, Odysseus, discovered Achilles and sent him to the war where
he killed Hector, the champion of the enemy. In a highly disre-

spectful act, Achilles dragged Hector behind a chariot to the Greek ships. Later, he was wounded in his vulnerable heel and died.

Apollo: Son of Zeus and Leto. One of the most beautiful of the gods, he is the musician (playing the lyre with which he is often depicted) of the deities, master archer, and healer (he taught men the art of healing). He is God of Light (he is associated with the sun), and God of Truth (he never spoke falsely). He killed the frightful serpent-monster Python with a silver arrow after a severe battle.

Argus: A monster with a hundred eyes who was slain when Zeus lulled him to sleep with a lyre.

Athena (*Minerva in Roman mythology*): Born full grown out of Zeus' head, she is the fierce and ruthless goddess of battle. She is the protector of civilized life, goddess of handicrafts and agriculture, and the tamer of horses for use by men (she invented the bridle). She carried her father's devastating weapon, the thunderbolt, but she is also regarded as the goddess of wisdom, reason, and purity. Her temple is the Parthenon, the owl her bird, and the olive (which she created) is her tree.

Cerberus: Hades' (see below) dog who prevented the living from descending into the infernal regions of Hades, and to prevent the dead from escaping. A terrible beast with three to fifty heads (depending on the legend), anyone wishing to pass by him had to appease him with a bribe. Orpheus (see below) lulled him to sleep with his lyre.

Daedalus: Ingenious Athenian craftsman who invented and constructed a labyrinth on the island of Crete to contain the fiercesome Minotaur (see below). When Daedalus fell out of favor with King Minos, he was imprisoned in his own labyrinth, from which he could only escape by flying. He invented wings for himself and his son Icarus (see below) made of wax. Icarus disobeyed his father's instructions not to fly too close to the sun and drowned when his wings melted, but Daedalus survived and went safely to Sicily.

Echo: Hera, chief goddess, believing that her husband Zeus was in love with a nymph, encountered Echo, whose bright chatter charmed her. Not finding Zeus' nymph, Hera decided to punish Echo by taking her voice away. However, Hera said, when someone spoke to Echo, she would have the last word. Echo fell deeply in love with Narcissus (see below) but because she could not speak to him, she could never attract his attention. In shame, she banished herself to a lonely cave.

Hades (*Pluto in Greek mythology*): Brother of Zeus and Poseidon, he is ruler of the nether (under) world. Wishing to marry Persephone, a virgin goddess of great beauty, against her mother's will, he carried her off as she was gathering flowers. He made her queen of the under world, named "Hades" after its ruler. Hades is depicted by Homer as a gloomy, sunless abode where the ghosts of the dead fly around like bats. The entrance to Hades is guarded by five impenetrable rivers (see "Styx" below).

Helen: Daughter of Zeus and Leda, Helen is the most beautiful woman in the world. Through trickery and by breaking his oath, Paris abducted Helen and took her to Troy, which started the ten year Trojan War.

Hercules: Son of Zeus and Alcmena. After Hercules' birth, Hera sent two serpents to devour him but he crushed them with his hands. He became the most valiant of men, but was tormented by Hera who drove him to madness. As atonement for killing his children, he submitted himself to twelve labors to benefit mankind. After his death by a poison cloak, given to him by his wife, he obtained divine honors for his good works.

Hermione: Daughter of Helen (see above). Hermione's father, Menelaus, promised Hermione in marriage first to Orestes before the Trojan war, and then to Neoptolemus (Achilles' son) during the war. She married Neoptolemus but bore him no children. Upon his death she married Orestes and had one son. Hermione also is a character in William Shakespeare's *A Winter's Tale* and John Milton's *Paradise Lost.*

Icarus: Son of Daedalus, who disobeyed his father's instructions, flew too close to the sun, fell to the sea, and drowned.

Janus: One of the oldest Roman gods, Janus is represented as having two faces, one looking forward and the other backwards (the month of January is named for him). He is credited with inventing the uses of money (Roman coins had his effigy on them). In times of war, the Temple of Janus was left open so he could assist the Romans.

Mars (*Ares in Greek mythology*): God of war and son of Zeus and Hera, both of whom detested him. According to the Greek account, he is a murderous coward who bellows with pain and runs away when he is wounded. The Romans admired him and depicted him in shining armor. His bird is the vulture and the dog his chosen animal.

Medusa: One of the three deadly Gorgons whose gaze

killed men by turning them into stone. Instead of hair, her head was covered with deadly snakes. With the help of the gods who loaned him a helmet that made him invisible, a belt buckle that served as a mirror (so he wouldn't have to look directly at Medusa's gaze), and wings for his feet, Perseus cut off Medusa's head.

Minotaur: Born from the union of a white bull and a mortal woman, this monster required the yearly sacrifice of youths and maidens from Athens. Finally confined in a labyrinth designed by Daedalus (see above), the Minotaur was eventually conquered by Theseus.

Narcissus: A beautiful youth, he saw his image reflected in a fountain and fell in love with himself. He would have nothing to do with the nymphs who desired him, and the goddess Nemesis vowed to avenge the scorned maidens. As Narcissus admired himself in a pool, he pined away and died. The nymphs whom he had scorned looked for his body but found only a new and beautiful flower which they named for him, the narcissus. It was this flower that Persephone was picking when Hades (see above) caused the earth to open, swallowing her to the under world.

Odysseus (*Ulysses in Roman mythology*): Bound by oath to protect Helen, he led the Greek expedition to reclaim her when she went with Paris to the city of Troy. After ten years, the Greeks won the war by tricking the Trojans with a wooden horse, and Odysseus attempted to return home to his wife Penelope (see below). His ships were blown off course, and for seven years he wandered the world, eventually finding his way home.

Olympus: Original legends held that the gods dwelled on

top of Mt. Olympus, the highest mountain in Greece, but this idea evolved into Olympus being in some mysterious region far above the mountain. The entrance to Olympus was a great gate of clouds maintained by the Seasons.

Pan: Inventor of the flute, Pan was a wonderful musician who created merriment everywhere he went, especially in woodlands, thickets, forests, and mountains. Part man, part goat, he has a goat's horns and a goat's feet. He played sweet melodies to attract nymphs whom he loved, but they always rejected him because he was so ugly.

Pandora: The first mortal woman, who was made of clay at the request of Zeus and who was endowed by each of the gods with a special gift. In revenge of Prometheus, who had stolen fire from Zeus and given it to mortals, Zeus gave Pandora a box full of evil spirits, believing she would marry Prometheus and the evil would be released upon him. Instead, she married another man, who opened the box and released all the evil upon the world.

Pegasus: A winged horse sprung from the blood of Medusa (see above) when Perseus cut off her head. Tamed by Minerva (see above) or Neptune (also called Poseidon, see below), Pegasus was given to Bellerophon to conquer the Chimera of whom Medusa was one (see above). When Bellerophon tried to fly to heaven upon Pegasus, Zeus sent a fly to torment the horse, causing the fall of his rider.

Penelope: Daughter of Icarus (see above), she was courted by many suitors when it was believed that her husband Odysseus (see above) would not return from the Trojan War. In order to forestall the suitors, she said she would choose a husband from among them when she had finished weaving a tapestry. Each

night she would unravel the
work she had completed during
the day in hopes that her husband
would return.

Persephone: Daughter of Zeus
and Demeter, she was abducted by
Hades (see above) to become queen of
the under world. Demeter, not know-
ing where she was, wandered the world seeking her. Out of pity
for Demeter's torment, Zeus allowed Persephone to spend six
months on Earth and six months in the under world. She is thus
associated with spring and summer, rebirth, and crop fertility.

Poseidon (*Neptune in Roman mythology*): Zeus' brother and
the second most powerful god, Poseidon is ruler of the sea,
where he had a magnificent undersea palace. Master of horses
(he gave the first horse to man), he calmed the seas by driving
his golden chariot over the waters. He is always depicted with
his three-pronged spear, which he uses to create storms at sea.

Romulus: The legendary founder of Rome and the son of
Mars (see above), Romulus and his twin brother Remus were
thrown into the Tiber river in an attempt to kill them at birth.
They were rescued and raised by a she-wolf, eventually conquered their foes, and laid the foundation for the city of Rome
that would become the capital of the western world.

Satyrs: Like Pan (see above), Satyrs were goat men, with the
ears, tail, and budding horns of a goat, although they were
sometimes represented with the tail and ears of a horse. They
were the companions of the god of wine, Dionysus, and thus
contributed to the merriment of festive occasions.

Sibyl: A fortune teller who asked for eternal life but forgot to ask for eternal youth. The sibyl usually wrote her prophecies on leaves which she left at the opening of caves.

Sileni: Part man, part horse, they walked on two legs, unlike the satyrs (see above) who walked on four legs. They are depicted on Greek vases, sometimes with horses' ears and always with horses' tails.

Sphinx: In the Greek legend, the sphinx is a monster with a woman's bust and a lion's body. She liked to find mortals, present them with riddles they could not answer, and devour them. She swore to kill herself if anyone could answer her riddle, "what animal walks on four legs in the morning, two legs at noon, and three in the evening." Oedipus correctly answered it ("man") and saved his kingdom.

Styx: One of five rivers separating the underworld from Earth, Styx possesses the water that the gods used to seal oaths, and whose waters possess magical powers (see Achilles above). Acheron, the river of woe, pours into Cocytus, the river of lamentation. An ancient boatman named Charon ferries the souls of the dead across these rivers where they will either be condemned to torment or sent on to bliss in the Elysian Fields, which is a heavenly place of perpetual happiness.

Thor: The Norse god of thunder and of the home, he presided over the weather and crops. His hammer, like Zeus' thunderbolt, created thunder. The English word "Thursday" is derived from his name.

Titans: The generation of gods before Zeus, the Titans were of enormous size and strength. Cronus (or Saturn) was chief of the Titans until Zeus, his son, dethroned him (this time is called "the twilight of the gods") and established a new generation of gods.

Venus (*Aphrodite in Greek mythology*): She is said either to be the daughter of Zeus and Dione, or to have sprung from the foam of the sea (there is a famous painting by Botticelli of Venus ascending from a shell). One of the Muses, she is the goddess of love and beauty who enjoys laughter. She moves in radiant light, and without her presence there is no joy. In some accounts, she is treacherous and malicious, especially as she deceives men. The myrtle is her tree, and the dove, sparrow, or swan her bird.

Vulcan (*Hephaestus in Greek mythology*): Although the only ugly god, and lame, he is kindly and peace loving. He makes armor, furnishings, and weapons for the gods, with the help of his handmaidens whom he forged out of gold. His workshop is said to be under a volcano, which he causes to erupt when his forge is hot. He is married to one of the three Muses, Venus (see above).

Zeus: Supreme ruler, Lord of the Sky, rain god and cloud gatherer, Zeus wielded the awful thunderbolt. He used lightning to express anger at his subjects and humans, and to secure their attention. His wife, Hera, jealous of the many children fathered by Zeus, often sought to deceive him and harass his children and their mothers.

— British Legends —

Arthur, King: Possibly derived from a blending of a chieftain from the fifth or sixth centuries and a Celtic god, the Arthurian legend evolved in both Britain and France over several centuries, adding such elements as the Knights of the Roundtable,

Arthur's betrayal by Lancelot and Guinevere, and Merlin's magic.

Beowulf: The hero from a tenth century poem, Beowulf wounds the monster Grendel and pursues Grendel's mother, a witch, back to her cave which is reached under water. Using an old sword, made by giants, that he finds in the cave, and protected by woven armor and God, he beheads both the witch and Grendel. Warned not to be boastful about his accomplishment, he surrenders the gifts the king has given him, returns to his home land, and receives part of the kingdom.

Brigadoon: Based on a mythical German village called Germelshausen in a story written by Friedrich Gerstäcker. The village was cursed to never change and to remain invisible. A musical and movie based on a book by Alan Jay Lerner changed the setting to the fictional Scottish community of Brigadoon which was enchanted long ago. Lerner may have been inspired by the thirteenth-century stone Brig o' Doon, the bridge Tam o'Shanter crossed to flee from witches. In the play, outsiders could see Brigadoon only one day every century, but any native who decided to leave Brigadoon would cause the magic to end, and everyone would die. If visitors chose to stay, they abandoned their modern lifestyles.

Excalibur: King Arthur's sword which he either drew out of a stone or which was given to him by Vivien, the Lady of the Lake (see below). When Arthur was mortally wounded, he ordered that Excalibur be thrown into the water; a hand rose from the water, caught the sword, and vanished.

Gawain and the Green Knight: Gawain beheads the Green

Knight, who picks up his head and instructs Gawain to meet him next Christmas Eve in a great castle, at which time he resists temptation by the Lord's wife, and is wounded by the Lord, but his life is spared.

Grendel: A monster who invades the beer hall, carries off thirty of the men, and haunts the hall for twelve more years, killing as he pleases. Beowulf (see above) is summoned to the country and battles both Grendel and his mother.

Guinevere: The best known legend of Guinevere is told by Alfred Lord Tennyson in "Idylls of the King" (1859), in which she declares her shame for betraying her husband and king through her love affair with Launcelot, exiles herself to a nunnery, meditates on her sin, falls prostrate at Arthur's feet, and spends the rest of her life heart-broken and contrite.

Launcelot: Stolen in childhood by Vivien, Lady of the Lake (see below), she returns him to the court of King Arthur when he reaches manhood to sow discord. Initially Arthur's most valiant and trusted knight, Launcelot and Queen Guinevere, King Arthur's wife, fall in love and betray their king. When their tryst is discovered, she is sentenced to die at the stake, but at the last moment Launcelot carries her off. Pursued by King Arthur and Sir Gawain (see above), Launcelot returns Guinevere to the king.

Merlin: Several accounts over several centuries explain Merlin in differing ways. The son of the devil in one legend and King Arthur's father in another, Merlin evolves as the young Arthur's tutor and mentor, and the king's magician. In Alfred Lord Tennyson's "Idylls of the King" (1859), Vivien induces Merlin to take refuge from a storm in an old oak tree, and entraps him there spellbound.

Percival: One of King Arthur's Knights of the Round Table, Percival's best known legend is his quest of the Holy Grail.

Shangri-la: Described in James Hilton's *Lost Horizon,* this is where people enjoy neverending peace and youthfulness.

Vivien, the Lady of the Lake: A supernatural figure, Vivien is depicted as sometimes benevolent toward King Arthur and sometimes malicious. The magician Merlin falls in love with her, and she variously entraps him or uses him to carry out her wicked schemes.

Vortigern: A legendary fifth century king of Britain who allegedly usurped the crown by inviting the warring Jutes tribe to England to help him overthrow the local Picts tribe. But after he married Rowena, daughter of the Jutes' leader, the Jutes refused to leave and overran the country. In the Arthurian legend, Vortigen planned to kill Merlin (see above), but his evil ultimately destroyed him.

Xanadu: A magnificent Chinese city founded by Kublai Khan in 1256, containing 108 temples, a walled inner city, and a large park. Made famous by the journals of Marco Polo, Xanadu became a symbol of imagination and utopia in Samuel Taylor Coleridge's poem fragment, "Kublai Khan."

— Fairy Tales —

Alice (*in Wonderland*): A little girl who dreams that she pursues a White Rabbit down a rabbit hole and there meets with strange adventures and odd characters, including the Duchess, the Cheshire Cat, the Mad Hatter, the King and Queen of Hearts, and the Mock Turtle. In the Looking-Glass House she finds the live chessmen, meets Tweedledum and Tweedledee, and Humpty Dumpty. The story ends with Alice shrinking the Red Queen into a kitten.

Anancy: A West Indian trickster character who most frequently appears as a spider in folklore and usually tries to outwit humans that he encounters.

Beauty (*from "Beauty and the Beast"*): An attractive young woman who falls in love with and unconditionally accepts the grotesque-appearing Beast. A prince who was cursed, he is gentle and generous to Beauty. He transforms back into his princely form and marries his beloved Beauty.

Cinderella: The step child of a wicked stepmother, Cinderella is forced into unreasonable labor while her step sisters are given luxuries. By magic, Cinderella attends the prince's ball but is told she must leave by midnight. When the clock strikes, she is transformed back into her servile condition, but the prince finds her shoe, a slipper, and searches throughout his kingdom for the foot that fits the slipper.

Grimm Brothers: German linguists, they recorded fairy tales never written down and analyzed the psychological messages the tales contained. Their tales have shaped all children's literature and inspired the German Romantic and English Victorian authors of adult literature. *Grimm's Fairy Tales* have subsequently been interpreted by twentieth century psychologists as the basic expression of a child's imagination, especially the elements of violence and evil.

Hansel and Gretel: Lost in the woods, these children find a gingerbread house that is the home of a wicked witch. Captured and threatened with their lives, the children eventually find their way to safety by following a trail of bread-crumbs that Hansel has dropped.

Little Red Riding Hood: Taking a cake to her grandmother, she encounters a wolf who learns of her mission, gets to grandmother's house ahead of her, eats the grandmother, gets in the grandmother's bed, impersonates the grandmother, and ultimately eats Red Riding Hood. In the German version of this French tale, the wolf coughs up the girl and she is saved.

Rumpelstiltskin: From one of Grimm's fairy tales, he is a goblin who taught the miller's daughter how to spin straw into gold for his own greed. When she asked how long she must work for him, he replied until she guessed his name, which he believed was impossible. He tore himself in two when she correctly guessed it.

Sleeping Beauty: The king's daughter, Sleeping Beauty is hexed to die by a spiteful fairy but another fairy converts the death hex to a hundred years sleep. In due course, a prince comes to awaken her with a kiss.

Snow White: A beautiful girl whose jealous stepmother, the queen, plotted to murder her because a magical mirror said that Snow White was the fairest in the land. Snow White escapes into a forest. Seven dwarfs rescue and nurture Snow White. The queen learns that Snow White is still alive and tries to kill her three times by using disguises. Snow White eats a poisoned apple and is kept in a glass coffin because everyone thinks she is dead. A prince falls in love with her and takes the coffin to his castle. Snow White awakens when a servant slaps her and an apple chunk is forced from her throat.

— Mythical Objects, Beasts, and Ceremonies —

Stone of Destiny: A block of sandstone that traveled around Europe and Egypt before arriving in Scotland in the ninth century, the stone was used in the coronation ceremony of Scottish royalty to identify the true king. It was located at the castle at Scone before English King Edward I stole it in the thirteenth century and placed the stone at Westminster Abbey. Scottish Nationalists seized the Stone of Destiny in 1950. The stone has been displayed at Edinburgh Castle since 1996.

Blarney stone: In the Castle of Blarney, in County Cork of Ireland, there is a stone that is difficult to reach. Legend holds that anyone who kisses the Blarney Stone will be given the art of flattery and telling lies.

Pooka: A Celtic sprite which represents both fertility and fear. Considered a trickster, a Pooka is a source for the word "boogeyman" and was derived from the name of the central European nature god Boga who was like Pan (see above). The Pooka sometimes appears as a sinister black dog.

Lindworms: Dragons with a snake-like body with two legs and unable to fly. Thirteenth-century adventurer Marco Polo claimed that he had seen lindworms on the Central Asian steppes.

Loch Ness monster: A large creature that is believed to live in Scotland's Loch Ness in the Highlands. Discussed in local legends for centuries, this sea serpent is considered an omen of misfortune. Scientists have used sonar to try to prove that the monster exists and have speculated that it is either an unknown type of animal or a prehistoric species believed to have been extinct.

ANALYSIS OF THE
MYTHOLOGICAL ALLUSIONS

— Potter As Myth —

The Harry Potter series includes both direct and indirect references and allusions to Greek and Roman mythology (see the preceding pages for profiles of the mythical figures in the following discussion.) Norse and other cultural mythologies are also suggested. Hogwarts could represent Olympus, the mountain-like home of the Greek gods and goddesses. Characters in the novels have similar names or traits as certain gods. Harry, Hercules, and Apollo slay snakes and are considered the greatest heroes of their worlds. Albus Dumbledore represents the all-powerful Zeus. Minerva McGonagall, as her name suggests, is Athena, protector of Hogwarts. Hagrid could be Poseidon because of his mastery of water. He is also representative of the giant Titan clan. He rages at the Dursleys like the Norse god Thor. Voldemort is Mars, the god of war.

James and Lily Potter could represent Vulcan and Venus. Vernon Dursley might be Hades, guarding dark secrets of the underworld, with Petunia as Persephone. Professor Quirrell is Janus, the god with two faces. The egotistical Gilderoy Lockhart is Narcissus, and Hermione serves as his doting Echo. A mythical character named Hermione married Achilles' son Neoptolemus. Percy and his girlfriend are Odysseus and Penelope. Peter Pettigrew could be Icarus who does not heed the warnings of Daedulus. Lupin could be the mythical twin brother of Romulus; the sons of Mars, they were raised by a wolf to become founders of Rome.

Harry Potter creatures also have mythical counterparts. Fluffy is Cerberus, the multi-headed dog guarding the underworld. The basilisk might be Medusa, whose glance turns people to stone. The centaurs resemble Pan, the goat man; the Satyrs; Sileni, the mythical half horse-half men; and Pegasus. Another creature who suggests characteristics of the centaurs, Snape, and Voldemort, is the sphinx, who has the body of a lion and the head of a woman. In legends, the sphinx asked travelers to solve riddles and would kill them if they could not solve the word puzzle. All of these monsters parallel the Animagi in Harry Potter; they retain a human's intellect but gain an animal's freedom to roam; in the process, they lose some of their sense of right and wrong.

Places in the Harry Potter series also have mythical roots. The chambers beneath Hogwarts are like Pandora's box, a forbidden container of potential trouble and misery. The tunnels resemble the River Styx that led to the netherworld or the labyrinth which restrained the bullish Minotaur. Above ground, Hogwarts, like Olympus, rises above common places and exists to stimulate the residents. Both mythical and Harry Potter characters try to avoid displaying excessive pride (called "hubris" by the Greeks), and not risk being humbled or destroyed by someone or something more powerful than them. Despite their efforts, most characters have a hamartia (ha-mar-TEE-uh), the Greek word for tragic flaw, which causes conflict and advances the plot.

— Potter as Legend —

Harry Potter is famous in his own time and reminds readers of other legendary characters both noble and notorious. Harry's ability to pull Godric Gryffindor's sword from the hat and out of the basilisk's mouth is like King Arthur pulling the sword Excalibur from a stone. The King Arthur legends share many similarities with the Potter series. Dumbledore is the wise magician Merlin. He guides Harry the way that Merlin counseled Arthur. Harry and Arthur undergo quests and tests of mental and physical agility. Dumbledore praises Harry for his humanity in sparing Pettigrew's life, which can be compared to the chivalry that Arthur displays in his daily conduct.

Dumbledore emphasizes that Pettigrew owes Harry his allegiance even though he is still allied with Voldemort. Harry and Pettigrew, despite being rivals who loathe each other, are bonded through Harry's act of mercy, and, at some crucial future point, Pettigrew will be forced to support Harry instead of Voldemort. Ron, Colin, Dean, Seamus, and Neville could be Harry's knights, supporting and defending him while quarreling among themselves for his attention. Ron, more specifically, might be Lancelot, Arthur's best friend, who ultimately betrays him over the love of Guinevere.

Hogwarts and surroundings are their Camelot, with the lake perhaps being the hidden, silent home of Vivien, the Lady of the Lake, whose parallel Harry Potter character is yet to be divulged. This setting is a paradise for the knights to yearn for when they are away from home. While Arthur searched for the Holy Grail—the cup Jesus drank from at the Last Supper—the

Hogwarts characters have a metaphorical grail in each story, whether it is finding the philosopher's/sorcerer's stone, saving Ginny's life, or securing Black's freedom. Percival, Arthur's most loyal knight, resembles Percy Weasley. Also, perhaps Arthur Weasley's sons are the knights of his round table and Ginny is the unfaithful Guinevere in a yet-to-be-developed love triangle.

Literary critics and historians have dismissed some King Arthur stories as untrue while admitting that others have a degree of validity because of recurring details and geographic sites that can be located. They have compared versions of verses written in the twelfth century by Chretien de Troyes and prose recorded in the thirteenth-century Vulgate based on oral accounts of the King Arthur legends. Arthurian motifs present in the Harry Potter series include caves, stones, dragons, and magical clothes, chess pieces, and trees. Numbers are used to indicate magic, such as the seven-league boots which enabled a person to cover seven leagues, or twenty-one miles, in one step. Merlin disguised himself as a stag to enter an emperor's palace much like James Potter transformed himself to gain freedom of movement.

The name Voldemort might have been inspired by King Vortigern, an overlord, who legends say arrested Merlin when he was a child. Vortigern planned to kill Merlin in order to use his blood to cement the mortar in a tower. Symbolized by a red dragon, Vortigern's evil ways ultimately destroyed him.

Other legends suggest parallels with the Potter novels. The basilisk reminds readers of Beowulf's hideous Grendel, or a sea monster described by generations of sailors. Hogwarts and Hogsmeade could be the Scottish Brigadoon or a version of mythical paradise and utopia depicted in many legends.

Hogwarts could also be the idyllic Xanadu where the thirteenth-century Mongolian emperor Kublai Khan luxuriously lived during summers. An unverified legendary source for Ron Weasley's name has been posted on a fan site. Supposedly based on an obscure and unspecified legend, Ron's name allegedly means "Running Weasel," an ancient warlord and gifted chess player according to this legend, who died because of an accident involving a rat that had been dyed yellow, as Ron attempted in Book I.

— Potter as Fairy Tale —

The novels also perpetuate fairy tale imagery. Like Cinderella, Harry escapes from abusive guardians who expect him to labor unceasingly, and he enters a magical world where he is the star and is the recipient of kindness and luxuries. Like Cinderella's chariot, Harry's magical escape is in a flying car. Hagrid, Molly Weasley, Dumbledore, or McGonagall are his fairy godmother. Hermione and Ginny might be Sleeping Beauty or Snow White who are awakened by Harry the prince. During examinations an "unnatural hush fell over the castle" as if the school was under a spell. Lupin also slumbers deeply on the Hogwarts Express as if enchanted, and Hermione is unable to awaken him. Only the arrival of the Dementors, represented by chilliness, rouses him from his unconscious stupor, but, ironically, the Dementors' Kiss, an act in the normal world that symbolizes warmth, causes the complete absence of a person's conscience, as in the "Kiss of Judas."

Harry also resembles Hansel as told by the Grimm Brothers, trying to outsmart the wicked witch as well as the carnivorous creatures in the forest in his quest for survival or metaphorical maturity. Harry and Hermione are like Hansel and Gretel when they venture into the Forbidden Forest. Their time in the forest represents an inner journey to discover self knowledge. Hagrid's hut reminds readers of the dwellings of fairy tale woodsmen. Hermione could also be the clever Beauty (of "Beauty and the Beast") who is enchanted by the fearsome Beast of Harry's alter ego. Harry is like the storyteller in renditions of "One Thousand and One Nights," realizing the longer he keeps Slytherin's heir talking the more time he has to live. Ginny's abductor is as persuasive as the wolf was to Little Red Riding Hood. Harry gazes into the Mirror of Erised much like Snow White's wicked stepmother questioned a mirror ("mirror, mirror on the wall") about her status in the kingdom. His use of Voldemort's name is like the Miller's daughter who says Rumpelstiltskin's name to free herself from neverending service of making gold from straw for him (coincidentally, the daughter is given three tries to guess his name, and she asks Rumpelstiltskin if his name is Harry before saying the correct name).

Other fairy tale elements include wands, warnings to stay on the path in the Forbidden Forest, and the use of a cloak to become invisible. Although Hogwarts and the wizard realm seem to operate with regard to rules, deviations from expected patterns enable character development to occur as they do in traditional fairy tales. Magic empowers and transforms ordinary people into remarkable beings. Characters seem removed from the normal cycles of life, but they observe seasonal change and they age like normal humans. However, Harry and Hermione can manipulate time, and the process of being transported back several hours is described as a haze of colors and suspension above the ground which helps readers suspend their belief to travel with them.

Harry and his friends are human chess pieces, alternating roles from pawns to the royalty. They suggest Alice's encounters in Wonderland, a modern fairy tale, or even the game board inhabited by enchanted pieces with which the Hogwarts students play. The mixture of living and dead people at the Deathday Party also seems like an event suited to Wonderland. The Harry Potter characters are aware of fairy tale elements. By staring intensely at him, Snape tries to make Harry confess that he went to Hogsmeade and Harry reacts by not blinking based on his encounters with the basilisk and Hippogriff. Snape dismisses Harry's pleas that Black is innocent as a "fairy tale" that had been "planted in Potter's mind."

The Potter series is based on many smaller lessons and stories that contribute to each novel's main plot. The messages taught in classrooms, on the Quidditch fields, and during adventures resemble Aesop's fables, which are cautionary messages about human behavior. Folklore is evident through the customs respected at Hogwarts and characters' actions. Aragog is the familiar folklore trickster Anancy trying to deceive and confuse Harry. The students' boasts, mostly untrue, about how well they flew on brooms before attending Hogwarts, are like tall tales that provide information about the values and aspirations of wizard culture. Harry Potter has also been addressed in urban legends (stories that seem to be true because the teller claims he knows the person involved, but the stories prove to be false although they do reveal cultural fears and interests) as fans speculate about future plots and circulate rumors on the internet and at playgrounds, schools, and libraries. As a result, Harry Potter has become part of a greater mythic saga that incorporates the information alluded to about wizard history prior to his arrival at Hogwarts, the addition of Rowling's fictional heroic tales, and popular speculation about Harry's post-Hogwarts' life.

— Mythical Objects, Beasts, and Ceremonies —

Stones are central to legends of diverse cultures. Mythical minerals, such as the magnetic lodestone, have the power to attract people. Other stones are believed capable of curing diseases. The Greeks and Romans worshiped sacred stones. Rocks were also revered through the building of pyramids. Ancient peoples tended pieces of meteorites as charms and marked boundaries with blessed stones. Memorials to fallen heroes and sites of Druid nature rituals were made from stone slabs. Stonehenge is one of the best known stone shrines.

The legendary Stone of Destiny, which could recognize the true king, was once kept at the site of a Dalriada fortress where Dunstaffnage Castle was later built in Scotland. Some stones, like the one at Blarney, are still accessible and promise luck to those who kiss it. In addition to positive characteristics, stones can also be considered negative, such as threats in fairy tales that evil people will be turned to stone.

The magical potions that develop wizard photographs and elixirs that promise immortality, courage, and bravery also have legendary sources. Crookshank's "bottlebrush" tail alludes to English mythology that says cats transport storms in their tails. McGonagall's transformation into a tabby is from English folklore in which witches disguise themselves as cats. Dobby reminds readers of a leprechaun, trying to trick Harry into obeying his orders. In fairy tales humans sometimes ride giant flying birds that resemble Hippogriffs.

The house animals have mythical symbolism which has a dual interpretation. Lions can be both brave and dangerous, and snakes can be evil and helpful. Hog imagery suggests a boldness and persevering fierce strength; the boar is the symbol of Clan Campbell, one of Scotland's most significant families. The warts suffix in "Hogwarts" could hint at the school's infectious nature among its residents. The owls represent a mythical duality. While many people respect owls for their wisdom, some superstitious cultures feared owls as prophets of death and despair. The Grim is like the Irish Pooka, a demon in the form of a black dog that attacks travelers. Lindworms are also supernatural creatures in early Irish lore. The Loch Ness Monster in the Scottish Highlands, first seen in the sixth century, may have a counterpart in the Hogwarts lake.

When Draco Malfoy saw Harry's floating head outside the Shrieking Shack, his experience resembles those that are chronicled in thousands of ghost stories describing strange apparitions and noises. Most of these tales were local folklore and were based on factual feuds, kidnappings, or malicious acts at prominent sites where Viking or Roman forts once stood according to legends. At Castle Grant near Grantown-on-Spey, Scotland, Lady Barbara Grant starved to death in a cupboard in the sixteenth century where her father had locked her to prevent her from seeing a man she loved. Other ghost stories tell about witches, treasure hidden in caves, omens, and  people walled up in castles. Sometimes visitors claim that they feel like pictures are watching them somewhat like the interactive portraits at Hogwarts.

Legendary characters celebrate holidays and victories on the battlefield with feasts similar to those Harry attends in Hogwarts' Great Hall. The tribes that settled Great Britain before the Middle Ages observed specific ceremonies that have evolved into modern holidays. While Harry and his friends indulge in Halloween mayhem, Celtic peoples observed Midwinter's and Midsummer's Eves when the living and dead could interact and cross normally rigid barriers, somewhat like Harry and his classmates being able to transverse the railroad station barrier on September 1 and and the last day of school in June. The Scottish people refer to the winter months as Dudlachd, meaning gloom (or deadlocked) which also hints of Dudley's name. Ironically, Harry prefers the winter's darkness over the summer's lightness because of his confinement to the Dursleys' home. May Day symbolizes a mock battle between winter and summer—evil and good—somewhat like Harry's annual confrontation with Voldemort in late spring. Like Romans at Lupercalia, Harry indulges at Hogwarts' farewell banquets to prepare for his summer fast without magic.

INTERPRETATIONS

Bruno Bettelheim analyzed how fairy tales enable children to express their fears and learn coping mechanisms. He believed that children endure more fear and terror than adults realized and he promoted reading fairy tales to release some of this emotional pressure. Bettelheim would have praised the Potter series for demonstrating how children can deal with oppressive situations and coexist harmoniously with frightening and loathsome people. Harry reinforces Bettelheim's thesis that struggle is inevitable in life and that eventual triumph is possible through cleverness and diligence. Harry reassures readers of all ages that they too will survive whatever challenges they encounter.

Rowling's use of myth and legend provide young readers with a comfort level that removes the story from their immediate lives while recalling fantasy characters and situations that are very familiar. Young readers may not know many of the mythological characters discussed in this section, but they recognize the symbolic importance of each, and the role each one plays in working out social, moral, and religious themes. Although she was trained in classical studies and is probably very aware of her use of allusion, it doesn't matter if J. K. Rowling did or did not consciously know that she was invoking particular mythological characters and situations. It is highly probable that the reason for the success of the Harry Potter series is the blending of archetypal patterns and symbols she has concocted. The invisibility cloak, for example, is a perfectly plausible symbol. All religions have incorporated "invisible" doctrines into their theology; just because you cannot "see" God doesn't lessen His presence; children often see things that aren't real. When they pull the covers over their heads, they disappear from the external world into their own realm. Cloaks, as costume, have been draped over magicians, wizards, kings, flying superhumans, and deities. Joseph's magical coat from the Bible is a recognizable symbol for many people. So for Harry's deceased father to have left him an invisibility cloak is archetypally true. We believe that Harry can disappear, but what makes this part of Harry's adventure interesting is that he is protected by the cloak only if he uses it correctly. As part human, he has every chance of exposing himself because of his own mistakes.

READING FOR RESEARCH

Bellingham, David. *Goddesses, Heroes & Shamans: A Young People's Guide to World Mythology.* New York: Kingfisher Books, 1994. Valuable encyclopedia for students.

Coghlan, Ronan. *The Illustrated Encyclopedia of Arthurian Legends.* Shaftesbury, England: Element, 1993. A beautifully illustrated guide to characters and motifs in the King Arthur legends.

Mercatante, Anthony S. *The Facts on File Encyclopedia of World Mythology and Legend.* New York: Facts on File, 1988. Concise, comprehensive reference source.

INTERNET RESOURCES

The Encyclopedia Mythica
   http://www.pantheon.org/mythica

Folklore, Myth and Legend
http://www.acs.ucalgary.ca/~dkbrown/storfolk.html

Fairy Tale Resource Page for Teachers and Librarians
http://www.ualberta.ca/~mshane/title.htm

Log on to **www.beachampublishing.com** for many additional projects, discussion questions, writing and research ideas, websites, and bibliography.

CHAPTER 10

ARCHETYPES AND BIBLICAL REFERENCES

"I don't believe people are looking for the meaning of life as much as they are looking for the experience of being alive." —JOSEPH CAMPBELL

"To listen to some devout people, one would imagine that God never laughs." —AUROBINDO GHOSE

Introduction

Much of the world's literature is derived from ancient stories that have become imprinted on our subconscious minds. From troubadours who preserved stories before people could write to Star Wars *characters, writers have known that by invoking certain images, symbols, or language from imprinted stories, they could evoke powerful emotions from their readers. Harry is, himself, a classic archetypal hero, and understanding his archetypal forebearers will explain much of his appeal to young readers who identify with the pleasures and perils of heroism better than most people.*

ARCHETYPES AND THE COLLECTIVE UNCONSCIOUS

Carl Jung, a psychologist, student of Sigmund Freud, and one of the foremost thinkers of the twentieth century, defined a concept he called "the collective (or universal) unconscious." He asserted that all modern beings retain patterns of their ancient ancestors, and that regardless of geography, race, or religion, all people everywhere share common fears and desires. Biologists have long recognized instinctual patterns in lower animals—the nesting of birds, the ritual dance of storks, the spinning of spider webs—and recent DNA discoveries confirm that except for tiny differences in DNA structure, all creatures are biologically similar.

Jung argued that the collective unconscious in society is expressed through "archetypes" that embody a primordial, preconscious, instinctual expression of mankind's basic nature. Because people undergo essentially the same kind of basic experiences, the expression of the collective unconscious is universal, and archetypes are as meaningful to remote tribesmen hunting for food in the jungle as to Wall Street executives fending off predators.

Anthropologists have discovered many universal motifs that support Carl Jung's proposition that all people everywhere share archetypal beliefs and experiences. Almost every culture has embodied in its legends, literature or religion similar stories or beliefs, such as the destruction of the world by flood, famine, plague, or earthquake; the slaying of monsters; sibling rivalries; and the Oedipus legend. Although the details vary greatly from culture to culture, the basic patterns are amazingly similar. These stories express mankind's reaction to essentially changeless situations, originating from experiences, attitudes and problems related to the universe, gods, survival, parents, and children. Every generation retells these ancient archetypes to interpret the world as they experience it.

HARRY AS ARCHETYPE

Almost all works of literature that have endured time tell the stories of archetypal characters. The phenomenal success of Harry Potter suggests that he and his world are reinterpreting ancient archetypes for a generation of young readers who may have been jaded by reality television but eagerly embrace their connection to their collective unconscious.

Lord Ragland, in his groundbreaking study of archetypes, *The Hero: A Study in Tradition, Myth, and Drama* identifies three principal categories of archetypes: characters, situations, and objects/symbols. His is a long list, but here are some of Ragland's observations, some of which appear in Harry and his world.

The hero in every culture experiences a series of well-marked adventures that strongly suggest a ritualistic pattern. Ragland finds that traditionally the hero's mother is a virgin, the circumstances of his birth are unusual, and at birth some attempt is made to kill him. He is, however, spirited away and reared by foster parents. Little is known of his early childhood, but as he nears maturity he returns to his future kingdom where he learns some of the secrets of his past. After a victory over the king or wild beast, he marries a princess, becomes king, and reigns uneventfully. After losing favor with the gods, he is driven from the kingdom and meets a mysterious death, often at the top of a hill. His body is not buried but resides in one or more holy sepulchers.

Situations which the archetypal hero endures include:

1. The quest. The hero searches for someone or some talisman (object) which, when found, will restore the health of the kingdom.
2. The task. To save the kingdom or win the hand of a princess, the hero must perform some nearly superhuman deed.
3. The initiation. The young hero entering puberty must survive a ritualistic act that transforms him into understanding the problems and responsibilities of adulthood.
4. The journey. The hero must seek information or truth through a perilous journey that often includes a descent into the under world.

5. The fall. The hero descends from a higher to a lower state of being that usually involves spiritual defilement and a loss of innocence. The fall usually results in the hero's expulsion from paradise and a penalty for disobedience.

6. Death and rebirth. The most common of all archetypal situations, this reflects the influence of the cycle of life and death, winter and spring, night and day.

MORAL STRUCTURE AND THE HOGWARTS SYSTEM

Although religion seems absent in the novels, Hogwarts and its inhabitants are rooted in moral settings and situations. Scholars who study the history of religion realize that people have expressed spirituality in many ways. Ancient peoples believed that animals, plants, and objects contained the spirits of gods who protected them. Groups such as Native Americans designated specific people to direct rituals and preserve myths about spiritual beliefs. The diverse religions that modern cultures practice emerged over thousands of years and are based on the teachings of spiritual leaders, including Jesus, Mohammed, Confucius, and Buddha. Some religious guides told their followers that God was kind and forgiving, while others depicted a more strict and intolerant deity.

Harry and the Hogwarts community reflect numerous archetypal patterns and religious values, although there is no mention of religion in Books I-III. Harry does not attend church in either the Muggle or magical worlds, nor do any of his friends, teachers, or family. If Hogwarts or Hogsmeade contain a chapel, or if the Dursleys' neighborhood houses a church or cathedral, they have not been mentioned in the series so far. Christmas holidays at Hogwarts are secular, and Easter is referred to mostly as a way to note advancing time in the school calendar. Students do not pray before meals or at bedtime. Bible study is not incorporated in the curriculum.

Despite the omission of religious ceremonies, Hogwarts and the magical world expect students and adult wizards to accept high standards of moral conduct, of how to live virtuously, dutifully, and purposefully to aid others and rid the world of evil. Good is emphasized in characterizations and plots. Children are encouraged to respect their elders, somewhat like the ancestor worship practiced in Asian and African religions.

The school song is like a psalm, praising and uniting the community. Professors resemble missionaries seeking student followers. The lessons and examples are reminiscent of biblical people and events which symbolize universal experiences of suffering and joy, defeat and perseverance, and hate and love. Both biblical and Harry Potter characters withstand hardships because of an angry God. The Bible tells about demons and sorcerers, unexplained wonders, and brutal tortures and murders—clearly defined archetypal experiences from every culture.

BIBLICAL ALLUSIONS

Because the Bible is the theological and cultural basis of western society, writers often retell its stories in fictional works, or make indirect references to it in order to suggest to readers some values or principles the Bible addresses. This is a time-honored use of allusion in literature, which Rowling also uses.

Archetypal stories narrate miraculous incidents similar to the phenomena Harry witnesses, as well as his struggle of good versus evil. Harry is marked as the chosen one by his scar, which resembles stigmata that sometimes appear on fervently religious followers. It could also be viewed as a brand of shame. When Cain murdered Abel, God placed a blemish on his forehead. Harry's scar is symbolically in the shape of a lightning bolt, hinting of the storms that terrified ancient peoples as signs of forthcoming disaster.

Harry's parental legacy signifies that he is the heir to the wizard kingdom, preparing himself for Armageddon and Resurrection. His initial visit to Diagon Alley, being immersed in wizard culture, could represent his initiation as the wizard world's appointed savior. He is assisted by his two closest friends, Ron and Hermione. Harry might be considered the prodigal son, returning to his true home. He also could be referred to as a messiah, apostle, or prophet within the wizard community because he spreads the message that good will ultimately triumph over evil.

Harry's nightmares include premonitions about evil somewhat like the dreams of Joseph and other biblical characters. As a toddler, Harry is saved from death when Hagrid transports him to the Dursleys' in a bundle of blankets, which recalls the basket used for infant Moses' escape when the Pharaoh ordered that all male babies were to be killed or the "swaddling clothes" in which the infant Jesus was wrapped. Harry is also a pious pilgrim, intensely pursuing his journey to find his identity and power to enact vengeance for Voldemort's crimes. Harry is like the potter that Jeremiah observed who continued molding his clay at his wheel until he created flawless jars. Jeremiah compared the clay to people, declaring that God was also a potter who toiled with his creations until he was satisfied they were ready for service.

Harry can also be regarded as a medieval crusader, draped in symbolic robes in quest of the Holy Grail. As a Seeker, Harry battles heretics during games of Quidditch. His accident symbolizes a fall from grace before he can rise again as a worthy spiritual leader. Avoiding the fate of Lot's wife who turned into a pillar of salt when she looked back at Sodom, Harry leaves the Quidditch field with his face forward, avoiding glancing to either side. He also evades the basilisk's gaze. Themes of betrayal, love, loss, and inner conflict permeate Harry's life as they do biblical characters' experiences.

GOOD VERSUS EVIL

Saints and sinners populate the pages of the Harry Potter series. Harry is surrounded by wise men and women, who were known as "magi" in the Bible. Thought to have been scholars, the wise men presented the infant Jesus with presents, somewhat like Harry's professors offer him material, intellectual, and emotional gifts. Dumbledore is wise like Solomon and shares wisdom with his students that mimic parables and proverbs. Lupin resembles the Apostle Paul whose letters offered advice and warnings.

Harry's parents suggest Christian symbolism. There are many James mentioned in the Bible, including two of Jesus' disciples.

Saint James, the brother of Jesus, was mar-
tyred for his beliefs somewhat like Harry's
father who died defending his principles.
Lily Potter's name represents her purity of
spirit as demonstrated by sacrificing her
life to save her son Harry. Lilies signify the
resurrection and ascension of Christ after his
crucifixion and a symbol of Easter.

Sirius Black somewhat resembles Job because of the suffering
he patiently endures resulting from false accusations and unjust
imprisonment. Black, confined to an island, also recalls John
the Divine who wrote the *Book of Revelations* while he was a
prisoner on the island of Patmos. Molly Weasley is a spiritually
strong, determined woman who, like biblical women, defended
their families from evil. Hedwig, named for a saint, uncom-
plainingly serves Harry and comforts him in times of stress.

Percy Weasley is like a Pharisee who strictly follows rules
while acting smugly superior. Harry and many of his classmates
might be described as Good Samaritans because of their acts of
kindness and generosity. The trio of Harry, Ron, and Hermione
suggest the power of three and the spiritual trinity.

Other biblical allusions include Voldemort as an archangel,
especially when he is referred to by the title "Lord." Harry wonders which of his classmates has betrayed him (like Judas) when
the diary is stolen from his room in Book II. The decadent,
greedy Dursleys seem to lack souls and emphasize how the term
"non-believer" gains new meaning as defined by wizards. Some
Muggles are like Scythians who were uncivilized and foreigners
within their communities. Aunt Marge cruelly suggests that

Harry is retarded, and nobody defends him at what proved to be Harry's "last supper" at the Dursley home.

Biblical sorcerers and witches are depicted as sinners. Paul visited the magician Elymas Bar-Jesus, the wizard of Cyprus, who tried to discredit him. The Samaritan Simon Magus was a sorcerer who tried to purchase more power when he was impressed by the apostles' abilities. He admitted his sin, but traditional legends claimed that he later started and spread heresy. Daniel slew the dragon Bel, a Babylon god described in the Apocrypha (early Christian texts not included in the New Testament), and his faith protected him when he was thrown in a lion pit, somewhat like Harry facing the basilisk.

SACRED PLACES

Even though Hogwarts is a secular site, it represents Harry's spiritual home where he is awakened to new awareness and understanding of himself and the world. Hogwarts enables Harry to see the possibilities of peace and harmony for both wizards and Muggles. Without his immersion in the Hogwarts community and commitment to its creed, Harry would have been powerless to confront evil that threatens not only himself but the world. Hogwarts is isolated like Essenes, a community where a sect prepared for the final confrontation between good and evil. The castle is a sanctuary like the community of Samaritans or a monastery. Dumbledore's office protects precious artifacts, the magical equivalent of the Ark of the Covenant encasing the Ten Commandments. Bill Weasley works at the Gringotts bank in Egypt, a central location of biblical events. The Chamber of Secrets could be the Garden of Eden with Harry as Adam, Ginny as Eve, and the basilisk as the seductive serpent. Ginny's fall from grace is the catalyst for the abandonment of the chamber and new order at Hogwarts. The hissing of the chamber's doors and the basilisk suggest ancient languages being released from the Tower of Babel. Hogwarts' chambers and the Shrieking Shack's upstairs room harbor evil, like biblical lion dens and torture rooms. The threatening message written on the wall in Book II resembles the message that Daniel translated for the Babylonian King Belshazzar, warning him that he would be punished for looting a temple.

The architecture of Hogwarts and other wizard sites parallels biblical structures. Hogwarts sits on a cliff above Hogsmeade; temples often sat on hills above populated areas. The wizard castle has stone gates, steps, towers, wells, and chambers like those described in the Bible and preserved by archaeologists. Hogwarts' walls resemble those surrounding cities in the Holy Land, and tunnels beneath the castle are like those used to protect early Christians from persecution. The cave Harry enters on his first night at Hogwarts are like the caves used to hide the Dead Sea Scrolls from the Romans or to bury the dead.

OBJECTS AND NUMBERS

Religious artifacts are often revered as sacred items. Many of these objects are enshrined for the devout to visit or used in prayer. Others have vanished, only present in biblical or scholarly descriptions. These sacred artifacts serve as symbols of religiosity. Several objects in the Harry Potter series suggest similar imagery. For example, when a novice wizard puts on the sorting hat, the experience resembles a baptism because the student is immersed in the hat and christened with a new identity.

The Bible tells about the Tree of Life which promises eternal life and the Tree of Knowledge which can make people aware of good and evil. Harry, like Eve, is tempted by metaphorical fruit, such as the Marauder's Map and the Invisibility Cloak, which results in his being transported closer to evil. The Invisibility Cloak, which Harry uses to explore and leave the castle, is reminiscent of the Shroud of Turin used to conceal Jesus' body after the Crucifixion.

Rocks are significant in the Bible. David killed the giant Goliath with a single stone. The disciple Peter's name means stone (or translated as "Cephas" in the Semitic language Aramaic). Satan tried to trick Jesus to transform stones into bread. Many biblical characters and martyrs were executed by stoning (a punishment still practiced in some countries). Stones were rolled in front of caves until bodies decayed. Tombstones are carved from rock, and one funeral custom involves visitors leaving a rock on the grave. Hogwarts was built on a mountain, and most strong biblical buildings have a rock for a foundation. Jesus is often referred to as the "rock" of the Protestant church.

Winged beasts like the Hippogriffs in Book III are often featured in religious imagery. Daniel had a vision of a flying lion and other creatures which he said warned of foreign invasion, similar to the Dementors surrounding Hogwarts. Job saw sea serpents which reminds readers of the giant squid that lives in the

Hogwarts lake and whose purpose in the stories has not been told yet. Fawkes is a phoenix which was a symbol in ancient Egyptian religions of the sun and rebirth. Christians later used phoenixes to represent resurrection and eternal life.

Biblical characters used coins made of valuable metals and stamped with unique designs like the wizard money Harry has. In addition to the Trees of Life and Knowledge, other plants were significant during biblical times. The biblical plants, like the Whomping Willow, were often named with descriptive words. For example, the Oak of Mamre marked the place where angels told Abraham that his elderly wife Sarah would give birth to a son. Biblical characters wore tunics, robes, and cloaks like the clothing students and teachers wear at Hogwarts. King Belshazzar promised scarlet robes, suggesting clothing like the Gryffindors' Quidditch uniform, as rewards to loyal followers.

Numbers are important to both Bible and wizard environments. There are four horsemen of the apocalypse (war, disease, hunger, death), traditional emblems of evil, and four houses at Hogwarts. Seven is a number used by Jews to designate perfection. Jesus performed seven miracles which people believed were signs that he was the son of God. Seven wonders of the ancient world were identified. And there are seven deadly sins (anger, covetous, envy, gluttony, lust, pride, and sloth). Hogwarts students devote seven years to their studies to battle such sins.

ARMAGEDDON

Timing is crucial in the novels. *Ecclesiastes* states that for every thing there is a season and a time, and Harry's life seems preordained. At the appointed time, he begins an exodus with several hundred children to Hogwarts. Harry witnesses and experiences strange events that sometimes border on the miraculous. Simultaneously, Voldemort and Black are both exiled, the former to the metaphorical wilderness and the latter to a fortress. During this time, Harry prepares himself for the final battle with Voldemort.

The Bible says that God told Adam and Eve that their descendant will damage a serpent's head to destroy evil, and Harry achieves this in Book II. The *Book of Revelations* chronicles Armageddon, the final confrontation of good and evil in which good prevails and Jesus returns to Earth. That narrative reveals that after one thousand years of peace, Satan will be freed but will die in a lake of fire before he can renew the conflict. At that time, everybody will face judgment from the book of life (resembling McGonagall's all-knowing book about the wizard world). *Revelations* offers clues and symbols for readers to interpret much like the Potter novels have information subtly embedded. Perhaps *Revelations* suggests how Book VII will conclude with Harry and goodness emerging victorious as Voldemort dies in the nearby lake.

READING FOR RESEARCH

Halverson, Dean C., ed. *The Compact Guide to World Religions.* Minneapolis, MN: Bethany House Publishers, 1996. Describes basic beliefs and practices of major religions.

Richards, Larry. *International Children's Bible Handbook.* Dallas, TX: Word Books, 1997. A comprehensive view of world religions.

Trimiew, Anna. *Bible Almanac.* Lincolnwood, IL: Publications International, 1997. Information about people, miracles, and other significant biblical events.

INTERNET RESOURCES

Religion Online
  http://www.religion-online.org/

Virtual Religion Index
  http://religion.rutgers.edu/vri/index.html

World Wide Study Bible
  http://ccel.wheaton.edu/wwsb/

Log on to **www.beachampublishing.com** for many additional projects, discussion questions, writing and research ideas, websites, and bibliography.

CHAPTER 11

HISTORY

"History is fables agreed upon." —VOLTAIRE

"There is no king who has not had a slave among his ancestors, and no slave who has not had a king among his." —HELEN ADAMS KELLER

INTRODUCTION

Just as authors use allusions to legends and mythology to suggest situations, themes, and the fate of characters, they also use historical events and people to develop plot. The sources of these events and people demonstrate a portion of the author's creative process, as well as explain the origin of the fictional realm. As a well educated British citizen, J. K. Rowling is certainly knowledgeable of her country's history, and whether consciously or subconsciously, she has a rich historical heritage that she uses to add layers of meaning and intrigue to her novels.

There has long been controversy among critics as to the validity of literary allusions. Some critics argue that if the author did not intentionally use allusion, then readers should not attempt to find parallels. Other critics argue that if readers recognize an allusion, it becomes part of the fabric of the novel whether or not the author intended it.

The following discussion of historical allusion in the Harry Potter novels presents historical precedents that some readers have recognized.

BACK IN TIME

The Hogwarts Express is a time machine transporting Harry and his classmates to different eras. Characters and situations in the Potter series are reminiscent of historical figures and events. Rowling uses some historic names, places, and occurrences to develop characterization. Somewhat like the wizard world, Great Britain has a complex history of internal dissent and militancy as well as external aggressiveness and warfare. Diverse groups have lived in Great Britain, ranging from ancient tribes, such as the Picts and Celts, to invaders that include the Vikings and Romans. The Druids and Stonehenge are the most recognizable symbols of ancient Britain. These peoples have all contributed to the British language, customs, and civilization.

British history is tinged with murders, betrayals, imprisonments, beheadings, riots, deceptions, intrigue, rescue attempts, assassinations, escapes, and sieges. Historic figures have declared allegiances in civil wars, scaled castle walls, assaulted fortresses with boulders launched from catapults, shot flaming arrows at rival troops, burned heretics and witches at the stake, suffered famine, fires, and plague, and dumped vats of boiling oil on enemies. Pretenders to the crown have disguised themselves (somewhat like Harry donning the Invisibility Cloak or his father becoming an Animagus) and been punished with confinement in dungeons or sessions in torture chambers (like the subterranean vaults underneath Hogwarts). Those who did not survive were buried in catacombs which were also like the chambers.

TIME PASSAGES

The historic details and allusions contribute to the reality of the Harry Potter series, which helps readers accept the fantastical as believable. For example, numerous British monarchs have had the names Harry and James, and Lily Potter might be Eleanor of Aquitaine. Eleanor was devoted to her son Richard the Lion-Hearted and sacrificed for his happiness much like Lily did for her son Harry. The lion imagery of the royals evokes symbolism of the Potters' allegiances to Gryffindor. Hogwarts, founded a millennium ago, during the ascent of the Middle Ages, resembles a medieval fortress, and the school's Great Hall is an architectural feature of most castles throughout Great Britain and Europe. The chambers recall images from ancient Greek history of the legendary maze restraining the monstrous Minotaur or from from Roman history in which horrific combat was staged between humans and beasts in the Colosseum. The Patronus could be a magical descendant of the Roman patronus who protected selected individuals in Britannia. In Books I and II, the chambers' protective devices are like the traps the Egyptians constructed in the pyramids to protect mummified royalty. The medieval atmosphere of Hogwarts is resplendent with the language, tools, weapons, parchment, alchemy, belief in bizarre creatures, and chivalric code of a thousand years ago.

Dobby's self-punishing behavior mimics medieval religious flagellants. His garment is like Roman togas or galley slaves' tunics, and Dobby mentions the Dark days when house elves were flogged before the "new dawn," or Renaissance, when Harry Potter "triumphed." Clumsy, forgetful Neville is a court jester, and Hermione, Harry, or Ron remind readers of Joan of Arc's determination to fight and sacrifice for her beliefs. The owls attend the wizards and witches like falcons served their medieval masters. Medieval chivalry is similar to the courtesy and honor codes practiced at Hogwarts. Fawkes self-immolates somewhat like his namesake Guy Fawkes who plotted to blow up the British parliament with gunpowder. The Filibuster fireworks refer to the long-winded speeches politicians deliver to delay and divert

opponents and also bands of pirates. Parliament and the Ministry of Magic are parallel counterparts.

The Potter novels could also be analyzed using the framework of modern history. The Chamber of Secrets eerily resembles the underground caverns where war prisoners were forced to labor on German munitions during the Holocaust. Harry and his friends are like the hidden Jewish children who were removed from their homes and assumed new identities to survive from being deported to certain extermination in death camps. Ghettos were closed communities, isolating Jews from other urban areas, and residents developed their own rules, survival tactics, and activities somewhat like Hogwarts. Slytherin's initials, S.S., suggest Nazi stormtroopers, and the moniker Ravenclaw is similar to the name of the Ravensbrueck concentration camp.

The Chamber was originally opened in 1942, reinforcing World War II comparisons, and Dumbledore defeated another powerful wizard in 1945, possibly alluding to Hitler's downfall. Buckbeak's hearing was on Hitler's birthday and his scheduled execution and Harry's and Hermione's assault on the Shrieking Shack occurred on June 6, the day of another legendary invasion when Allied troops landed at Normandy in 1944. Their desperate offensive maneuver into the Shrieking Shack and chambers are like Allied troops taking a stand at Dunkirk in 1940 before ultimately evacuating. Harry, Hermione, and Sirius Black fly on Buckbeak somewhat like World War II glider pilots quietly maneuvered to battle zones. When Harry, Ron, and Hermione are in the chambers and the Shrieking Shack, their situation is reminiscent of the prisoners trapped in the Black Hole of Calcutta. Quirrell's turban hints of Middle East imagery and strict religious beliefs that fuel Holy Wars.

HISTORICAL FOOTNOTES

The wizard children are moved from London to the countryside by train, just as British children were evacuated and dispersed to rural homes to avoid German bombing raids during World War II. Many of these war refugees may have embarked from King's Cross station, which was built during Queen Victoria's reign. Harry's ride is also like the children on the orphan trains in the United States who were transferred from urban to rural places. Dumbledore's demeanor and diplomatic wisdom resembles that of Sir Winston Churchill. The stories also parallel Cold War themes of evil, power, threats, devastation, and division. Like countries, people are conquered, controlled, and devoured by evil powers as represented by Ginny, saying that the heir of Slytherin "took me over." Because he is a werewolf, Lupin was denied employment and blacklisted like McCarthy-era communists, and he acted like a World War II conspirator by remaining passive and justifying his silence. Sirius Black could be misunderstood and falsely accused like "The Man in the Iron Mask," exiled like Napoleon, trapped like the infamous princes in the tower, or a prisoner of war in the Gulag or Siberian labor camps forced into labor in that permafrost region which symbolizes the Cold War. He is rescued like a war hostage held in a remote location.

The secret tunnels between Hogwarts and Hogsmeade resemble those used by American, North Korean, and Vietnamese soldiers in the American Civil, Korean, and Vietnam Wars to exit prisoner of war camps or infiltrate areas. The clandestine features of this tunnel are reminiscent of the Underground Railroad which helped American slaves escape to freedom in the nineteenth century. Azkaban suggests London's Newgate Prison (approximately the same age as Hogwarts), the Parisian Bastille, or most likely Alcatraz, an island penitentiary near San Francisco, California. Neville's loss of passwords mimics Confederate General Robert E. Lee's "lost order" which Union troops found during the Civil War. While the Confederate note told Union forces where enemy troops were heading, Sirius Black's use of Neville's list provided the people at Hogwarts a major clue about his location on the grounds. Just as Harry explores Hogwarts while everyone else sleeps, much of Scottish history happened under the darkness of night such as Mary, Queen of Scots, marrying the Earl of Bothwell at 4 a.m.

The howler messages hint of the term "Red-Letter Day" which historically meant a happy celebration of a feast or holiday. The idea of not speaking an archenemy's name has a historical precedent when the MacGregors massacred the Colquhouns at the Battle at Glenfruin in 1603, causing the name MacGregor to be banned in certain regions, like Voldemort's. Also, historic figures and events were referred to by colors such as the Black Prince, Black Dinner, and Black Plague. The goblin Red Caps could refer to the Royal Military Police that have guarded Scotland. Many factual aristocratic names sound almost as nonsensical as the fictional names Rowling devised for her characters.

READING FOR RESEARCH

Blackburn, Bonnie, and Leofranc Holford-Stevens. *The Oxford Companion to the Year.* New York and Oxford: Oxford University Press, 1999. Extensive coverage of calendar history and day-by-day analysis of holidays and significant events in numerous cultures.

Davidson, James West, and Mark H. Lytle. *After the Fact: The Art of Historical Detection.* 4th ed. Boston: McGraw-Hill, 2000. Shows readers how to conduct historical research through case examples, including the Salem witchcraft trials and a study of indentured servitude. Suggests methods to reconstruct events, look for visible and invisible clues, and assess evidence and sources.

Weitzman, David. *My Backyard History Book.* Illustrated by James Robertson. Boston: Little, Brown and Company, 1975. This excellent resource is filled with ideas for history projects that encourage readers to understand their families and communities. These activities help readers relate personal and local historical concepts to broader historical events. Includes instructions to build models and other crafts.

INTERNET SITES

History
http://www.thehistorynet.com

Do History (Historical Toolkit)
http://www.dohistory.org/on_your_own/index.html

The History Sourcebook Project
  http://www.fordham.edu/halsall/index.html

Log on to **www.beachampublishing.com** for many additional projects, discussion questions, writing and research ideas, websites, and bibliography.

CHAPTER 12

SCIENCE

"Imagination is more important than knowledge. Knowledge is limited. Imagination encircles the world." —ALBERT EINSTEIN

Introduction

Although the Potter series seems to lack science and technology, the books actually are filled with scientific undertones. Ironically, while Harry and his peers appear to shun technology, which is identified as being part of the despised Muggle culture, the stories appeal to readers immersed in a technology-distilled environment.

SCIENCE AT HOGWARTS

Harry rarely watches television or plays computer games, and it is odd that readers would embrace his non-technological life. Of course, Dudley has access to these state-of-the-art electronic devices, but he is loathsome to readers. Nobody at Hogwarts surfs the internet or communicates by e-mail. (One explanation for this might be that the use of these systems outside academia was not widespread until the mid 1990s, after Books I through III are set.) However, like a stereotypical mad scientist, Arthur Weasley enjoys tinkering with technology, using magic to enhance a car. The castle is an engineering achievement. Students study applications of astronomy, botany, and chemistry. They combine herbs and animal-based substances to make potions. The fantastical creatures they learn to control and bizarre plants parallel genetically engineered food and livestock. Zoology is of interest because of the wild and domesticated animals at Hogwarts. Optics is crucial for understanding photography and mirrors; lenses have been manipulated for centuries to create magical illusions, and reflections in people's pupils were the source of the term "evil eye." The students are affected by weather extremes. Geology and metallurgy are present in the form of stones and metals, particularly wizard money, that the students encounter around the castle. The petrification of students in Book II also demands a scientific explanation, such as understanding how wood is fossilized. Since ancient times, some humans have believed that precious gems and metals can cure illness and extend life spans.

Health and nutrition are incorporated in the students' hearty meals and recurring infirmary visits. Physics is an integral part of the Potter novels because the characters attempt to control time. Lunar cycles and moon phases regulate activity at Hogwarts. Measurement of time is also crucial for preparing potions and traveling. One of the British units of measurement is the hogshead, a fitting measurement for Hogwarts.

Although not considered credible by modern standards, astrology, connected with pioneering astronomical observations, was a significant science during the Middle Ages and Renaissance, and astrological aspects such as predictions permeate the Hogwarts culture. The moving wizard pictures rely on a specially concocted potion to achieve that effect which is similar in appearance to java movement in internet images. Interestingly, the term wizard has been used to describe outstanding factual scientists. Thomas Edison was called the "Wizard of Menlo Park" (where his laboratories were located). Renowned botanist George Washington Carver was known as the "Wizard of Tuskegee," and eighteenth-century astronomer and mathematician Benjamin Banneker was also labeled a wizard because of his genius and talent.

ALCHEMY AND CHEMISTRY

The science most clearly related to the Harry Potter series is chemistry in the form of alchemy. Chemists study the composition of matter and how it changes. The comprehension of chemical processes was enhanced by early alchemists' experiments which built a foundation for chemistry, which would eventually be recognized as a science in the seventeenth century. Medieval scientists practiced alchemy, hoping to produce gold from less valuable metals. In addition to trying to manufacture gold, alchemists desired to develop potions, known as elixirs, to ensure good health and extend life spans. Ancient writers stated that animals, such as stags, lived hundreds of years after drinking such liquids, proving that potions worked.

Founded in Egypt, alchemy was practiced throughout the Mediterranean regions and as far away as China. Ancient Greek and Roman writings discussed alchemy. Empedocles, in the fifth century B.C., stated that all objects consist of water, air, fire, and earth, establishing the basis for alchemy theory. The idea of making gold appealed to ancient peoples, including Caligula, a Roman emperor, who ordered his servants to transform a sulphurous type of arsenic into gold. In the fifth century A.D., Zosimus the Theban attempted similar work based on his knowledge that sulfuric acid dissolved metals. He was the first person to mention the philosopher's stone. Early alchemy was controversial, and Emperor Diocletian demanded that books about such experiments be burned.

Aristotle's idea that matter naturally attained perfection

formed the basis of alchemists' beliefs. Alchemists hypothe-
sized that because the earth created gold from imperfect metals that they should be able to replicate this process. Because
of its mystical nature, early alchemy was associated with magic
and astrology. The *Summa Perfectionis (Summit of Perfection)*,
written by the Arabic scientist Geber, was the first significant
publication addressing alchemy methods. Arabic alchemists
said that metals were composed of mercury and sulfur which
inspired European alchemists, most notably Roger Bacon,
Albertus Magnus, Andreas Libavius who wrote *Alchemia,* and
Philippus Paracelsus, who said that the salt, sulfur, and mercury of compounds represented earth, air, and water.
Paracelsus believed that one unknown element was the source
of these other elements. He called this the "alkahest" and
thought it was the philosopher's stone.

Referred to as "philosophers" because science in the Middle
Ages was known as natural philosophy, alchemists, such as

Nicholas Flamel who lived in the fourteenth century, focused on producing a philosophers' stone which they believed could magically convert substances into precious metals such as gold or silver. Flamel supposedly converted mercury into gold in 1388 and lived to be 116 years old. Scholars say that Flamel pretended to be an alchemist to disguise the source of his vast wealth through moneylending and questionable business ventures.

Historically, these scientist-philosophers distilled a form of mercury and purified it with salt and vinegar. Then, the mixture was placed in a crystal vase and heated over fire. The alchemists labeled the melted substance as "liquor." When boiled in a white vase, lighter colored liquor supposedly became silver, and red liquor turned into gold. The process was complicated and lacked scientific validity, frustrating alchemists who repeatedly failed to manufacture desired products.

Despite the physical impossibilities of chemically producing gold from lesser elements in the Middle Ages, legends about the wondrous abilities of alchemists circulated. Woodcuts pictured alchemists and illustrated alchemy manuals. In 1386, Chaucer referred to the alchemists and the philosopher's stone in the "Yeoman's Tale" (from *The Canterbury Tales*). Alchemists divided into two groups: one evolved into scientifically-grounded chemists, while the other focused on metaphysical aspects that resulted in alchemy being considered a fraudulent activity practiced by charlatans to deceive people. During the Middle Ages, alchemists were motivated by greed and control. Both European and Asian cultures embraced the idea of using powder, usually described as being black, as a philosopher's stone to turn objects into gold. This color imagery reinforces motifs of darkness and the intersection of good and evil in the Harry Potter novels, such as Sirius Black being depicted as sinister but actually metaphorically becoming Harry's golden mentor. Some modern scientists consider alchemy to be a useful methodology, and twentieth-century book titles and other references to alchemy signify that the subject is chemistry-related.

Hogwarts could be considered a metaphorical philosopher's stone which initiates Harry's metamorphosis from an insecure child into an empowered wizard. His professors and Hagrid are symbolic alchemists. The Egyptians stressed that alchemy abilities should not be used for personal gain but for altruistic and spiritual purposes. Like astronauts who develop pharmaceuticals in space that are impossible to manufacture on Earth, Harry and his friends may devise an elixir to cure some plague in their parallel world.

READING FOR RESEARCH

Harre, Rom. *Great Scientific Experiments: 20 Experiments that Changed our View of the World.* Oxford: Oxford University Press, 1983. Historic accounts of significant scientific accomplishments.

Scientific American. *Scientific American Science Desk Reference.* New York: John Wiley & Sons, Inc., 1999. A comprehensive source of scientific and technological definitions, explanations, sources, and biographical material. An essential reference for children to consult.

Vecchione, Glen. *100 First-Prize Make-it-Yourself Science Fair*

Projects. New York: Sterling, 1999. Ideas for a wide variety of experiments and displays.

INTERNET RESOURCES

Alchemy
  http://www.levity.com/alchemy/index.html
Science Sites
  http://kidscience.about.com

Log on to **www.beachampublishing.com** for many additional projects, discussion questions, writing and research ideas, web-sites, and bibliography.

CHAPTER 13

MAGIC AND WITCHCRAFT

"I don't believe in magic" —J.K. ROWLING

"If you ban all books with witchcraft and the
supernatural, you'll ban three quarters of
children's literature." —J.K. ROWLING

Introduction

Humans have been entranced by magic for centuries. Since the Egyptian conjurer Dedi beheaded animals then supernaturally healed them in 2700 B.C., magic has been credited with causing miraculous occurrences or blamed for disastrous tragedies. Illusions have entertained and confused audiences. The performance of magic tricks crosses cultural and time barriers. Throughout history, incidents of magical phenomena and the associated activities of sorcery and witchcraft have sparked both ecstasy and hysteria among populations worldwide. White magic is considered good and used for healing, while black magic is evil and intended to maim or murder. Harry Potter relies on white magic to defend himself, while Lord Voldemort fights with black magic.

HISTORY OF MAGIC

Four types of magic are practiced in the modern world and in the Potter novels. 1) Sympathetic magic involves wish fulfillment using symbols such as voodoo dolls or fingernail clippings or hair, like Harry, Ron, and Hermione use for the Polyjuice Potion in Book II. Also, the consumption of an animal or use of its hair, bones, or skin is believed to empower people, such as the unicorn hair in wands or Voldemort drinking unicorn blood. 2) Divination involves gaining knowledge through various practices such as Trelawney's reading tea leaves. 3) Thaumaturgy encompasses alchemy and sorcery, such as potion making. 4) Incantation is the recitation of spells to achieved desired effects, such as Harry illuminating his wand with the word "lumos."

Words suggesting magical influence or bewitchment, such as "charmed" and "spell," are a part of most languages. The term magic can mean enchantment, occultism, and mysticism. Magicians have also been referred to as conjurers, witches, sorcerers, and wizards. Cultures, both past and present, incorporate magic and witch symbols in art, literature, and advertisements to signify such wide-ranging themes as joyfulness and danger.

Magic represents attaining the impossible. People are vicariously empowered and thrilled by magicians' mastery and control of the surreal. Audiences can peripherally experience danger without directly confronting it. Magic seems to be an intrinsic part of human behavior. Humans want to be tricked and astounded so that they can question the natural order of their world and their basic beliefs. As society has become more industrialized and reliant on technology, many people sense their community has been demythologized, or stripped of mystery and wonder, and they feel empty. Magic helps fill their spirits with a sense of surprise, astonishment, and bewilderment about their external surroundings and internal self.

The earliest references to magic were associated with religious belief systems to explain the unknown. The three Wise Men were magi, or scholars, who were associated with performing feats unfamiliar to the average person. Magi is the source of the word "magic" and represents Persian priests whose rituals had astrological and occult elements. The Bible mentions miraculous events sometimes credited to magicians. Celtic druids worshipped nature in religious applications of magic. Greek and Roman magicians created optical illusions in underground chambers by using concave mirrors and incense smoke

(thus inspiring the saying "smoke and mirrors" to describe a person's deceptive actions). Early scientists also were considered magicians because of their mysterious activities, specifically alchemy (see Chapter 12, Science). Because people could not understand experimentation with metals and other objects, they labeled the scientists as sorcerers who magically transformed substances.

Magic gave its practitioners authority because of their access to knowledge unavailable to other people. Many magicians dramatically demonstrated their tricks to crowds, and magic gradually became part of theatrical performances, circuses, and sideshows. These conjurers became equated with thieves, ruffians, and sorcerers during Queen Elizabeth I's reign. Reginald Scot's *The Discoverie of Witchcraft* was published in 1584 to explain magicians' techniques in an effort to prevent them from being executed as witches.

Although magic is presented as a serious endeavor to be witnessed with respectful, hushed, focused attention, some magicians use humor and comedic interludes to intensify the more sobering tricks. Rowling notes that most of the magic in her books is serious but admits to playing up the juxtaposition of humor and solemnity which represents the vast differences between the humorless but amusing Muggles and the witty but somber wizards. She especially likes to portray magic backfiring on its users such as Ron Weasley coughing up slugs when he tries to cast a spell on Draco Malfoy. Such inexpert attempts at magic make the Hogwarts wizards seem more human than supernatural and more childlike than adult. Magic is often associated with the imagination of children at play. Powerless and dependent, children's creativity strengthens their autonomy and sense of self. Through magic, children can envision fantastical places and things and imagine controlling their own destiny, correcting injustices, and disarming bullies.

THE PRACTICE OF WITCHCRAFT

The word "witch" has varying meanings according to the time and context of its use. Before the twentieth century, "witch" was an accusation, identifying a person as wicked, deceitful, and a threat to the community. Many people labeled as witches were executed or severely punished based on flimsy evidence of their supernatural nature. By the late twentieth century, the word "witch" implied a member of an organized group that practiced pagan beliefs of nature worship. Often called Wicca (meaning sorcerer or prophet), these witches considered their activities to be a religion. Modern witches share many rituals created by early witches. Historians believe that witchcraft emerged from ancient fertility cults that were a folk religion worshipping multiple gods and predating Christianity. These cults and Christianity coexisted through the Middle Ages.

For centuries, witches have been featured in literature, popular culture, and in songs and folktales. Artifacts, such as defixiones, or curse tablets, and archeological sites, such as British-Roman cemeteries with decapitated witches, perhaps to silence their spells, provide clues about attitudes exhibited toward witches. All cultures throughout history have believed in some form of witches. Beliefs shared by many of these groups suggest that witches are fallen angels who use their supernatural powers to injure people or destroy property, to cause storms, to become physically stronger, to predict the future, to fly, to become invulnerable to destruction, to cast love spells or hexes, and, most significantly considering the Harry Potter series, to transform into an animal such as a werewolf like Lupin or become invisible. Such shapeshifting gave humans enhanced sensory abilities and diminished their conscience, enabling them to perpetuate evil acts if instincts and desires took over reason.

Witches were blamed for triggering nightmares and madness. They were believed to be most active at nighttime, ride broomsticks (or fly in baskets in Africa), have animal familiars including owls, use wands, and have birthmarks that indicated they were witches (like Harry's scar). Also, Halloween is a significant holiday for Hogwarts, witches, and Druids, who celebrated Samhain, which was the final day of the Celtic calendar. Witches are featured in folklore and Shakespeare's plays, Lucius Apuleius' *The Golden Ass,* Homer's *Odyssey,* Virgil's *Aeneid,* Nathaniel Hawthorne's *The House of Seven Gables,* and Arthur Miller's *The Crucible.*

While most ancient people believed that magic was an essential part of life, some contemporaries and later generations expressed differing views toward witchcraft. The Code of Hammurabi forbade witchcraft, and the first recorded witch hunt was begun in 367 by the Roman emperor Valerian. Initially, the Christian church only punished witches with penances. When the church became stronger, ecclesiastical authorities resisted secularism, heresy, and witchcraft. A few Europeans tolerated suspected witches because they thought their spells were amusing or comforting, but most people targeted witches for horrendous tortures to test their purity and force them to confess and identify other alleged witches. Many people agreed to confess because they were promised that they would be pardoned, but inquisitors often betrayed their captives.

In New England, the Puritans viewed witches as completely evil beings who acted according to the commands of their master, Satan. Interestingly, most cultures believed that wizards had overwhelmed the Devil (like Harry defeating Voldemort), and that witches were less powerful than their magical counterparts. The Puritans considered witches to represent a trial of their faith in God and cited the book of Exodus from the Bible: "Thou shalt not suffer a witch to live." Such beliefs enabled the Salem witch trial hysteria to rage out of control. The founders of Hogwarts built the school in an isolated area far away from Muggles to avoid such persecution of magical people.

As early as the thirteenth century, Roger Bacon, a Franciscan monk and alchemist, was charged with using black magic. An advocate of developing the philosopher's stone to sustain life, Bacon also conducted scientific experiments that caused people to become suspicious of him. He was imprisoned, and his books were burned. Bacon was an inspiration to many sixteenth-century magical practitioners such as Dr. Johann Faustus, the subject of Johann Spies' biography, *The History of Dr. Faustus, the Notorious Magician and Master of the Black Art*, Christopher Marlowe's play, *The Tragical History of Dr. Faustus*, and Johann

Goethe's epic poem, *Faust,* which described a Sabbat at Brocken, the Harz Mountain's highest peak in Germany.

WITCH HYSTERIA

Witchcraft became a felonious offense by English common law in 1541 and was supported by monarchs including Queen Elizabeth I. During his reign, King James I initiated a vendetta against suspected witches. The author of the treatise *Demonology,* James had presided over Scottish witchcraft trials. The English Parliament enacted a strict anti-witchcraft law in Great Britain and its colonies to please James. Men became professional witch-seekers, testing people suspected of witchcraft by seeing if they felt pain if a suspected Devil's mark was pricked or had animal familiars such as dogs and cats. These witch hunters earned financial rewards for every witch they identified who was convicted. Many of the targeted witches were elderly, female, widowed, or sick with epilepsy or another illness which caused seizures that were mistaken for satanic possession. These individuals were often considered economic burdens on local communities and made into scapegoats by irate, intolerant, insecure neighbors.

From the fourteenth through the seventeenth centuries, millions of Europeans died during witch hunts sponsored both by governments and churches. In preliterate, superstitious societies, people readily blamed witchcraft for causing misfortunes, including the plague, instead of understanding the cause of their illness, such as parasites or viruses. Accusers also believed that witches carefully selected their enemies to suffer curses. Lady Alice Kyteler's witchcraft trial in 1324 was the first one recorded in

England; her wealth was presented as evidence of her demonic possession. Joan of Arc was called a sorcerer because of her religious visions. Afraid of her power, her tormentors imprisoned her and tried her for heresy, saying that she was a witch because she heard evil voices. Like many witches, Joan of Arc was later proven innocent of witchcraft charges and posthumously exonerated.

The book *Malleus Maleficarum (Hammer of Witches)* published in the late fifteenth century guided witch hunters and judges to prosecute witches after Pope Innocent VIII issued the *Summis Desiderantes,* ordering that witches be purged and appointing inquisitors. In that century, Torquemada, known as the Grand Inquisitor, sentenced almost one hundred thousand people as witches in Spain. He targeted Jews, Moors, and other minorities that he considered undesirable. Martin Luther, who founded Protestantism, stated that all witches should be burned,

escalating the frenzy. A person's denial only intensified accusations, and doubters were intimidated to join persecutors in their attacks. Outbreaks of plague and famine increased people's anxiety, exacerbating witch-hunting activity to punish perceived wrongdoers. Family members sometimes turned against each other with witchcraft charges.

The violence of the fifteenth century heightened during the next one hundred year period. Agnes Waterhouse, the first English woman executed as a witch, was hung in 1566 at Chelmsford. A widow, Waterhouse was charged with souring butter and ruining crops. More than half a million women were executed during the witch hunt craze. Powerless because they were uneducated and could not own property or hold office, women relied on men to take care of them. In misogynistic societies, elderly and infertile women were considered unworthy of food and were often victimized. Because some self-described witches served as healers, they often performed midwifery and were persecuted if infants or mothers died. Physicians who based their practices on astrology, the study of celestial phenomena, instead of science blamed witches for the deaths of patients.

The British Witchcraft Act of 1735 stated that people could no longer be prosecuted for witchcraft unless they pretended to practice magic. The Enlightenment replaced fantastical belief systems with rational thought, and mysticism, astrology, and sorcery were considered more as superstitious behaviors rather than valid endeavors. Persecution resembling the witch hunts has occurred sporadically. Often described as witch hunts, these organized attacks were staged against specific groups targeted for their beliefs, ethnicity, or religion and who are demonized as being evil.

Two major examples are Adolf Hitler's systematic extermination of European Jews and other minorities in the 1930s and 1940s and Senator Joseph McCarthy's political assault on American communists in the 1950s. Hitler manipulated Germans' fears about poverty and starvation after World War I to reinforce anti-Semitism. When synagogues were burned on Kristallnacht (a word evoking eerie images of evil characters in the Harry Potter series) in November 1938, Jews were relocated to ghettos or forced labor camps. By the end of World War II, more than six million Jews (including two-thirds of Europe's Jewish population) had been killed during the Holocaust.

WITCHCRAFT TRIALS IN AMERICA

In 1648, Margaret Jones, a healer, was the first person found guilty and executed as a witch in the Massachusetts Bay Colony. Approximately 344 people were killed based on witch hunts in New England between 1620 and 1725. Four out of five victims were women. Witch hunts were most frequent in the colonies of Virginia, Pennsylvania, and New York. The Salem, Massachusetts, witch trials are the best known in American history. Girls accused both women and men in that community and nearby villages, including in Connecticut, of bewitching them. The girls stated that the slave Tituba, originally from Barbados, had taught them voodoo and how to tell the future. Hundreds of people were imprisoned and tried, and fourteen women and six men were executed. Four others died in jail.

A backlash resulted in petitions and testimony supporting the good characters of the accused. People began claiming that the girls were lying and playing a game. Reverend Increase Mather, president of Harvard College, warned that innocent people might be killed and demanded that the trials stop. Massachusetts Governor Sir William Phipps ceased all witch hunt activity, pardoned the accused, and publicly apologized. Some historians have suggested that the Salem witch trials were sustained by people envious of the victims' commercial successes. Other scholars note that a microfungi found in rye bread caused ergotism which caused visions, spasms, and delusions similar to the behavior exhibited by the girls. This fungi is similar to lysergic acid diethylamide (LSD) which can make people highly suggestible to seeing things and repeating ideas told to them.

"McCarthyism," also called America's "witch hunt," refers to the efforts of Senator Joseph McCarthy to expose and rid the United States of communists. Politically motivated, McCarthy played on American's fears about threats to capitalism, such as inflation and labor conflicts. McCarthy announced that some federal employees were communists who posed treason and espionage risks. He never provided proof of his accusations, but the media relayed his charges in newspapers and on television. McCarthy began to release blacklists, mostly his political rivals. Some vulnerable targets named names to avoid being listed by McCarthy. Although Senator Margaret Chase Smith denounced McCarthy's tactics, she was ignored. At least 7,000 federal employees lost their jobs. Hollywood actors and screenwriters also were blacklisted. People who plead the Fifth Amendment and refused to cooperate were arrested for contempt. Many dissenters lost their jobs, were humiliated publicly, and even committed suicide. The climate of distrust

resembled that of other witch hunts in which people projected
their fears and sinister characteristics on others who were
deemed as outsiders and severely punished them to justify the
accuser's perceived sense of righteousness. Such behavior permitted atrocities like Auschwitz and My Lai to occur.

TRICKS OF THE TRADE

Magic became a favored amusement by the seventeenth century. Anonymous street performers clad in star-patterned robes,
somewhat like those worn at Hogwarts, demonstrated simple
magic tricks for passerbys. On stages, magicians amazed audiences with mystical illusions and sleight of hand. People made
false assumptions and illogical conclusions about what they witnessed. Magicians relied on skills of dexterity, agility, memory,

or technological and scientific knowledge to create deceptive maneuvers to entertain people. Sometimes trained animals, musical accompaniment, or dramatic presentations enhanced magical tricks. Many illusions were based on an understanding of natural phenomena, careful use of lighting and shading, or the manipulation of specially designed props to make people appear to levitate or disappear. Several magicians had worked as clockmakers, learning how to operate minute mechanical switches and gears. Some magicians divulged the secrets of their magic on stage and in books and popular magazine articles. Oriental and Egyptian costumes made magicians appear to be exotic, and many conjurers wore turbans like Quirrell's.

Optical tricks manipulating light to create illusions had been a favorite device since ancient times. In 1863, John Nevil Maskelyne built a wooden cabinet with mirrors that were carefully placed to reflect so that a person placed inside seemed to vanish. This cupboard caused people to disappear like the Dursleys' cupboard concealed Harry. Acoustics also were useful for magic. Ancient magicians developed talking heads, such as Orpheus at the temple of Delhi, which listeners thought spoke to them but were really voiced by speakers using tubing. Harry hearing the basilisk is like this magic trick. Magicians relied on electromagnetism to trigger devices such as trap doors to switch people with animals and other tricks. In 1769, the Hungarian Baron Kempelen of Pressburg designed a chess puzzle, concealing a player who moved the pieces with magnets, which was popular throughout Europe. Less scientific magic included spirit-writing in which magicians such as John Henry Anderson, known as "The Wizard of the North," appeared to read audience members' minds and answer questions sealed in envelopes. He relied on assistants who wandered in the audience and gave him the correct answers.

Magicians were often referred to as wizards in advertisements and promotional literature. John Wyman, Jr., known as "Wyman the Wizard," was a popular American magician who performed for prominent people like President Abraham Lincoln. Jonathan Harrington was a New England ventriloquist who threw his voice in the hardware store where he worked. In 1859, he started an annual Fourth of July conjuring show for Boston children. In that city's public garden, Harrington, who combined comedy with magic, was joined by other magicians, including notable showman P.T. Barnum. Richard Potter was one of the most interesting early American magicians. He performed ventriloquism, hypnotism, knife swallowing, and fire-related tricks. Potter was the first person to demonstrate the Hindu Rope Trick, ascending an unanchored rope into the sky. Potter Place, New Hampshire, was named for Richard Potter, whose former residence has a stone which reads: "In Memory of Richard Potter, the Celebrated Ventriloquist, Aged 52 years. Died Sept. 20, 1835."

By the twentieth century, magicians appeared on Broadway, films, and television. Considered famous showmen, they were like movie stars. Harry Houdini was an especially dramatic and stylish escape artist, and the timing and suspense involved in his performances foreshadow Rowling's page-turning plots. Harry Blackstone, Sr., Doug Henning, and David Copperfield all contributed to public awareness and appreciation of magical illusions. By the turn of the twenty-first century, television stations featured shows that focused on illusions and revealed magician's secrets. This was reminiscent of the discrediting of Lockhart and practitioners of Spiritualism in the 1920s. Houdini exposed how mediums feigned to contact spirits during seances.

POTTER MAGIC AND CONTEMPORARY SOCIETY

Magic and witchcraft in the Harry Potter series are equated with imagination. Harry and his peers are empowered by magical abilities that enable them to defend themselves against evil. The contrast between the magical world of Hogwarts and the unimaginative setting for Muggles emphasizes how magic can expand a person's vision and expectations of himself and others. Magic is restricted in the proximity of Muggles because nonmagical people might abuse it. Wizards and witches practice their magical techniques and are careful not to use magic carelessly or irresponsibly. Although they often use white magic for fun, specifically in Quidditch matches, young wizards and witches recognize that magic has often been misunderstood by people who are scared of nonconformists and lack the imagination to comprehend the unknown. Instead of being used subversively, magic connects children with adult mentors and helps them achieve maturity and insights unavailable to most non-magical children.

The evils presented in the Harry Potter series parallel modern horrors. Cults, gangs, ritual sacrifices, and vandalism plague communities around the world. Newspapers and television tell people daily about despots and disasters. Movies contain violent images of warfare on battlefields and in neighborhoods. People have access to information about making bombs and suicide methods on the internet. Halloween has been banned in many places. The college town of Iowa City, Iowa, has enforced restrictions on children dressing as witches or devils or wearing clothing with those images at schools. Teachers and librarians who defend literature with magical themes are often fired. Witch hunts continue in modern society. In 1994, one hundred women were accused of witchcraft and murdered in South Africa. Men and women had been burned for practicing witchcraft two years earlier in Kenya. Lightning bolts which killed eighteen soccer fans at Puerto Lempira, Honduras, in 1995 and an entire soccer team of eleven players at Kinshasha in the Democratic Republic of Congo in 1998 were blamed on witchcraft. Believing in sorcery, people often performed magical rites in attempts to influence who won and lost soccer games.

Modern witches proclaim to practice pagan rituals of nature worship, such as observing the solstices and initiating new members. Known as "Wicca," this witchcraft is not Satanic. Wicca witches honor the feminine and seek to improve the Earth. Like their ancient predecessors, they understand the role of natural energy to achieve creativity. Wicca is also referred to as "Craft," and these Neo-Pagans consider it a religion which connects humans with the universe. They seek peaceful solutions to social problems to achieve order from chaos. Similarly, shamans and pagans recognize seasonal changes and spiritual renewal. Valued by their communities, shaman, or medicine men, are associated with evil spirits that those cultures consider essential to encounter in order to challenge demonic forces. Witches are common through Asia, Africa, and parts of Latin America. Witchcraft is also practiced in America's Appalachia, and the Amish people of Pennsylvania paint hex signs on their barns to protect them from witches.

Magic and witchcraft have become a part of mainstream culture. Adaptations of "The Sorcerer's Apprentice," written by Lucian of Samosata in the second century, have appeared on stage and movie screens, especially as the Disney film, *Fantasia*. Other movies have pagan and witch themes, including *Dragnet* and *The Wizard of Oz*. Television shows such as "The Worst Witch," "Bewitched," "I Dream of Jeannie," "Charmed," "Sabrina, The Teenaged Witch," and "Buffy, the Vampire Slayer" all have magical themes. Comic strip witches include "Broomhilda." Sports teams are called the "devils" or "werewolves." A major internet service provider in the United Kingdom is named "Demon." Role game players pretend to use magic in "Dungeons and Dragons" and sorcery-themed computer programs and arcade contests. Haunted houses terrify patrons at Halloween. Paris' Le Theatre du Grand Guignol was known for displaying exceptionally realistic and grotesque scenes.

Terms and images addressing magic and witchcraft are incorporated in expressions and advertising. Some people consult astrologers, mystics, and psychics for personal and professional guidance. Rowling, however, does not believe in magic no matter how enchanting her writing is. Because of critics' concerns about the possible persuasiveness of the series' appealing magical lifestyle, Rowling emphasizes that she has not met any child interested in becoming a witch because of reading the novels. Harry's, Ron's, and Hermione's magical role as wizards and witches is to inspire readers' imaginations and interest in literature.

Reading for Research

Davies, Owen. *Witchcraft, Magic, and Culture, 1736-1951*. Manchester: Manchester University Press, 1999. A scholarly account of witchcraft in Great Britain, discussing aspects such as the popularity of Wicca in modern society.

Jay, Ricky. *Learned Pigs & Fireproof Women*. New York: Villard Books, 1986. An entertaining account of bizarre magical performers and animal assistants.

Meltzer, Milton. *Witches and Witch-hunts: A History of Persecution*. New York: The Blue Sky Press, 1999. A children's book which effectively covers the history of witchcraft and modern witch hunts against targeted groups. Includes transcripts of related documents.

Internet Sites

Magic Sites
http://magic.about.com

Magical Pasttimes: The On-line Journal of Magic History
http://www.uelectric.com/pastimes/index.html

Society of Young Magicians
http://www.magicsym.org/

Log on to **www.beachampublishing.com** for many additional projects, discussion questions, writing and research ideas, websites, and bibliography.

CHAPTER 14

LITERARY QUALITIES

*"I think it's wrong to think of adult books as 'real
literature.' Real literature can be for people of nine
and that's what I'm trying to write."*
—J.K. ROWLING

*"People have said the humour is very adult,
but I do think they underestimate children. Certainly,
some of the kids I've met have got every joke and even
if they haven't, it doesn't actually matter. It annoys me
that people think you have to dumb down for
children."* —J.K. ROWLING

INTRODUCTION

Joanne Rowling has been praised by important literary critics for her exceptional imagination and her craft, and she has won numerous awards, including a nomination for the prestigious Whitbread Prize that acknowledges Britain's highest literary achievement. This chapter analyzes some of her accomplishments.

TIMELESS TALES

The Harry Potter novels are reminiscent of literary classics that have nurtured humans' thirst for adventure and the macabre in storytelling that is both entertaining and instructive. The stories are allegories commenting on social and political conditions. They seem to transcend time, being rooted in ancient narrative techniques of tales that were orally transmitted to crowds, tragi-comedies performed in Greek or Elizabethan theaters, or nineteenth-century novels serialized in popular periodicals. Harry's stories could have been told by the pilgrims of Geoffrey Chaucer's *The Canterbury Tales*, the plague refugees in Giovanni Boccaccio's *The Decameron*, or aired as a modern soap opera on radio or television. They could have been whispered around military campfires or sung by buffoonish court jesters. Their timeless literary attributes can be credited to their foundation on mythology, legends, and literature as old as the Bible (see Chapter 9, Mythology, Legends and Fairy Tales; and Chapter 11, Archetypes and Biblical Allusions).

Whether such epic lore is told in poetic cycles, performed in musical rounds, scripted in scenes and acts, or read from a book, its emphasis on mystery, adventure, and banishment of evil is universal to all cultures and eras. Rowling's literary style is analogous to elements contained in fictional and factual historical stories. Sometimes satirical and alluding to corrupt or misguided political, social, or cultural figures, Rowling's stories are reminiscent of Shakespearean dramas that revolve around insider humor and moral dilemmas often created and worsened by the suffering characters.

The complexities of the Potter novels' structure, plots, characterizations, language, and themes inspire further intensive and elaborate analysis of each component. All of Rowling's diverse literary motifs can be integrated in the unifying concept that imagination is the true source of magic to comprehend, coexist with, and cultivate humanity.

LANGUAGE AND HUMOR

Rowling's sense of humor and history create a literary style unique to Harry Potter. Her playful use of words and names—penning puns that are obvious and somewhat overly corny at times while others are more sophisticated blends of intellectual insights, sarcasm, and wit—allows her to invent a setting both funny and frightening. The jargon unique to the Potter novels, including the bureaucratic names of decrees and warnings issued by the Ministry of Magic, adds to the concept of a contained fantastical world receptive to supernatural occurrences and bizarre dwellers. Considered a closed society, the wizard realm is depicted through language and tone that seem exclusive, welcoming only individuals deemed to have magical potential. Yet Rowling's literary techniques design Hogwarts to be inclusive, inviting readers to become part of the story.

Her figurative use of words creates a believable setting populated by recognizable inhabitants who share common human traits in addition to their extraordinary talents. Some people "tower" over others, and the words "paralyze" and "paralysis" frequently describe physical limitations as well as emotional indecision. Words are powerful, magically creating desired effects or defending their speakers from harm. Harry realizes that words can also be weapons. The descriptive passages of the castle's exterior and interior appearance personify Hogwarts. Readers feel that they have been immersed into the school's culture and should hurry to class or Quidditch practice. Details further enliven the Hogwarts community because readers can see the tortoise shell with the teapot pattern or the mouse whiskers on the snuffbox that had been transformed. Readers vicariously travel to Diagon Alley to gather required school supplies, gaze at the Firebolt, watch the monster books fight, and eat wizard delicacies. Rowling's words personify actions such as footsteps that "died away," reinforcing the death imagery that cloaks Hogwarts.

BRITISH AND AMERICAN ENGLISH

Rowling's innate British humor enhances the wordplay in the series. Translated editions alter some of the British words and phrases so that readers belonging to other cultures can understand the meaning that Rowling intended. Most of the British words for food, actions, and spoken expression, however, have remained as they appear in the British editions. For the American editions, editor Arthur A. Levine asked Rowling to choose words and phrases more familiar to American readers. They developed a vernacular that represented the British nature of the novels but which American readers could follow. In addition to aiding comprehension, this translation resulted in Harry and Hogwarts seeming more realistic to readers in the United States who lack experience and awareness of boarding school and British culture.

The title was the most obvious change. In Great Britain, Harry sought the philosopher's stone, referring to the activities of medieval alchemists, including the real Nicholas Flamel, and their attempts to create a philosopher's stone to turn other metals into gold. While many British readers would have been aware of this historic background, American readers might have misinterpreted the word "philosopher" as someone who ponders the meaning of thoughts instead of a scientist experimenting with magic. Rowling decided to substitute the word "sorcerer" in the American edition so that readers would be aware that the book was about magic and not mistake its contents for being about something uninteresting and even boring. Other slight changes in the American novels involved editing traditional British spellings, such as removing the "u" in "colour," and including a table of contents that groups the chapter titles together.

Specific words were substituted, such as "vacation" for "holiday," "mail" for "post," "subway" for "underground," "closet" for "cupboard," "trashcan" lids for "dustbin" lids, and "schedule" for "timetable." Foods often are the same, and Harry consumes crumpets in both British and American editions. British expressions such as "git" and "nutters" are uttered in both countries. Some words and phrases are intended to sound like children's slang and italicized to emphasize those words. Some wordplay is lost in the translations though. The British "Sellotape" becomes "Scotch tape" in the United States, and readers miss out on the pun of "Spellotape" being used to patch a broken wand. Many invented names, especially for candies, were not changed because they accentuate the novels' fantastical qualities.

WIZARDRY WORDS

Book reviewers have described Rowling's words as casting a spell to enchant readers. The passwords and magical instructions all seem appropriate to the situation or desired objective, or they are nonsensical to reinforce the absurdity of a character or moment. Names of people, places, and objects often have double meanings. Harry is often harried. Some names seem like insightful derivations, such as Granger perhaps being inspired by the word "Grangerize" which is an eponym describing how James Granger, author of the *Biographical History of England* (1769), tore out pictures from published texts to use for illustrations in his books, somewhat like Hermione dissects books for information to solve mysteries.

Sniglets are words that are not in the dictionary yet but may someday be included because of popular acceptance and use. "Munchkin" from *The Wizard of Oz* is an example. Someday, "Quidditch" and "Muggle" may define more than a game played on broomsticks and dull people because readers will expand its meaning to incorporate familiar applications in their environment. The invented words prevent readers from assigning unrelated traits to characters and activities. If the Dursleys had been called Philistines or Boeotians, they might seem more exotic to readers. Many of the names and words sound phonetically like other words. For example, a computer spell check of the name Hagrid suggests the word "highroad" and Weasley is associated with the word "weasel." The exact naming of people, especially of evil individuals, is crucial to confront and successfully challenge them. Many myths, legends, and fairy tales have purported that you cannot control a person or cast a spell over a person until you've learned his secret name.

Rowling inspires wordplay. *The Daily Telegraph* best seller list included alliterative descriptions of the Potter novels and rhymes: "Bored boy becomes boarder," "Oppressed orphan summoned to secret school," "Potter puzzled by petrified pals," "Warped warlock harries Harry" "Escapee's escapades worry wizards," "Snatched from suburbia by sorcerers, "School: yells, bells and spells," "Is Potter's pursuer friend or fiend?" and "Sorcerer's school in state of siege."

The Potter novels encourage readers to understand the precise definitions of words, differentiating between jealousy and envy, suspicion and concern. Some words have double meanings. The school motto and other words have Latin foundations, appropriate for an English boarding school where Muggle students would study ancient languages. Names indicate personality types, such as peevish Peeves, or properties, such as the Floo powder flying Harry to another destination. Some names share prefixes with words that have definitions resembling characterizations, such as Malfoy being a malefactor or malevolent.

NAMES

Perhaps Rowling's most effective stylistic device is the use of names. Like Dumbledore and Harry, she recognizes the power of a name and deliberately identifies people, items, and places by monikers that reveal aspects of their personalities and traits, either by describing the namesake or ironically depicting opposite characteristics than would be typically expected. Such contrary names provide humor to lessen the fear that might otherwise be provoked by those characters or reinforce their malevolence. Some names are anagrams and provide clues to riddles posed in the stories or serve as red herrings to distract readers.

Chapter titles succinctly offer symbolic references and sometimes misleading clues that add to the growing sense of suspense. Rowling's literary use of names with double meanings exposes the dual nature of wizards and related events and activities as being concurrently good and evil. Characters' first and surnames are sometimes alliterative, such as Severus Snape and Cho Chang, and mostly rhythmic, adding to the literary tone of their depiction, especially when read aloud. Harry sometimes seems like a younger version of the spy James Bond who skillfully evades antagonists who have descriptive names like Harry's enemies.

Although the origin of Rowling's names may seem far-fetched to some readers, her clever inventions of so many unique names strongly suggests a pattern that she uses for combining word definitions to form names. Some, such as "Quidditch" and "Muggle," can be interpreted by understanding the components, either through phonetic interpretations or linguistic examinations. For example, "quid" is slang for money, a piece of a chewy substance, or part of the Latin phrase "quid pro quo." That phrase means an exchange of items or compensation for a loss. It also is the title of a medieval tract that was distributed to medieval herbalists and apothecaries. The word "ditch," meaning a hole in the ground for drainage, irrigation, to defend land, or to abandon something or crash land. Combined with definitions of "quid," Quidditch might indicate the ferocity of the competition compared to trench warfare or its value to players being equivalent to money or property.

"Muggle" could be misread as muffle, muddle, or middle, suggesting someone who is confused, inept, or mediocre. The derivative "mug" suggests someone who makes faces, seeks publicity, or assaults others, all characteristics of how the Dursleys and other mortals are portrayed. Muggle also suggests "muggy," meaning unpleasantly humid and suffocating. Other names, such as Hedwig, Dumbledore, and Snape, have factual, and often appropriate, origins; Hedwig is the name of a saint, Dumbledore an old English term for bumblebees, and Snape an English geographical site. Some names suggest roles. For example, the Ministry of Magic's abbreviation MOM hints of that organization's constant monitoring of wizards and witches, while the Defense Against the Dark Arts position, or DADA, alludes to the patriarchal (fatherly) tendencies of those professors. Both of these surrogate parents are instrumental to Harry's adventures.

FICTIONAL FRAMEWORK

The Potter novels may seem formulaic because the stories feature characters representing extremes of good and evil. Through skillful characterizations, readers identify with the appealing protagonists and despise their foes. Intriguing but hazardous predicaments induce anxiety because the enemies appear to be outwitting the heroes. The novels seem to conform to the classic fantasy structure of a quest cycle beginning in a normal setting, then transferring to the fantasy realm where the conflict is resolved so the protagonists can return home. Harry Potter, like archetypal heroes, must undergo an apprenticeship and successfully complete a quest, interacting with fantastical inhabitants much like those Alice encounters in Wonderland, to earn respect from his fictional companions and readers. During this educational period, Harry must learn from his adventures and enrich his community with his skills as a form of gratitude.

The novels intermix familiar ideas, figures, and scenes with startling phenomena innovative to readers who are both adults and children, although older readers are more likely to understand the clever asides and comments. However, Rowling does not condescend to her readers, and she crafts complex sentences and selects precise vocabulary to complement her fabricated words. Nor is she patronizing, expecting readers to research her allusions. Rowling manages to balance elements of humor and horror to set a shaky tone in which readers are unsure of their own comprehension or fluctuating action. This illusionary nature makes readers feel they have magically become part of the book.

PLOT DEVELOPMENT

Another stylistic technique is Rowling's ability to scare readers and create suspense by carefully pacing the plot to keep Harry and others in jeopardy for long durations and providing cliffhanger chapter endings. Within the novel, stories intertwine confusing clues and tantalizing twists somewhat like the convoluted tunnels underneath the school. Confrontations are not rushed and are fully developed, often repeating key statements and concepts that clearly illuminate what each combatant's complaints, motives, and ambitions are. Exciting events which foreshadow more sinister occurrences build tension and intensify as the plot nears its climax.

By the conclusion of each book, Rowling neatly resolves the divergent story lines that are all related to the primary plot, and the fluidity of her prose encourages readers to devour the novel in one sitting despite the book's length, and then reread passages to determine where hints were hidden. Foreshadowing includes the fight between Arthur Weasley and Lucius Malfoy, Ginny forgetting her diary, and Harry thinking the Hogwarts Express resembled a snake while he flew above it in the car.

OUTSIDERS

Being an outsider is an important stylistic characteristic in the Potter novels, especially because an omniscient narrator removed from the action is telling the story. The trio of heroes are all misfits in some form despite their varying backgrounds and they feel restricted by societal expectations and limitations.

Harry feels isolated from his parents' legacy. Ron does not always feel comfortable with his family. And Hermione never feels secure that she truly belongs at Hogwarts. Other classmates also question whether they should be included in the wizard realm, sensing that they exist on the periphery.

Solitude, seclusion, and loneliness lead to acceptance, admission, and fellowship symbolized by Harry's movement from confinement to freedom, flying away from his tormentors in Book II. Harry, although embraced as a part of Hogwarts, often stands on his own, which is symbolized by him because he is the only student who can hear the sinister voice and is marked by the lightning bolt scar. He is in effect quarantined from the Dursleys' hatefulness even at traditional family holidays such as Christmas when they contact Harry only to remind him how much they despise him, inoculating him against feeling any affinity for them.

Each of the characters discovers previously unknown attributes and qualities that help them form their identity and participate as a valued member of the community. They each have painful episodes they have to cope with and preconceived prejudices they must overcome. Each realizes his or her inner strength and how to utilize them to achieve their purposes. They have to rely on themselves because of the hesitancy of adults to believe their warnings and assist them.

VOICE

Voice is also a powerful literary tool in the novels, and the dialogue seems authentic for each character, such as the thick dialect uttered by Hagrid, offering insights to supplement omniscient passages. Harry symbolically loses his voice when confronted with unfair accusations, yet he is the sole person who can hear the sinister utterances of the chamber's monster. Intentional deafness, such as Draco Malfoy ignoring people he considers to be his inferiors, symbolizes racism. Harry understands and speaks Parseltongue, a reference to the grammatical dissection of language, and his voice opens the chamber. Evil is personified by vindictive voices that are chillingly cold, while friendly, supportive voices are soothingly warm, and the warmth versus cold imagery extends to other depictions of good and evil.

MAGIC

The literary motifs of magic and secrecy dominate the novels. The illusionary and deceptive natures of magic accentuate themes of enchantment. Rowling distinguishes between knowledge of and actual ability to practice magic as emphasized by inept wizards and resulting in different levels of sorcerers. Harry Potter stories offer readers the opportunity for wish fulfillment by designing a fantasy world where they can identify with characters that are popular, successful, and empowered. Magic is possible because of imagination, which is equated with power. Spells can be used for vengeance, to reduce burdensome tasks, for practical uses such as defense against attackers, or other applications. Again, Rowling applies her poetic sense of words by naming spells and charms to indicate their purpose, such as "Expelliarmus" which disarms an opponent, or to describe their results such as "Tarantallegra," which makes someone's legs jerk like a spider. Harry learns that magic is accessible to everyone if they know where to look for it, and by understanding and accepting their personal truths. Arthur Weasley explains that keys magically shrink but Muggles say they are lost because they do not want to admit they have witnessed magic. By combining realism and fantasy, Rowling effectively provides her readers escapism through the plausible ventures of the fictional actors who are rewarded for challenging and conquering their abnormal circumstances and opponents.

HIDDEN IDENTITIES AND FAMILY

By giving characters dual personalities, Rowling shows how people and actions often are more complex than superficial appearances suggest. There are characters whose intentions are ambiguous, deceiving Harry with how he senses their seemingly virtuous and well-meaning nature. Rowling plants subtle clues about potential villains, such as their efforts to control others. The literary representation of passivity and assertiveness underscores the idea that obtaining and wielding power influences whether an innately good person will be tempted by wickedness or rendered ineffective by withstanding such enticements or if an already flawed person will become more damaged. This puzzle must be pieced together with fragments of knowledge and misinformation to enable resolution with mysterious antagonists.

Magic is able to reveal the truth about characters and situations and expose their facades and masks. Invisibility is an important motif because it conceals evil, such as the blank diary pages, but also represents how good characters are metaphorically unseen because they are overlooked. Harry's father's invisibility cloak ironically intensifies Harry's presence instead of diminishing him because he can traverse more areas of Hogwarts.

Harry learns about the subtleties of people who seem brave and loyal but are also cowardly and malicious. He senses that simply because some characters do not exercise dark powers that does not mean they lack such potential. He acknowledges the differences between right and wrong can be difficult to distinguish, sometimes overlapping, and that he risks making detrimental decisions because of vague or false information and his inability to detect impostors. Because Harry often opts to ignore school rules in his pursuit of justice, he becomes embroiled in situations that have a contradictory outcome, and this unpredictability reinforces the literary theme of duality, which complicates and pushes the plot toward its conclusion. Harry realizes that he not only has the ability to perform magic but also has the capacity to make choices. He learns that the power of love can overcome opposition, and that family bolsters a person's strength.

Rowling uses family as a literary device. Harry's quest is to seek vengeance for his parents' death and to resolve his feelings of rootlessness. Two of Harry's friends, Hermione and Ginny, represent his mother, and his efforts to save them symbolizes his grief and desire for redemption because he wishes that he also could have rescued his mother. Just as Rowling experienced an epiphany about her life's purpose when her mother died, Harry begins his search for self-identity and meaning when he learns who his parents were and how they died.

He surrounds himself with images that represent his parents, such as the moonlight that glows comfortingly yet illuminatingly through his turret window and is the backdrop when he is rescued by the Weasleys, and again when Dobby realizes he is free. Harry explores his internal conflicts, especially his desire to belong to his family despite the agonies inflicted on him by the Dursleys. He wants to compensate for his childhood miseries and be connected to people and places beyond his sphere and time, both physically and emotionally, especially his deceased parents. By coming to terms with his past, Harry is able to live in the present and prepare for the future. He is replenished through love for himself, others, and his community; he is fortified by love's power and protective forces.

GENDER

Gender is another important literary device. Although each character is identified as male or female, most characters could be borderline androgenous, exhibiting personality traits ascribed to both females and males, as embodied in such characteristics as kindness and aggression. The pipes and stone tunnel leading to the Chamber of Secrets are like the birth canal, and the Chamber, although considered evil, could also be regarded to be womb-like and nurturing, ultimately protecting Ginny and Harry. The Weasley's flying car expands to accommodate its passengers and their luggage, suggesting the womb.

In most literature, wands are associated with phallic symbols, with Ron's bent wand indicating his impotence at magic. His vomiting slugs shows his lack of control over his changing body. Also, Harry's broken right arm temporarily incapacitated him much like Ron's wand hindered him, slowing his maturity. Harry averted his gaze from the snake's blinding stare, protecting his eyesight, symbolic of his enhanced perception which was restored by the motherly Molly Weasley when she repaired his eyeglasses in Diagon Alley.

Mythologist Joseph Campbell would consider the chamber to be a netherworld where the hero would be helped by supernatural guides, as when Fawkes assists Harry. Psychological analyses of the stories might see them through Freudian suggestions about sexuality and repressed desires, or Jungian imagery in which the stairways, tunnels, and tomb-like chamber represent Harry's fears and introverted personality. The Chamber could be depicted as containing imagery of the internal agony and conflict an individual endures within their psyche.

COLOR

Colors are important to the literary style of the Potter novels. In British history and culture many people, places, and events are identified by color, such as the Black Chapel from King Arthur lore and the Black Knight from Edward Eager's *Half Magic* (1954). In the Potter series, shades of red represent goodness, such as the Gryffindors' scarlet robes (a color associated with royalty), Harry's red ink, and the crimson Hogwarts Express train. The Weasleys have red hair, sometimes described as flaming, the same color as the roof of their house which shelters them, and characters blush, showing red faces when embarrassed or flattered. Blood is important as a life force to resist the poison of evil and also as the definer of social rank. Red also denotes badness. Villains' eyes sometimes have "an odd red gleam." The sun is described as ruby and blood red, indicating the degree of evil at Hogwarts. The Quaffle, which is necessary to score goals in Quidditch, is a large red ball. Fire is sometimes described as being blue, and the bird-keys in one chamber in Book I have feathers that are bright jewel colors. The Knight Bus is purple, a derivative of the primary colors red and blue which sometimes indicates royalty, as Harry is regarded in the wizard world.

The Slytherins' robes are green, and the basilisk's skin is a "vivid, poisonous green." Harry recalls a green light when his parents were attacked. Green also has good connotations because it is the color of ink used on Hogwarts' correspondence and Arthur Weasley's garments. Snape dons black robes which also drape Ginny in the chamber, sometimes symbolizing their participation in dark magic. White does not necessarily indicate innocence or the absence of evil. Lucius Malfoy's fists are described as white, and Harry feels "white-hot pain" when he is wounded. White snow blankets Hogwarts, confining its inhabitants, both good and evil, to suffer each other's company. Aragog has "milky white" eyes, and Ginny's catatonic face resembles white marble. The benign Hufflepuffs wear canary yellow Quidditch uniforms.

METAPHORICAL MATERIALS

Metals are significant, showing the symbiotic reliance of the wizards on the mortal world. Metals also reinforce the alchemy foundation of the wizard's training, with some metals regarded as signs of strength, decay, or other traits associated with astrological signs of good and evil. Metal cauldrons are used to boil potions. The Dursleys' preferred academic institution, Smeltings, indicates the act of separating metals which can symbolize elitism. Percy's prefect badge is silver as is Tom Riddle's service trophy. Laboratory tools are silver and brass, and dining utensils and Fawkes' perch are gold, the valuable metal that alchemists tried to make using the philosopher's stone. Wizard money consists of precious metals with such names as sickle, like the metal agricultural tool, and galleon, referring to Spanish sailing vessels filled with riches.

Plants and stones are also important images. The Whomping Willow is malevolent, and the Mandrakes' vocalizations can kill, but mandrakes also are the antidote to restore transfigured people and animals that have been cursed. Hogwarts has oaken doors, creating comforting earthy images, while the Forbidden Forest is home to thorny bushes that grab intruders' clothing and prevent them from fleeing. Harry's mother's name was Lily, a symbol of rebirth and peace, whose beautiful flower blooms aloft a tall stem reaching toward the light. Lilies are held in esteem, while his aunt's name Petunia suggests something plain, hardy, mediocre, low to the ground, and taken for granted.

The Hogwarts castle is constructed of marble and stone. The targeted students are petrified, which is a form of fossilizing organic tissue, usually plants. Teachers are sometimes "stony-faced" when confronted with displeasing situations. Precious stones include emeralds as snake eyes in a bas-relief in the Chamber of Secrets and egg-sized rubies on Godric Gryffindor's sword. Students buy protective amulets made of metals and stones to ward off evil.

NUMBERS

Numbers also seem to be symbolic, especially the numerals 2, 3, 4, 7, and 8. Two is significant because of the duality occurring throughout the book in the form of two worlds and two sides of people as well as the symbolism of the Weasley twins and the double attack on Hermione and Percy's girlfriend Penelope (perhaps comatosely waiting for her Odysseus—Percy—to return to her). The trio of Harry, Ron, and Hermione suggest the power of three and the spiritual trinity. Harry fatally wounds the basilisk on its third strike. Hagrid knocks on the front door of Hogwarts three times when Harry first arrives there in Book I. Students are divided into four houses at Hogwarts which is also the number of seasons and horsemen of the apocalypse, traditional emblems of evil. The Dursleys' address is the numeral four, and Harry's arrival made their family consist of four people.

Students attend Hogwarts for seven years, and there are seven players on each Quidditch team. The Gryffindors' House Championship win was the first time they had defeated the Slytherins in seven years. Sirius is imprisoned on the seventh floor of Hogwarts (Harry locates the office by counting to the thirteenth window on that level) Seven children were born to the Weasley family, and the spiders have eight eyes and legs. Thirteen people died from a single curse blamed on Sirius Black. In addition to exact numbers, references to quantities reinforce characterizations. Size indicates the degree of a person's or thing's malevolence. The Whomping Willow, Aragog, and basilisk are exaggeratedly large, while Harry is considered small for his age.

TEMPERATURE, TIME, AND SEASONS

Movement upward symbolizes ascension toward sanity and goodness, while movement downward suggests descent into madness and evil. Gliding and floating can be peaceful—the flying car or Hagrid's flights—or ominous like Snape's bat-like motions. Fire symbolizes rebirth and purification, and water represents danger. Temperatures are also a barometer of malevolence. Characters and rooms seem icy when they are sinister and warm when they are benevolent. The weather worsens as evil intensifies and improves as goodness prevails.

Seasons are associated with activities. Summer is the interim in which Harry must suppress his magical nature and feels most depressed; autumn brings his rebirth and return to Hogwarts, followed by the hibernation of winter in which he busily pursues schoolwork. Spring brings sporting and academic success when, renewed from his winter's rest, he is most potent to vanquish whoever torments him or threatens the school.

A reference to a Quidditch match being the worst game in three hundred years suggests to readers how wizards perceive time and their age. Dawn signifies new beginnings such as the timing of Harry's arrival at the Burrow. The wizards celebrate traditional Muggle holidays, and the Christmas vacation assures the trio sufficient time to prepare the potion they need to trick Draco Malfoy. Halloween is the anniversary of the attack on the Potters, but the holiday, not the murder, is accentuated as one of the school's favorite pastimes.

READING FOR RESEARCH

The Merriam-Webster New Book of Word Histories. Springfield, MA: Merriam-Webster, Inc., 1991. Valuable reference for learning the origins and applications of words.

Rawson, Hugh. *Rawson's Dictionary of Euphemisms and Other Doubletalk: Being a Compilation of Linguistic Fig Leaves and Verbal Flourishes for Artful Users of the English Language*. New York: Crown Publishers, 1995. An entertaining discussion of synonyms, antonyms, euphemisms, slang, and jargon.

Rees, Nigel. *Why Do We Say?: Words and Sayings and Where They Come From*. Poole, Dorset, and New York: Blandford, 1987. Explains etymology of popular words and phrases.

INTERNET SITES

The American-British British-American Dictionary
http://www.peak.org/~jeremy/dictionary/dict.html

A Word A Day
http://www.wordsmith.org

The Word Detective
http://www.word-detective.com

Log on to **www.beachampublishing.com** for many additional projects, discussion questions, writing and research ideas, websites, and bibliography.

CHAPTER 15

MORAL AND SOCIAL CODES

"If you're writing about evil you genuinely have a responsibility to show what that means."
—J.K. ROWLING

"Seven blunders of the world that lead to violence: wealth without work, pleasure without conscience, knowledge without character, commerce without morality, science without humanity, worship without sacrifice, politics without principle."
—MAHATMA GANDHI

INTRODUCTION

Many of the hundreds of reviews of the Potter novels have focused on Harry as a role model. He confronts adversity in an honest and honorable manner, he strives to help those in need, and he seeks to live by a code of conduct that is just and good. But he is also a prophet within his world, and it is not enough that he live by a code that is not worthy of his esteemed place; he must decipher good from evil within himself and then within the social structure he has inherited in order to exemplify moral and social codes that others will follow.

LIFE LESSONS

Rowling's characters learn lessons about social issues during their interactions with family members, teachers, friends, and adversaries. Perhaps Rowling's most difficult challenge is creating Harry as an example of morality and correct behavior for the millions of readers, both young and mature, who follow his series. A daunting task for a young boy, Harry is not only accountable to himself but also has to set standards for present and future generations. He is acutely aware of his role in society, whether he is living within the confines of the Muggles at the Dursleys' home or savoring his freedom at Hogwarts. His sense of fairness and justice is well developed.

Believing that people should be treated equitably, Harry combats favoritism and elitism through his reactions to hostile classmates and professors, and his performances on the Quidditch field. Although he disobeys some school and Ministry of Magic rules when he feels he is justified, Harry, for the most part, tries to function within the system instead of adding to its possible disintegration. Hogwarts and mortal schools experience similar cliques and stresses such as snobby students versus geeky pupils, academic pressures and incentives to cheat, and the competitive nature of team sports within the school and against rivals at other schools. Harry tries to uphold Hogwarts' honor in all of his endeavors.

Even though he is still a child with youthful wants and dreams, Harry comprehends the idea that work and commitment are necessary to succeed and reach goals, and that being given privileges and possessions only weakens people's character as evidenced by Draco Malfoy. Harry, Ron, and Hermione demonstrate self-discipline to excel at their studies to become effective wizards. They also recognize the value of teamwork and cooperation, thinking of the well-being of their peers, Gryffindor house, and the Hogwarts community, more than they regard their individual ambitions and desires. The magical trio realize that study and knowledge are more powerful than magic, and they learn to nurture and rely on their intelligence instead of the illusions of sorcery. Although Harry lacks Hermione's genius, he regards being smart as an important attribute and attempts to master his class work, even in courses taught by loathsome professors such as Snape.

SOCIAL PROBLEMS

In Book II, racism is central to the plot. An informal hierarchy among wizards is revealed in which controversial castes are assigned to sorcerers based on their pedigree. Pure-blooded wizards are considered to be the best wizards, while those with any Muggle blood are referred to by such derogatory labels as mudbloods, alluding to their mixed heritage. Wizards with ancestors who have magical powers but who lack sorcery skills themselves are rudely referred to as Squibs. Many wizards with sanctioned family backgrounds indulge in bigotry against Muggle-born members of the community, even calling for their extermination in scenes eerily reminiscent of World War II's Holocaust, Stalin's purges, or ethnic cleansing in 1990s Yugoslavia. Or they do not publicly condemn racist wizards, passively allowing such ostracism to mushroom out of control.

Acknowledging his own Muggle mother, Harry is appalled by any form of hate crime possibly being initiated, and his power, fueled by love and compassion, saves wizards with less prestigious pedigrees from losing their lives and opportunities to use their magic productively. Harry heeds Dumbledore's advice that choices exceed talents in each person's character development. Perhaps his sense of social responsibility will alert readers to harmful prejudices they hold or encounter and embolden them to voice their concerns.

Book III addresses the damage caused by false accusations and rumors. This novel also reveals how a joke can emotionally scar targets of misguided humor. Although he seeks to avenge his parents' murder, Harry is a humanitarian who is willing to consider Black's and Pettigrew's pleas instead of reacting hastily and emotionally. Harry also respects how his actions will affect other people. When he decides not to kill Pettigrew, Harry says that he does not want his father's friends to become accomplices to murder. Harry intellectually recognizes that prison is the most

appropriate punishment for
Pettigrew. In his confrontations with Lord Voldemort,

Harry also fights fairly despite his antagonist's tricks. Such ruses
emphasize the manipulative, deceitful, and overwhelming
nature of evil. Harry's resourcefulness and ability to understand
people to respond justly, and to forgive symbolize why he is
esteemed by his fictional peers and real-life readers.

ROLE MODEL

As a role model, Harry exemplifies socially admirable behavior such as respect for his elders, peers, and younger children,
even people who annoy or deride him. Harry is courteous, using
titles to address adults, including Lord Voldemort. He and his
classmates deal with verbal abuse and sometimes physical
assaults with clever remarks or proactive behavior that confuse
and distract their attackers. Harry has a sense of civic responsibility, understanding his role within his community and how he
must cooperate for the common good of that society.

Harry is particularly empathetic toward animals, revealing
his sense of humanity toward all life. He cares for other people
and is not self-absorbed or greedy, sharing his belongings and
abilities. Despite the Dursleys' apathetic mistreatment, Harry
strives to be dutifully decent toward them because of his familial allegiances. He is devotedly loyal to his friends whom he
supports even when personality conflicts arise.

Harry summons bravery to battle foes even though he is often
afraid, and he tries to do what he believes is right even if he is

ridiculed, risks losing something he treasures, or faces danger. He aims to be an uplifting leader of his classmates, inspiring them to compete better in classes and on the Quidditch field. Reinforcing the concepts of altruism and tolerance for people who are different, Harry, although he is not perfect, exhibits ethical and personal traits most parents wish their children would emulate. He serves as a model for good etiquette, and his life story serves as a parable for children coming of age in the next millennium.

OBJECTIONS BY CONCERNED PARENTS

Popular response to Rowling's series has not been entirely positive. In the United States, parents in several states requested that the novels be withdrawn from public schools libraries. They also asked for teachers to stop reading the books to students and incorporating them into lesson plans. The most publicized protest was in Columbia, South Carolina, and coincided with Rowling's American book tour. The parents protested to school boards that the books contained too much evil, were too dark, and glorified sorcery and the occult, which they argued was irresponsible because of increasing cases of violence at schools. They also argued that the books promoted witchcraft, specifically Wicca (which is never mentioned in the books), which they said was a religion and the reason why the books should be removed from schools because of separation of church and state.

The conservative Christian organization, Focus on the Family, posted its concerns about the novels on a web site. Some ministers preached about the evils of the novels, saying that the series' popularity was proof of satanic support. Other preachers defended the series for emphasizing courage, loyalty, and love. The protestors emphasized excerpts from the books taken out of context that they thought proved their objections but they ignored passages in which Harry, Dumbledore, and other characters talked about how they loathed evil. Such misleading use of citations fueled misinformed reports that the Harry Potter series was inappropriate for children. Despite censors' efforts, the novels were not effectively banned in the United States. Most challenges were addressed locally without restrictions being implemented.

Banning attempts, however, resulted in international publicity and articles discussing the Puritanical nature of some Americans. The media distorted some aspects of the banners' efforts, and the parents' fears, misunderstanding, and unfamiliarity of fantastical children's literature perpetuated rumors. Rowling defended her books, asserting that no fans had expressed interest in becoming a witch and saying that children realized that the books are fantasies not reality. Both she and her publishers announced that they did not intend to change characterizations and themes to accommodate censors. Some schools, such as those in Zeeland, Michigan, initiated a policy requiring students to obtain parental permission to check out the novels. Other schools required librarians to dismantle Harry Potter displays and insisted teachers remove the books from reading lists and storytime.

READING FOR RESEARCH

Alexander, Jenny. *Bullying: Practical and Easy-To-Follow Advice.* London: Penguin, 1998. Suggests useful ideas for coping with taunts.

Baldridge, Letitia. *Letitia Baldridge's More Than Manners! Raising Today's Kids to Have Kind Manners and Good Hearts.* New York: Scribner, 1997. Insightful guide to teaching children how to act with respect for people and their community and how to deal with a variety of situations.

Lewis, Barbara A. *The Kid's Guide to Social Action: How to Solve the Social Problems You Choose And Turn Creative Thinking into Positive Action.* Minneapolis, MN: Free Spirit Publishing, 1998. A valuable source to guide children who want to stop or change negative situations into positive activities.

INTERNET RESOURCES

The Southern Poverty Law Center's Teaching Tolerance Program
    http://www.splcenter.org/teachingtolerance/tt-index.html

The Golden Rule
    http://www.fragrant.demon.co.uk/golden.html

Muggles for Harry
    http://www.mugglesforharrypotter.org

Log on to **www.beachampublishing.com** for many additional projects, discussion questions, writing and research ideas, websites, and bibliography.

CHAPTER 16

ILLUSTRATIONS AND FOREIGN EDITIONS

"My favorite cover is the American one."
—J.K. ROWLING

"Harry Potter is the most popular part of my work.
But it's a very small part." —MARY GRANDPRÉ

Introduction

In the Harry Potter series, the illustrations, both cover and internal art, convey meanings. All of the editions published in Great Britain and most of the foreign versions depict Harry on the cover. Sketches at the beginning of chapters portray significant characters or incidents. The illustrations as a group provide symbols crucial to each book's plot and offer clues to plot twists. The art effectively communicates information about the series' themes, characters, and conflicts.

BRITISH EDITION: BOOK I

While she was writing Book I, Rowling drew detailed sketches of the characters, particularly Harry, Dudley, and Dumbledore. Although her art was not published with the books, she showed them during a 1999 "60 Minutes" interview. Bloomsbury Publishing commissioned Thomas Taylor, a British illustrator, to create the cover design for Rowling's first book. His edition focuses on the front of a red steam engine bearing a green sign with yellow letters proclaiming that it is the Hogwarts Express. Stars swirl in the black steam. A streamlined modern train sits in the background.

A befuddled Harry stands to the right of the Hogwarts Express beneath an antique sign that says it is platform 9 3/4. Harry pensively touches his right hand to his chin. His scar zigzags down his brow. His shirt, jacket, and backpack resemble normal school clothes. On the back cover Dumbledore, depicted as a thin, bearded and mustached wizard in striped pants and a purple robe, smokes a long pipe and clutches a thick book with a pentacle on it. The title page features the regal-appearing Hogwarts crest and motto, foreshadowing the role of the four houses and the characteristics of their members.

BRITISH EDITION: BOOKS II AND III

Cliff Wright illustrated Books II and III. His depiction of Harry is more realistic than Taylor's somewhat cartoonish Harry. On Book II's cover, Harry, Ron, and Hedwig are flying in a turquoise-blue car which dominates the scene. The Hogwarts engine and one and a half cars are visible in the lower left corner. The red train's smoke could easily be confused with the clouds around the car, showing the boys' being connected to the action below. The train is about to disappear into a tunnel, symbolizing how Hogwarts is separated from the mortal world. Both boys are smiling, and Hedwig is stretching, a wing forming the backdrop of each boy's head. The back cover depicts Hogwarts. The castle is geometric, formed of rectangular shapes connected by suspension bridges and featuring cylindrical turrets at almost every corner. Roofs have scalloped edges, and turrets twist into points almost like upside-down ice cream cones. Hogwarts foundation is concealed by fog.

Book III's cover is less colorful and more sinister. The bland coloring of Buckbeak blends into the yellow of the full moon. Splashes of red on Harry's clothing and his scar are in stark contrast to the yellowish-brown beast. Harry and Hermione almost merge together with their dark hair and cloaks. Harry's determined stare contrasted with Hermione's open-mouthed grimace make them appear to be almost a two-headed human.

The back cover shows a salivating wolf with milky-white eyes. The drab color of this beast also seems to camouflage him, almost like Lupin conceals his werewolf nature by not wearing fancy clothing.

Adult editions feature black and white photographs of trains and cars or an artistic image of the Hippogriff. While the British children's editions have vivid colors and rounded images, almost like a comic book, the adult covers are more sharp, linear, and focused. Both versions provide images true to the series' plots. The Canadian editions use the same children's artwork as the British.

AMERICAN EDITIONS

Rowling has expressed her preference for the American illustrations. Artist Mary GrandPre' has applied her style, which she refers to as "soft geometry," to the dustjackets. A graduate of the Minneapolis College of Art & Design, GrandPre' admits to being influenced by Walt Disney movies. She tries to create illustrations that have a film-like animation quality so that readers' repeatedly sweep their eyes across her art and see new details in characters' expressions and backdrops. Using pastels, GrandPré's style is soft and playful.

COVER: BOOK I

Book I shows Harry flying underneath an arch and between two columns. The lettering in the title looks like it has been carved in the stone. On all of the books, Harry's name is styl-

ized, with the "P" looking like a lightning bolt. His left hand is extended to
catch the Snitch. Hogwarts sits to the right,
depicted as a grouping of spires. Fluffy is
hidden in the castle design. A unicorn
darts to the left. Smudges beneath
Harry suggest figures of other broomstick flyers. Harry's gaze is averted as he
keeps his eyes on the winged Snitch,
which appears almost cherubic. His jeans, sneakers, and striped
rugby shirt look like casual schoolboy attire, accentuated by his
scarlet cape. Gold stars dot the purple sky, and the steps to
Hogwarts end at a grassy field that is bordered by evergreens.
Stretching the dustjacket out, readers see an owl clutching a letter in its talons and a silver-bearded wizard in a purple cloak.
His half-moon glasses suggest that this is Dumbledore.
Geometric shapes and a key decorate the backdrop, and the
missing stone possibly could be concealed in the masonry. The
dustjacket flaps reveal drapes tied away with gold cords from
the stage where Harry is performing, and the mysterious leg
and hand of an individual holding a candle.

COVER: BOOK II

Book II has more intense colors, contrasting the scarlet
Fawkes with the tan chamber walls. Two green snakes line the
walls and other serpents (two with colored eyes) form a bas
relief on the pipes. The title is splashed across the stone wall like
the message Harry sees after Mrs. Norris is petrified. A torch

illuminates the center of the picture. Harry, Ron, and Ginny are being pulled upward by Fawkes whose extended wings dominate the top of the dustjacket. Three feathers float toward the tiled floor as the children ascend. While Harry, sword at his hip, watches Fawkes, Ron, holding Harry's cloak, gazes at his sister who clutches his hand. They all seem gleeful and unafraid. Framed by Harry's arms and Fawkes' tail, a twisted pile of serpentine sections oozes from an opening in the wall. A black cat, possibly a feline relative of Mrs. Norris, arches its back in fright against a starry backdrop. In the far right corner, a basilisk's sinister eye with a slim vertical pupil stares at the reader.

COVER: BOOK III

The panoramic view presented by the illustrations on Book III's dustjacket provides hints about the contents. Harry and Hermione are centered on the front cover. They seem to be enjoying their flight on Buckbeak, who also looks cheerful for a Hippogriff. Hermione is holding the rein that guides Buckbeak. Buckbeak's wings are outspread like Fawkes' on Book II and the owl's on Book I, symbolizing their movement toward freedom. The American Buckbeak is not as drab as the British version, appearing silvery like Pegasus and with dapples on his hindquarters, hinting of his vigor. The trio is framed by a window with Sirius Black's scruffy shadow appearing in the lower left corner. The title resembles the writing on a pirate's map which is significant because Harry is like a pirate smuggling treasure in the form of Black from the castle.

A rat and its looming shadow sit outside the window to the

right. The left portion of the dustjacket shows Dementors just a few feet away from the window. The closest Dementor's bony hand eerily clutches at a stone, and the rolls of its gaping hood are highlighted. In the background, a werewolf darts from the castle, and a shadowy cat sits under the curlicues of the Whomping Willows branches. A silvery, almost transparent stag stands beside the lake, its image reflected on the water. On the hill above the stag, there is a small building, possibly Hagrid's hut, with smoke drifting from its chimney; one window is illuminated. A crescent moon, instead of the story's essential full moon, drifts in the starry twilight sky. Sloping evergreens contrast with the purple, blue, and pink hues of the sky. Where Harry, Hermione, and Black are pictured, there is glowing lightness almost like a halo. The Dementors glide through darkness.

INSIDE ART

The American editions feature black-and-white illustrations on the title pages and at the beginning of each chapter. The title page illustrations incorporate images that set the mood and suggest what the story will include. Book I's title page pictures a castle that looks like a woodcut of a medieval town. The stone walk, spanning what appears to be a moat, leads readers into Hogwarts and the book. Book II is more revealing of the ensuing plot. Eyes peer menacingly from a chamber, and a spider's large shadow looms between snake-wrapped pillars. A single feather has floated to the ground. In Book III, Sirius, a rat, and the willow tree are contained within a window's arch.

The interior illustrations are rounded, resembling the contents of a snow globe or cameo. They are miniature representations of characters and events. Each artfully shaded caricature is packed with details. A chocolate frog sits next to Dumbledore's wizard card, Gilderoy Lockhart's teeth sparkle, and Aunt Marge floats like a parade balloon. Each tableau alerts readers to a significant person or situation that will occur in that chapter. The text is further enhanced by artistic use of fonts to simulate letterhead and handwriting unique to each character. Smudges show where Hagrid's tears fell on his letter. Stars decorate page corners and frame page numbers.

FOREIGN COVERS

Each country's artist chose to portray Harry, Hogwarts, or a representative character differently. Illustrated by Ien van Laanen, Book I published in the Netherlands shows only one of Harry's feet, part of his leg, his scarlet robe, and the broom straws. He is passing across a glowing full moon, and a wingless Snitch is zooming past him in the opposite direction. A realistic-appearing white owl with an expressive face is featured on the back cover, holding a letter with a red wax seal in its beak. The Dutch edition of Book II shows the flying car from behind. Both have dark backgrounds.

The German edition, illustrated by Sabine Wilharm, is more stark, and sinister. The children and chess pieces remind readers of Edward Munch's painting "The Scream." Harry looks like he could be slightly deranged, and the backgrounds for the first two books are busy and crowded with details. Book III's

German cover contrasts with its simplicity of Harry against a snowy backdrop with a wolf trotting toward him, its shadow touching his back. Green trees line the path's sides, pairing life and death imagery. The back covers have illustrations connected to the ISBN bar code. On Book I, Hedwig is tugging at the code as if she were trying to deliver it, and, on Book III, a rat is looking at the bar code.

In contrast, the French covers by Emily Walcker are almost childlike and innocent because of their simplicity. Harry, Ron, and Hermione are the same size and are dressed in witch attire unlike other editions that show the characters in normal clothes with a cloak as an accessory. The buckles on their hats look like something the pilgrims would have worn. The lines that form the children's features are spare like a comic strip character's expressions. Their cheeks are rosy, and Harry does not have a scar on his forehead. A wide-eyed Hedwig is caged in the French cover of Book I. Hermione holds a book; Harry clutches a stick and Hedwig's cage; and Ron's freckles dominate his cheeks. A witch flies above the castle. On the back cover, Hagrid is drawn like a cartoon character and looks like Paul Bunyan.

On the French cover of Book II, Ron and Harry are apprehensively peering down a dark tunnel with a menacing chain attached to the wall. Harry's wand lights their way. The back cover illustrations again are cartoonish. Draco Malfoy has slits for his eyes and mouth as he sneers from his broomstick, and Gilderoy Lockhart smiles like he's starring in a toothpaste commercial. Book III shows Harry and Hermione riding Buckbeak. Harry looks thrilled, while Hermione seems agitated. Buckbeak appears determined to escape. Other smaller illustrations on the back covers of the French editions depict Remus Lupin like Mister Rogers wearing a sweater, holding a book, and suffering dark bags under his eyes. Sirius Black resembles a stereotypical movie villain, wearing dark clothes and furrowing his heavy brows. He has sideburns and a five o'clock shadow. The interior illustrations in the first two books (none appear in the French Book III) cleverly combine the chapter numerals with the person's or object's shape. Each drawing represents something that occurs in that chapter.

Scandinavian editions have more fantastical styles. The Swedish cover for Book I shows Harry in a scene like a fairy tale image. Looking more mature than on the other covers, Harry stands in the center of a chaotic scene filled with people and animals. He floats above the crowd, Hedwig on his shoulder, and sparks shoot from his feet. The Hogwarts Express is behind him, filling the background with steam. Denmark's edition looks like a landscape from a picture book. Harry is flying above the castle on Book I's cover, and Book II reveals the castle through a broken passage. Harry stands, holding his sparkling wand aloft, and the back of an observer's head is in the lower center. The edition of Book I from Finland shows the trio in bold colors and with sharp, gawky features standing in front of chess pieces that are holding weapons and exhibiting sour expressions.

Book I from Iceland prints the author's name as Joanna Rowling and shows a Harry significantly different than other versions. Almost macabre, he is blushing, appearing somewhat feverish, and wearing a formal, striped tie. His scar is bigger, redder, and more pronounced. Harry stands in front of the Hogwarts Express, and the background is an unnatural red, dotted with stars. The Norwegian edition was published with GrandPre's art on Book III and a Norwegian title. The Korean version also used the Book III American cover art accented with Hangul lettering.

The Japanese edition features original art by Dan Schleshinger that is dark and foreboding. The silhouette of a broom rider is centered over a full moon. Hogwarts' gargoyle-emblazoned turrets are shaped like the spindle that pricked Sleeping Beauty. A ghoulish character with yellow eyes watches from a tower. Hedwig dominates the cover and contrasts with the stark images in dark blue and the yellowish brown castle. Harry's arm is around Hermione's shoulder as she waves to the flying witch. They are both blonde and wearing pointed hats. Blue outlines reveal creatures with fangs, bulbous eyes, scaly tales, and veined wings lurking in the shadows. The internal illustrations are much cruder than in the American and French editions. They are simple black and white line drawings, and buildings and human shapes tend to be geometric. The chapter illustrations also are representative of plot developments, and they convey a sense of characterization. For example, goblins have long, tapered fingers and thin, sharp noses.

The books published in Italy have a light pastel appearance. On Book I, Harry and a giant rat are playing chess, and the black and white squares draw the readers' eyes to the intersection of the boy and beast where the queen waits. The cover of Book II shows Harry flying on an open book somewhat like the Danish edition. The Spanish cover for Book I is a photograph of a man dressed like Merlin who is standing flush right on a pale purple backdrop that is plain compared to other editions. On the Spanish cover of

Book II Harry is holding a sword and defending himself against a large, coiled, green snake which has its mouth open preparing to strike. Fawkes is flying up from the bottom center of the cover. The chamber is gray and appears stark and sinister.

READING FOR RESEARCH

Dalby, Richard. *The Golden Age of Children's Book Illustration.* London: M. O'Mara Books, 1991. Addresses the history of artwork designed specifically for children's books.

Feaver, William. *When We Were Young: Two Centuries of Children's Book Illustration.* London: Gollanez, 1976. Overview of the role of art published in children's books.

Whalley, Joyce Irene, and Tessa Rose Chester. *A History of Children's Book Illustration.* London: J. Murray with the Victoria and Albert Museum, 1988. Provides information about significant achievements in the field of children's literary art.

INTERNET SOURCES

Mary GrandPré
http://www.MaryGrandPre.com

Art
http://artforkids.about.com

Art History Resources on the Web
http://witcombe.sbc.edu/ARTHLinks.html

Women Children's Book Illustrators
   http://homepage.fcgnetworks.net/tortakales/illustrators/
   index.html

Log on to **www.beachampublishing.com** for many additional projects, discussion questions, writing and research ideas, websites, and bibliography.

SECTION III

~

TEACHING HARRY

CHAPTER DEVELOPMENT: DETECTIVE QUESTIONS FOR WIZARD SLEUTHS

This section poses questions from each chapter of the first three novels. They are designed to help readers recognize themes, ideas, and literary development. Teachers and parents can use them for stimulating class discussion, or playing quiz games with avid Potterites. Teachers may want to copy selected questions onto work sheets or flash cards so that students can play games with each other. The summary at the beginning of each chapter—synopsis, setting, themes, symbols, related myths/legends, and vocabulary development—provide teachers and parents with a thumbnail lesson plan and ideas for discussion and writing assignments.

At the end of Chapters 17, 18, and 19 are Projects and Activities, Discussion questions, and Developing Writing and Critical Skills for the novel in general rather than for individual chapters. Generally, the projects and activities are for younger readers, the discussion questions for intermediate readers, and the writing assignments for more advanced readers. Researching the related myths and legends and analyzing the themes present in the summary make excellent assignments. These myths and how they are reflected in the Potter novels are briefly explained in Appendix B: More Myths and Legends.

Hundreds more projects, discussion and writing questions, arranged chapter-by-chapter, can be found on the Beacham Publishing website, **www.beachampublishing.com**

CHAPTER 17

HARRY POTTER AND THE PHILOSOPHER'S/ SORCERER'S STONE

DETECTIVE QUESTIONS FOR WIZARD SLEUTHS

"It is not so much our friends' help that helps us as the confident knowledge that they will help us."
—EPICURUS

"Access to power must be confined to those who are not in love with it." —PLATO

"Success is not measured by the position one has reached in life, rather by the obstacles overcome while trying to succeed." —BOOKER T. WASHINGTON

OVERVIEW

An orphan, ten-year-old Harry lives with his aunt Petunia Dursley and her husband Vernon and son Dudley. The first chapter describes events on Halloween night a decade before when fifteen-month-old Harry was delivered to the Dursleys's doorstep. Three mysterious people—a giant-looking man, a cat-woman, and an elderly man in a purple cloak—commented about the sad death of Harry's parents and debated whether he should live with his mother's sister. During that day, strange people had roamed the city streets, and owls filled the skies. The unimaginative Vernon Dursley thought he heard Harry Potter's name mentioned but tried to ignore what was happening around him. After wishing Harry luck, the odd trio tucked a letter into his bundle of blankets and said goodbye. The next morning, his Aunt Petunia Dursley discovered Harry.

Enduring a miserable existence, Harry suffers because of his restrictive and often abusive guardians who deny him basic comforts and kindnesses. They tell him that his parents died in a car wreck which also caused the scar on his forehead. Harry sleeps in a closet underneath the stairs where he often dreams of flying motorcycles and green lightning flashes. Unaware of his magical heritage, Harry does not understand why strange things happen to him, such as his hair growing long overnight, or why a snake talked to him at the zoo. Isolated and friendless, he is surprised when letters start to arrive addressed to him. Vernon prevents Harry from seeing the letters, which makes him angry. Curious, Harry schemes how to read a letter before Vernon can intercept it. As a result, Vernon forces everyone to flee from the house.

Stuck in an island hut with the Dursleys, Harry despairs. The arrival of Hagrid, the giant man who had brought him to the Dursleys' house, changes Harry's situation and outlook. He tells Harry that his parents had been a wizard and a witch who had been murdered by an evil archenemy named Lord Voldemort. Voldemort had also tried to kill Harry but somehow Harry had resisted the attack and stripped Voldemort of his powers. Because of that, Harry is famous in the wizard world. Hagrid fends off the Dursleys and prepares Harry for his first year at the Hogwarts School of Witchcraft and Wizardry. Through shopping sprees and initiation rites, Harry undergoes a transition from an ordinary boy into a phenomenal protagonist.

Although the first Harry Potter novel includes an adventure, the book's primary purpose is to establish a framework for readers to recognize the characters, settings, and rules that will continue in future volumes of the series. Terms unique to the books, such as "Muggles" indicating non-wizards, are defined. Readers learn the uses of enchanted objects and how Harry travels to Hogwarts. Harry's friends and enemies, both students and professors, are identified. Harry learns more about his role as the heir to a magical legacy.

Although not a brilliant student, Harry is talented at Quidditch, a wizard sport. Between games, classes, and quarrels with classmates and teachers, Harry solves puzzles to locate the stolen Philosophers's/Sorcerer's Stone, which promises eternal life, ironically in contrast to Harry's daily reminder of his parents' death. Harry confronts Voldemort, learns to trust his intuition and abilities to tackle what may appear initially to be impossible obstacles. After a decade of rejection, Harry also begins to trust people and enjoy teamwork and comradery. He realizes that passivity allows evil to thrive and he decides to take action to combat it. The themes of hope, loyalty, and family highlight Harry's growth in this first book as he seeks wisdom to prepare him for his fate.

CHAPTER DEVELOPMENT: DETECTIVE QUESTIONS FOR WIZARD SLEUTHS

See Appendix B: Mythical and Legendary Characters Cited in Section III for a brief explanation of the myths and how they are reflected in the Potter novels.

– Chapter 1: The Boy Who Lived –

Synopsis: Harry is rescued after his parents' murder
Setting: Dursley home, Vernon Dursley's office, bakery
Themes: love prevails, sacrifice, salvation, celebration
Symbols: blankets, cloaks, lightning, shooting stars, owls, green, flowers
Myths/legends: Hercules surviving the snakes' attack as a child

Vocabulary Development:
astounding: amazing and surprising
craning: stretching the neck in order to see
exasperated: irritated and angered
McGuffin: a mystery that does not really exist except to confuse
pinpricks: tiny spots
ruffled: disturbed, not smooth

tawny: brownish-yellow color
tyke: small child

1) Why do the Dursleys consider themselves to be normal? Why do they believe magical people like the Potters are abnormal? How familiar are the Dursleys with the Potter family?

2) For what reasons do the Dursleys think Dudley is an extraordinary child and that Harry is not? What is their opinion of imagination?

3) In what ways does Vernon Dursley ignore the strange people and animals he sees? How does he express his fear of the unknown and concerns that people might learn that his wife's sister was a witch?

4) Why do the wizards and witches continue to risk discovery by and interaction with the Muggles after Lord Voldemort was vanquished by Harry?

5) Explain the roles of Albus Dumbledore, Minerva McGonagall, and Rubeus Hagrid in the transfer of Harry from Godric's Hollow to Privet Drive. Why do you think they decided to leave Harry with his aunt's family instead of finding a wizard home for him? How does Harry's fame in the wizard world influence Dumbledore's decision?

— Chapter 2: The Vanishing Glass —

Synopsis: ten years later, Harry speaks to the snake on Dudley's birthday

Setting: Dursley home, zoo

Themes: freedom, self-expression, rebirth

Symbols: spiders, pigs, rats, flying, serpents, green light, food, motorcycles

Myths/legends: Ericthonius, the half snake man

Vocabulary Development:

carousel: a carnival ride, a merry-go-round

gibber: talk nonsensically

hoodlum: young street tough

mad: insane

maniac: wild-acting person

revolting: disgusting

shrill: high-pitched noise

tantrum: display of bad temper

vigorously: energetically

wolfing: eating very fast

1) How did the Dursley home change and stagnate during the decade that Harry lived there?

2) Why do the Dursleys celebrate Dudley's birthday but not Harry's? What is the significance of Harry's and Dudley's birthdays being so close together?

3) Why are the Dursleys reluctant to say Harry's name?

4) How are Dudley's friends similar to the students Harry later encounters at Hogwarts?

5) Which of the Dursley's rules does Harry break and how is he punished?

6) Why does Harry empathize with the boa constrictor?

— Chapter 3: The Letters From No One —

Synopsis: Harry receives mysterious letters
Setting: Dursley home and car, hotel, and island hut
Themes: escape, evasion, connection with others
Symbols: messages, time, television, storm, island, gray, seaweed
Myths/legends: Mercury delivers news

Vocabulary Development:
boaters: a hat with a wide brim
knickerbockers: trousers ending just below the knee
knobbly: bumpy
maroon: a dark red color
parchment: a kind of crisp paper
pelting: hitting; also a slang reference to the arrival of a lot of owls
porridge: oatmeal-like, cooked cereal
tailcoats: style of coat with extended back
trodden: stepped on
whelk: type of snail

1) How does Petunia's and Dudley's trip in London to buy items for the school year at Smeltings foreshadow Harry's shopping spree in Diagon Alley?

2) Why are the Dursleys are unable to understand Harry's sense of humor?

3) Why does Vernon Dursley enter Harry's cupboard for the first time? Why does he decide to move Harry to the smallest bedroom?

4) To what extremes do the Dursleys go to trying to evade delivery of Harry's letters and how does this alter their daily habits? Why do they think the letters might prove more detrimental than Vernon losing wages from missed work while traveling to evade the letters?

— Chapter 4: The Keeper of the Keys —

Synopsis: Harry meets Hagrid who tells him the truth
Setting: island hut
Themes: nurturing, deceitfulness, distrust
Symbols: gun, birthday cake, food, storm, owl, umbrella, pink
Myths/legends: Apollo tells the truth; Zeus throws thunderbolts

Vocabulary Development:
clouted: hit
cowering: shrinking in fear
dratted: expression of annoyance

foghorn: a loud horn blown to give warning in fog
gargoyle: a fantastical carving, usually ugly
incredible: unbelievable
outrage: vicious act
quailed: draw back in fear
scandal: disgraceful act
scuttled: hasty flight
stumped: puzzled
trances: dazed state

1) How does the timing of Hagrid's knocking weaken the Dursleys's reactions? Why is the storm a symbolic backdrop to his arrival?

2) Why does Harry apologize to Hagrid when he admits that he does not know what Hogwarts is?

3) Describe the emotions of Hagrid, Harry, and Vernon when Harry is told about his parents and learns that he is a famous wizard. Why is it symbolic that this happens on Harry's birthday? How does this information affect readers who finally are told that Harry is a wizard after reading three chapters of hints?

4) Hagrid introduces Harry to magic by sending a letter to Dumbledore via owl and defining the word "Muggle." How does this embolden Harry to confront Petunia about why she withheld information from him about his parents being a wizard and witch?

5) How does Petunia's slip of the tongue alert Harry to the facts about their deaths? Why does Hagrid decide to tell Harry about his legendary role in the vanquishing of Voldemort?

6) What details of Hagrid's story illuminate clues provided in the first chapter? What gaps remain to be clarified?

7) Why does Harry question Hagrid's veracity? What proof reassures Harry that he is a wizard?

8) What is significant about Hagrid using magic to enact revenge on the Dursleys? How does Hagrid's secret bond him to Harry?

— Chapter 5: Diagon Alley —

Synopsis: Harry buys school supplies and is introduced to wizard culture

Setting: Underground, Leaky Cauldron, Diagon Alley stores

Themes: friendship, trust, self discovery

Symbols: dark, light, gold, caves, goblins, railway, robes, wands, owls, books, feathers, unicorns

Myths/legends: Midas hoards gold

Vocabulary Development:

apothecary: pharmacy

babble: meaningless talk

billowing: fabric blowing out in the wind

bungler: one who does something badly

clambered: climbed

collapsed: fell, could not continue

escalator: moving staircase

gleamed: shone

hurtled: to move forward with great force

infernal: hateful

miniscule: tiny

peculiar: strange

pewter: an alloy, or mixture, of tin with lead, brass, or copper

phials: glass tubes

puncture: make a hole

quivered: trembled

ravine: a deep crevice in earth

savaging: attacking

scrambled: climbing with hands and feet

stalactites: a mineral deposit hanging down from the roof of a cave

stalagmites: a mineral deposit rising up from the floor of a cave

1) What is the significance of the contents of Hagrid's pockets?

2) Why is Hagrid proud that Dumbledore trusts him with Hogwarts' business transactions at Gringotts?

3) When Hagrid explains the Ministry of Magic's purpose, why does he say magic is hidden from Muggles and "we're best left alone"?

4) How do Hagrid and Harry help each other in unfamiliar settings?

5) What are people's reaction to meeting Harry? What clues to future events are provided in this chapter?

6) Why does Hagrid treat Harry as an equal? When does he treat him like a child? When does Harry act like the adult and Hagrid the child?

7) How does Harry react to the unique world he enters through the Leaky Cauldron courtyard?

8) Why does Harry think of Dudley when he visits the Potter vault at Gringotts and meets Draco Malfoy?

9) How do the stores in Diagon Alley meet both practical and fantastical needs and desires? How do Harry's purchases advance the plot?

—Chapter 6: The Journey From Platform Nine and Three-Quarters —

Synopsis: Harry leaves the Muggle world and learns about the Gringotts break-in

Setting: King's Cross Station, Hogwarts Express, Hogwarts

Themes: movement, transition, adventure, self-reliance

Symbols: train, luggage, food, twins, rat, toad, yellow, mountain, lake, path, boats, woods, castle, tunnel, three, ivy, pebbles, oak

Myths/legends: Odysseus explores the world

Vocabulary Development:
compartment: small room in a train
disgruntled: cross and upset
dud: fails to perform
goggle: stare
prefect: a student school official
ruddy: reddish
sniffy: disdainful and snobbish
tinge: faint color
turret: a tower at the top of a castle

1) How does Harry discover where Platform Nine and Three-Quarters exists?

2) Who does Harry meet on the platform and on the Hogwarts Express? What does he learn on this journey about the wizard world, the theft at Gringotts, and himself? What does he teach Ron about Muggles?

3) Why does Harry think the unknown is preferable to the Dursleys?

4) How do Harry and Ron reassure each other? What is the basis of their friendship? How do they react to Hermione Granger?

5) Why is the wizard candy significant?

6) What is symbolic about the movement of the first year students from the train to the castle?

— Chapter 7: The Sorting Hat —

Synopsis: Harry is selected a member of Gryffindor house

Setting: Hogwarts Great Room and Gryffindor Tower

Themes: decisions, vulnerability, belonging

Symbols: ghosts, candles, music, stars, hat, silver, gold, turban, secrets, dormitory, dream

Myths/legends: Lachesis decides others' destinies

Vocabulary Development:

airily: lightly

blubber: cry noisily

bowlers: a style of hat

chivalry: gallantry

cunning: clever

drone: monotonous sound

èclairs: a kind of pastry

flagged: identified

gales: rain with high winds

just: fair

magnificent: grand

meringue: a baked whipped egg white dessert

miffed: annoyed

nitwit: fool

oddment: peculiarity

queasy: sick

sleek: streamlined

swaggered: exaggerated walk

toil: work

treacle: molasses-like
tweak: pinch

1) Why does Harry compare the entrance hall's size at Hogwarts to the Dursleys's house?

2) What do the first year students fear about the sorting ceremony? Why is the ghosts' presence in the chamber significant?

3) How do the characteristics of the Hogwarts Houses suggest future plot developments? Why does the sorting hat assign some people quickly and others, like Harry, require more time? What do the students' conversations at the table reveal about their characters?

4) Why does Harry's scar burn when Snape looks at him?

5) What does Dumbledore's speech reveal about him? What rules does he issue? What rules are implied? What is the purpose of the school song?

6) Why does the turret seem like home to Harry? Why does he have a nightmare and what does it suggest may happen to him?

– Chapter 8: The Potions Master –

Synopsis: Harry attends his first classes and learns more about the bank break-in

Setting: classrooms, Snape's dungeon, Hagrid's hut
Themes: discouragement, confusion, nurturing
Symbols: school, cauldrons, home, corridors, ghosts, secret passages, monsters, owls, plants, newspaper, dog
Myths/legends: Lares and Penates

Vocabulary Development:
cheek: acting sassy
cozy: material placed around a teapot
dunderheads: stupid people
fungi: plural of fungus, a type of plant without green chlorophyll
rickety: shaky
seeping: fluid oozing
shimmering: glittering
simmering: very hot
ward: patient area in a hospital
zombie: walking dead

1) How do the ghosts and Hogwarts students and staff help and hinder Harry on his first day of school?

2) What classes does Harry take, and who teaches them? Where are the classrooms located? How do the professors react to Harry being their student?

3) Why is Snape so contemptuous of most students? What are his attitudes toward magic and people who attempt to practice it? How does Neville's incompetence affect Harry?

4) What information does Hagrid provide when Harry visits his hut? How does Harry's curiosity about the Gringotts' theft and Hagrid's evasive comments about Snape initiate the book's mystery?

— Chapter 9: The Midnight Duel —

Synopsis: Harry learns to fly and meets Fluffy

Setting: flying field, Hogwarts Great Hall, trophy room, and forbidden corridor

Themes: impulsiveness, despair, hope, treachery

Symbols: sky, forest, broken arm, sport, moonlight, halls, cat, dog

Myths/legends: Icarus and Daedalus test their wings

Vocabulary Development:

beckon: signal to come

flattened: made less high, squashed flat

gloatingly: delightfully mocking; feeling of great, often malicious, pleasure

hobbled: limped

hovering: flying in the same spot

javelin: spear

mingled: mixed

numbly: without feeling

quaver: tremble

shrilly: a high pitched, thin sound

toppled: made lower, brought down

wake: path

wrenched: twisted

1) How does Draco's maliciousness change Harry's life? Why can he be considered as a substitute for Dudley as Harry's primary peer antagonist? How does the tension between these two characters advance the plot?

2) Why do the students boast of exaggerated flying feats? What does their flying ability symbolize for wizards and witches? Why does Harry worry that he will fail at flying?

3) What do Neville's Remembrall and broken wrist foreshadow?

4) How does Harry comfort himself when he thinks that he will be expelled?

5) Why does McGonagall introduce Harry to Oliver Wood as "Seeker" and not by his full name? Why is she willing to bend the rule forbidding first year students from having brooms at school? How does the mention of his father affect Harry?

6) What is Draco's true intention when he challenges Harry to a duel?

7) Why does each student break the rules and roam Hogwarts at night?

8) How does Peeves' behavior cause the students to discover the guard dog and the trapdoor? How does this experience bond Harry, Ron, and Hermione? How does it divide them?

— Chapter 10: Hallowe'en —

Synopsis: Harry and Ron subdue a mountain troll

Setting: Great Hall, first floor girls' bathroom

Themes: courage, friendship, teamwork

Symbols: gift, hoops, balls, wings, gold, fouls, club (as weapon or tool), purple, monsters, odor

Myths/legends: Achilles's heel; Minotaur

Vocabulary Development:

askew: crooked

berserk: crazy-acting

bolted: suddenly ran

chortled: laughed

flick: quick, light movement

jostled: pushed

reeled: staggered

substitutes: in place of

swish: sound of moving fabric

wafting: floating

1) How do Harry and Ron perceive the previous evening's events the next morning? Why does Harry tell Ron about the package Hagrid retrieved from Gringotts?

2) What do the different models of brooms represent about the students who use them?

3) Why are the Quidditch rules important? What does each ball and position symbolize?

4) How are the events in class and at night on Halloween at Hogwarts pivotal to the plot? How do they strengthen Harry's, Ron's, and Hermione's friendship?

5) What are the professors' reactions to Harry and Ron knocking out the mountain troll to save Hermione?

— Chapter 11: Quidditch —

Synopsis: Harry plays in his first Quidditch match
Setting: Gryffindor common room, Quidditch field, Hagrid's hut
Themes: loyalty, perseverance, competition, victory, deceit, truth
Symbols: cold, fire, bloody wound, noise, lion, red, green
Myths/legends: Nemesis's pursuit of justice

Vocabulary Development:
chappie: slang for a young man
diversion: something to distract attention
jinxing: causing bad luck
lurch: sudden movement forward
wheedled: pleaded and begged

1) How does winter alter Hogwarts?

2) Why is Harry Gryffindor's "secret weapon"? How do his supporters and rivals prepare him for his first game? How does Quidditch change Hermione?

3) What does Snape's limp represent? How does his confisca-

tion of the Quidditch book result in Harry learning more about the stolen Stone? How do Ron and Hermione react to his news?

4) Why is Quidditch so important to Oliver Wood? What strategies does he insist his players implement? How does Lee Jordan's commentary advance the plot?

5) When Harry's broom goes out of control, how do people in the stands react? What saves him? How does this change Hermione's opinion of Snape?

6) Why does Hagrid defend Snape? How does he unintentionally divulge information to the children when he is lecturing them? Why is Harry so assertive in this conversation with Hagrid? How does the suspense in this chapter build tension and excitement?

— Chapter 12: The Mirror of Erised —

Synopsis: Harry sees his parents reflected in the mirror, which is his greatest desire
Setting: Gryffindor dormitory, corridors, library, classroom
Themes: family, generosity, sharing, joy, isolation
Symbols: presents, sweaters, food, cloak, books, mirror, dark, light, blood, green, reflections, socks
Myths/legends: Echo admires Narcissus

Vocabulary Development:
boats: serving dishes for gravy

chipolatas: sausage, particularly served during the Christmas season

crumpets: an unsweetened cake

engulfed: covered with water

festoons: decorations

keen: sharp

luminous: shining

paisley: a design pattern with curved shapes

taunting: teasing

transfixed: stunned

trifle: a dessert of cake, fruit, and custard

tureens: large bowls to serve food

whittled: method of carving wood figures with knife

1) Why is Hagrid upset that Harry, Ron, and Hermione are researching who Nicolas Flamel is? Why are some areas of the Hogwarts library forbidden and what does this foreshadow?

2) Why do Harry and Ron stay at Hogwarts for Christmas? What advantages does this give them that students who go home, such as Hermione and Draco, miss? How do holiday activities prepare Harry and Ron for future confrontations with enemies? What are Ron's strengths?

3) How are Harry's Christmas gifts crucial for plot and character development? What does Harry receive that Ron covets?

4) How does the Invisibility Cloak empower Harry? How does it weaken him? Why is it important that he is alone during his initial use of the cloak?

5) Why is the Mirror of Erised both appealing and disheartening? How does the mirror change Harry's personality and his goals?

6) How does Ron react to Harry's news about the mirror? What does he see? Why do the boys fight and what does this reflect about them? How do Mrs. Norris's patrols interfere with their plans?

7) Why does Harry risk a third trip to see the mirror despite warnings from Ron and Hagrid? What does he learn about Dumbledore and invisibility during his first conversation alone with Dumbledore? What does Dumbledore mean when he says "It does not do to dwell on dreams and forget to live, remember that"?

8) Why does Harry question Dumbledore's truthfulness when he asked him what he saw in the mirror? What made Harry bold enough to ask that personal question but not to inquire who had given him the Invisibility Cloak?

— Chapter 13: Nicolas Flamel —

Synopsis: Harry, Ron, and Hermione search for information about Nicolas Flamel

Setting: Gryffindor common room, Quidditch field

Themes: self-defense, achievement, discovery

Symbols: stone, gold, elixir, red, white, hood, curses, threats

Myths/legends: Ponce de Leon's search for the Fountain of Youth

Vocabulary Development:
brooding: in a bad mood
erupted: burst out
mystified: puzzled
somersault: acrobatic trick
strained: tight, tense

1) What do Harry's renewed nightmares represent?

2) How is the name Nicolas Flamel revealed? Why is he is significant to the plot? What would each student do with the magical Stone?

3) What do the fight in the stands and the action on the Quidditch field have in common? Why does Neville join the fight? How does Snape's refereeing affect the match's outcome? How does Harry think the victory redefines him?

4) What does Harry think the conversation he overhears between Snape and Quirrell in the Forbidden Forest means? How does this information heighten the tension as Harry realizes that an attempt to remove the Stone will occur soon?

— Chapter 14: Norbert the Norwegian Ridgeback —

Synopsis: Hagrid raises a baby dragon
Setting: library, Hagrid's hut, Hogwarts' tallest tower
Themes: secrecy, frustration, determination, nurturing, illegal
   activities

Symbols: dragon, egg, heat, black, orange, fire, fangs, window, bite, teddy bear, flying

Myths/legends: Atlas and Prometheus

Vocabulary Development:

bated: holding your breath when excited or anticipating an event

furling: unrolling in the wind

grappling: trying to get a hold of something or someone

jig: type of dance

loomed: threatening presence

stifling: hard to breathe

stoat: weasel

tartan: plaid

trowels: gardening hand tool

1) How does preparation for examinations parallel Harry's efforts to thwart the theft of the Stone?

2) What does the rule against dragons symbolize? Why does Hagrid break this rule? How does this affect Harry, Ron, Hermione, Neville, and Draco?

3) How does Hermione convince Hagrid to explain how the Stone is protected? Is this true to her character? Why is the information about the enchantments and their creators crucial to plot development? Why does Hagrid think it is impossible for anyone to steal the Stone?

4) What is the significance of Ron's dragon-bitten hand, Charlie's note, and the book Draco borrowed?

5) How does Norbert's escape foreshadow later rescue missions in the Potter series?

6) Why is Harry careless with his Invisibility Cloak?

— Chapter 15: The Forbidden Forest —

Synopsis: Harry, Hermione, Neville, and Draco serve detention in the woods
Setting: McGonagall's office, classrooms, Forbidden Forest
Themes: resentment, shame, irony, sarcasm, punishment, fear, courage
Symbols: hourglass, monsters, sparks, red, white, black, gold, path, arrow, unicorn, blood, cloak, Jupiter, Mars
Myths/legends: Chiron, Sileni, and Satyrs are half man and beast

Vocabulary Development:
alibis: claims of being elsewhere than the scene of a crime
bellowed: roared
blundering: clumsy
centaur: a creature that is half-man and half-horse
crossbow: weapon which shoots arrows
dappled: spotted
furor: anger
livid: enraged
oaf: fool

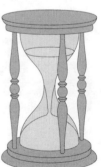

sapphires: blue gemstones
strode: taking long steps
whisked: rushed

1) How does McGonagall react to the students' disobedience? Why does she misunderstand their intentions? Why does Neville feel betrayed?

2) How do the Gryffindors treat Harry, Ron, Hermione, and Neville after they learn the house lost so many points because of their infractions? How do the Slytherins and other houses respond to the news?

3) Why does Harry decide to stop investigating mysteries? How does each character change after his/her punishment? Do they seem more grownup or childish?

4) Why does Ron want to resume efforts to protect the Stone? Why do Harry and Hermione refuse?

5) Why is Filch so eager to send the students into the Forbidden Forest for their punishment? Why isn't Hagrid more protective? How does each student express his fear?

6) How do the centaur's cryptic comments advance the plot? What is the result of Neville's false alarm? Why is Harry so sensitive to noises and feels like he is being watched?

7) What does the dead unicorn symbolize? What is its purpose

in the story? Why are all of the centaurs but Firenze so aloof? How does he enlighten Harry? Are the facts or the predictions that he shares with Harry more important?

8) Why does Ron become so agitated when Harry speaks Voldemort's name in the forest?

9) Why was Harry's Invisibility Cloak returned after his experiences with the hooded figure?

— Chapter 16: Through the Trapdoor —

Synopsis: Harry, Ron, and Hermione solve magical puzzles in the chambers

Setting: classrooms, Hogwarts grounds, Hagrid's hut, Gryffindor common room, chambers

Themes: self-confidence, intelligence, common sense, bravery, sacrifice, trust

Symbols: heat, examinations, squid, stranger, trapdoor, music, flute, dog, plant, birds, keys, white, black, chess, troll, fire, poison, owl

Myths/legends: Cerberus guards the underworld; Argus

Vocabulary Development:
batty: confused
bungled: to do badly
creepers: a vine type of plant; a nervous feeling
cringed: shrunk with fear
flailing: hitting wildly

flared: suddenly enlarged
fret: worry
logic: reasonable thinking
nettle: stinging weed
sweltering: hot
tentacles: arms of a squid or octopus
tumbled: fell

1) Why is Harry more concerned about the Stone than the others? Why does he think his scar hurts?

2) What does Harry remember about Hagrid's conversation regarding how he got Norbert? What did Hagrid divulge to the stranger in the pub which he then reveals accidentally to Harry, Ron, and Hermione?

3) Why do Harry and his friends not know where Dumbledore's office is located? Why are they so assertive when speaking to McGonagall and demanding to contact Dumbledore? How do they react when they encounter Snape on the grounds?

4) How does Harry justify the risks to protect the Stone when Ron and Hermione are reluctant? What does this transformation reveal about Harry's character development? How has his vendetta against Voldemort intensified? What boosts Hermione's and Ron's confidence?

5) Why does Harry feel justified to cast a spell on Neville? How do the trio outwit Peeves and Mrs. Norris?

6) How is each enchantment necessary to lead to the next stage of the adventure? How can the trio detect that someone had preceded them? How do they solve each problem and whose abilities are most useful at each step? What sacrifices are necessary?

7) Why does Hermione think friendship and bravery are more important than magical skills? Why does Harry doubt that he can defeat Voldemort without Dumbledore's assistance?

— Chapter 17: The Man With Two Faces —

Synopsis: Harry encounters Professor Quirrell in the final chamber

Setting: chamber, infirmary, Great Hall, Hogwarts Express, King's Cross station

Themes: betrayal, greed, power, duality, deceit, respect for self and others, emotional and physical pain, loss, death

Symbols: stone, mirror, turban, red, blood, infirmary, presents, names, candy, photograph album, green, silver, clothing, train

Myths/legends: Poseidon gives the Minotaur to Minos; two-faced Janus

Vocabulary Development:

detest: dislike

hygienic: clean

knack: ability

loathed: hated

scurrying: moving quickly

sidled: timidly approach from the side

spasm: seizure

swooping: coming down quickly

1) Why is Harry shocked by who he finds in the chamber? What revelations does Quirrell offer that explain mysterious events throughout the book? Are his answers satisfactory?

2) How does Quirrell plan to find the Stone? How does Harry try to prevent the mirror from revealing the Stone's location?

3) What does Harry learn about his father and Snape? What new information does Quirrell tell him about Voldemort?

4) How does Quirrell differentiate between good and evil, power and weakness?

5) Why does Quirrell tolerate Voldemort's abuses? Does Quirrell's tone seem confessional?

6) How does Harry react to Voldemort's torments? How does he defend himself? Why does he think he sees the Snitch?

7) Why does Dumbledore return in time to save Harry? What wisdom does he share with Harry? How do his comments and refusal to answer some of Harry's questions set up future plots? What does Harry realize about himself based on his experiences and Dumbledore's insights?

8) What does the revision of points for House championship represent? How does this moral victory prepare Harry for his

transition back to the Muggle world? How has Harry changed while Vernon Dursley remained the same?

PROJECTS AND ACTIVITIES FOR BOOK I

1) Write a fictional sports article about a Quidditch game or an interview with a player. Share your stories with your classmates.

2) Make a terrarium using moss and other plants similar to those mentioned in the novels.

3) Visit the zoo, especially the reptile house. How many boa constrictors does the zoo house? Write an essay about your experiences and include some information about boa constrictors.

4) Write a report about how garlic has been used as a magic potion throughout history. Mention superstitions and legends about garlic.

5) Write a thank you letter from Harry to Molly Weasley, Ron, Hermione, Hagrid, or the Dursleys for his Christmas gifts.

6) Design a sweater for the Hogwarts House that you would like to be a member of.

7) Play a recorder, which is probably most like the flute Harry used to enchant Fluffy. What tune would you play to make

Fluffy sleep? What melody would you play to accompany the school song?

8) Tape pictures of words, people, or things on a mirror to indicate what you would wish to see in the Mirror of Erised.

9) Design and make a cloak for either daily wear, as a Quidditch uniform, or to resemble Harry's invisibility cloak.

10) Polish and paint a stone to look like your idea of the Philosopher's/Sorcerer's Stone.

11) Mold clay to make a dragon and decorate it with paint. Name the dragon and write a brief description of what type of dragon it is, where it lives, what it likes to eat, and other habits.

12) Use a poster board to make a game about the Forbidden Forest. Draw several paths for players to move around on the board. Create tokens to represent characters, and design cards with different rewards and punishments. Write down the rules. Find dice, a spinner, hourglass, or any other objects you need.

13) Design a puzzle similar to the one with potions that Hermione solves (but do not use anything poisonous or foul tasting) to test your classmates' logic.

14) Find conversations that Harry overheard and write down your original interpretation. Then compare them to the truth that is later revealed.

15) Write an essay about what you think would happen if you discovered that you were famous and went to another school where everyone knew your story except you.

DISCUSSION FOR BOOK I

1) How do you think the story would have differed if Harry had always known he was a wizard and would attend Hogwarts?

2) Do you think Dumbledore was telling the truth when he said socks were his desire when he looked in the mirror? Was he being practical or concealing secrets?

3) What do sports symbolize?

4) Was Hermione justified to cast a spell on Neville?

5) Were the other students' reactions to Harry's, Ron's, Hermione's, and Neville's punishments justified?

6) Why wasn't Hagrid protective of Harry when he served detention in the Forbidden Forest because he was caught helping Hagrid's dragon Norbert escape? Was this true to Hagrid's character?

7) Discuss why Harry's friends did not pursue the stolen Stone as seriously as Harry.

8) Why did Ron sacrifice himself during the chess game in the chamber? Was it necessary?

9) What was significant about Harry confronting Quirrell alone?

10) Was it fair for Hagrid not to divulge information about Fluffy until Harry and his friends tricked him?

11) What is revealed about Hermione when she says that friends and bravery are more important than book learning?

12) Should Harry trust any of the information that Quirrell told him?

13) Does the magic seem plausible or are there inconsistencies that detract from the plot?

14) Should the Stone have been destroyed?

15) Why didn't Dumbledore vanquish Voldemort forever? Why is this considered Harry's task and nobody else's? Is no one else powerful enough or are they honoring Harry's right to avenge his parents' death?

16) Why didn't Dumbledore intervene in the rift between Harry and Snape?

17) Was it fair for Dumbledore to award so many points that the Gryffindors replaced the Slytherins as house champions?

DEVELOPING WRITING
AND CRITICAL SKILLS

1) Write a paper about mirror and reflection imagery in another novel.

2) Compare the role of sports in the Potter novels with other literature that feature sports. How do sports influence characterization, tone, and plots?

3) How does the first Potter novel provide insight into the development of a boy? Provide examples that show how Harry changes in this book.

4) Write a critical essay commenting on the centaur and unicorn community and how these mythical beasts communicate with each other and with humans. Compare this to other works of literature in which animals represent political and cultural ideologies.

5) Discuss the roles of scars and physical markings, both permanent and temporary, in literature. Explain how the mark's symbolism—ranging from good and evil–is perceived by the community.

6) Prepare a paper on fire imagery in the Potter novels, comparing events in the first book with later developments in the series.

7) Write about the theme of love as power in this book. Compare Dumbledore's philosophy of spiritual love empowering people with Quirrell's message promoting greed.

CHAPTER 18

HARRY POTTER AND THE CHAMBER OF SECRETS

DETECTIVE QUESTIONS FOR WIZARD SLEUTHS

"How glorious it is—and also how painful—to be an exception."
—LOUIS CHARLES ALFRED DE MUSSET

"Tell me what company thou keepst, and I'll tell thee what thou art." —MIGUEL DE CERVANTES

OVERVIEW

This sequel chronicles twelve-year-old Harry's second year at Hogwarts. The theme of tolerance is emphasized, and Harry boldly defends both friends and foes from a sinister presence hidden at the school. Prior to school starting, Harry is bewildered because his best friends, Ron and Hermione, have not contacted him all summer, even on his birthday. Harry despairs that he might never see them again. The boorish Dursleys are as horrible as ever, and Harry fears that he will never return to Hogwarts, which he considers his haven. To prevent business associates from seeing Harry, the Dursleys threaten him to stay hidden in his room where a self-flagellating house-elf named Dobby warns Harry that he must not attend Hogwarts because something horrible will happen there.

After a disastrous quarrel between Harry and Dobby which repulses the dinner guests and alerts the Dursleys that Harry will be expelled from school if he casts spells near Muggles, Harry is locked in his room like a prisoner and told that he will not be permitted to attend Hogwarts. Rescued by the Weasley brothers in a flying car, Harry manages to reach Hogwarts despite various obstacles. At school, he deals with both hateful and fawning classmates as well as nurturing, sinister, egotistical, and benign professors. Harry encounters conflicts and challenges that test his character and self-confidence.

When students lacking pure wizard ancestry start to become unexplainably petrified and Harry hears voices that no one else detects, he realizes he must solve the macabre mystery to save not only himself and the students and faculty but the school itself. With the help of Ron and Hermione, Harry learns the history of the Chamber of Secrets and the monster it contains, which is threatening the school after a fifty year hiatus. The trio prepare to vanquish the evil presence.

Only the heir of one of the school's founders, Severus Slytherin, knows where the chamber is and how to open it. Scary situations occur that cause the terrified Hogwarts community to suspect Harry is the vicious culprit descended from Slytherin who is tormenting the school. Experiencing self-doubt and confusion about his identity and personal history, Harry undergoes a series of trials to reach new levels of comprehension and ability to counter the dark forces which envelop the school. Despite his mental and magical agility, Harry stumbles into a trap set by his vengeful archenemy and relies on his faith in himself and his mentor, Albus Dumbledore, the school's head wizard, to survive.

CHAPTER DEVELOPMENT: DETECTIVE QUESTIONS FOR WIZARD SLEUTHS

See Appendix B: Mythical and Legendary Characters Cited in Section III for a brief explanation of the myths and how they are reflected in the Potter novels.

— Chapter 1: The Worst Birthday —

Synopsis: Harry is falsely accused of using magic on his birthday
Setting: Dursley house and garden
Themes: blame, repression, invisibility, isolation, emotional and physical starvation

Symbols: owl, green, sunburn, garden, manure, food
Myths/legends: Merlin's imprisonment by King Vortigern

Vocabulary Development:
clutches: in someone's control
padlocked: imprisoned
rapturously: joyously

1) Why is the word "magic" forbidden in the Dursley home? How is Harry punished for saying it?

2) Why are the Dursleys ashamed of Harry and exclude him from their social activities?

3) Why does Harry conceal the fact that he is not supposed to use magic when he is not at Hogwarts?

4) How is Harry punished for scaring Dudley?

5) Why are the Masons important to the Dursleys?

— Chapter 2: Dobby's Warning —

Synopsis: Dobby tells Harry not to return to Hogwarts
Setting: Dursley house
Themes: foreboding, vengeance, control, kindness
Symbols: elf, letters, pudding, owl, charm, mop, barred windows, soup, dream, zoo, moonlight
Myths/legends: Androcles and the lion

Vocabulary Development:
banshee: a female spirit who makes a wailing sound
brandishing: to wave a weapon or object in a threatening manner
falter: hesitate, quit
flay: to beat
nimbly: easily, with little effort
relenting: giving in
valiant: brave

1) Why does Dobby cry when Harry is polite to him?

2) How does Dobby try to make Harry take his warnings seriously?

3) How do the Masons react to the owl?

4) Why is Harry punished both by the Dursleys and the Ministry of Magic? Is this unfair? How does news that Harry is not supposed to use magic at home change Vernon Dursley's treatment of Harry? How do the Dursleys justify treating Harry like a prisoner?

5) What do Harry's selfless acts toward Hedwig symbolize? What does his dream about being an underage wizard in the zoo mean?

— Chapter 3: The Burrow —

Synopsis: Harry escapes from the Dursleys's house
Setting: the flying car, the Weasleys' home
Themes: liberation, rebellion, freedom, exhilaration
Symbols: flying, car, blue, pink, red, orange, green, chickens,
   ghoul, kitchen, gnomes
Myths/legends: Camelot

Vocabulary Development:
audible: can be heard
cheekily: to act sassy
clattering: noisy
compass: instrument to find direction
cowered: shrunk back in fear
dodgy: shifty
faltered: hesitated, stopped
fancies: wishful thinking
fiasco: failed event
gibbering: nonsensical
loophole: exception to avoid rule
revved: make an engine roar
rubbish: garbage, nonsense
ruddy: reddish
straggling: falling behind
tinkering: attempt to fix
tumbledown: in disrepair
twiddled: played with

1) What alerted the Weasleys that Harry might be in trouble?

2) How do the Weasley twins, Fred and George, apply Muggle methods to free Harry? Why is magic necessary to rescue him?

3) Why is Hedwig's screech symbolic? Would Harry feel as free if Vernon Dursley had not witnessed his departure?

4) Why does Harry suspect that Draco Malfoy sent Dobby to him?

5) How do Harry's experiences living with the Weasleys expand his awareness of what being a wizard entails? How do the Weasley parents and siblings represent what Harry's life might have been like if his parents had survived? Why do they rarely discuss Harry's family?

— Chapter 4: At Flourish and Blotts —

Synopsis: Harry encounters Gilderoy Lockhart, and Arthur Weasley and Lucius Malfoy fight

Setting: Diagon and Knockturn Allies

Themes: disruption, relocation, scheming, misunderstanding, grandiosity, hostility

Symbols: badge, books, powder, fireplace, soot, dark, glasses, opals, hand, poison, noose, bones, cauldron, newspaper

Myths/legends: Procrustes's insistence on conformity

Vocabulary Development:
abashed: embarrassed

ambled: walked slowly

awkward: clumsy

bombard: attack

brawling: fighting

bristling: stiff with anger

dingy: greyish, dirty

flea-bitten: in bad condition

gingerly: carefully

haggle: bargaining

ingenious: very clever

jaunty: spirited

marmalade: a kind of fruit preserve usually spread on muffins or bread

meddlesome: interfere in other's affairs

paddock: fenced area

pince-nez: a style of eye glasses attached to the nose

plunderer: thief

prudent: careful

quelling: to put an end to

scruffy: untidy

stampeded: ran away suddenly

sulky: unhappy

1) Why is Arthur Weasley so interested in Harry's experiences living in the Muggle environment?

2) What is significant about Harry's visit to Knockturn Alley and the information that he overhears? Why does he need to be rescued by Hagrid?

3) How do Hermione's parents interact with the Weasleys?

4) Why is Harry embarrassed by Gilderoy Lockhart's promotional stunt?

5) Why do Arthur Weasley and Lucius Malfoy fight? How does this set a sinister mood for the start of school?

— Chapter 5: The Whomping Willow —

Synopsis: Harry and Ron fly the car to Hogwarts
Setting: the flying car, Hogwarts grounds, Snape's office, Gryffindor common room
Themes: traveling, obstruction, resourcefulness, pride, hubris (excessive pride)
Symbols: fireworks, diary, car, train, sky, tree, blue, green, barrier, heat, wand, laboratory specimens
Myths/legends: Medusa with snaky hair like tree branches immobilizes her prey

Vocabulary Development:
aquamarine: a light blue-green color
boughs: tree branches
cajolingly: coaxed
cavernous: huge cave-like room
flouted: show contempt
gnarled: twisted and rough
innumerable: too many to count
moors: open land

pummeled: pounded
reckoned: dealt with
sacked: fired
sumptuous: extravagant
swig: to drink
triumphant: to win or succeed
trundled: rolled
walloped: hit and beat
wobble: unsteady

1) What personality characteristics do Harry and Ron share with Arthur Weasley?

2) Why do Ron and Harry decide to fly the car to school? What other options do they contemplate?

3) What is significant about Harry getting a lump on his head and Ron's wand breaking when the car hits the Whomping Willow?

4) How does personification of the car, tree, and Hedwig enhance the story?

5) Why does Snape seem delighted by the boys' misfortune? Why does Harry think Dumbledore's restrained disapproval is worse than any punishment administered by Vernon Dursley? How do the Hogwarts students react to Harry's and Ron's arrival?

— Chapter 6: Gilderoy Lockhart —

Synopsis: Ron receives a Howler, and classes begin

Setting: Hogwarts Great Hall and classrooms

Themes: accountability, egoism, hero worship, fraud

Symbols: letters, plants, earmuffs, beetles, blue, photographs, pixies, chandelier

Myths/legends: Narcissus gazes at his reflection

Vocabulary Development:

antidote: a cure to reverse poison or an evil spell

bedraggled: untidy

budgies: small type of bird such as parakeets

compost: organic mixture of soil and manure to grow plants in

disgruntled: cross and upset

immobilizing: stops movement

inquiry: question

jovially: in good humor

kippers: a type of fish such as salmon or herring

laden: carrying a load

nonplussed: unable to act, think, or speak; bewildered

pandemonium: excessive noise and activity

rampaging: violent behavior

rapt: complete attention

rifled: to ransack or plunder

roguish: naughty; playfully mischievous

scathing: heated and scornful

traipsed: to walk about idly or intrusively

transfixed: numbed to inactivity; motionless

trestle: railroad bridge
tufty: has bunches of hair, twigs, or other protruding material
turquoise: blue-green color
twinge: sudden pain

1) How does Ron's Howler increase Harry's guilty feelings?

2) Why does Lockhart think Harry intentionally flew the car to gain publicity?

3) What does Harry learn in his first classes?

4) Why does Colin Creevey want to photograph Harry? How does this provoke Draco to behave?

5) What happens in Lockhart's first class that suggests that he is incompetent?

— Chapter 7: Mudbloods and Murmurs —

Synopsis: Harry learns that some wizards are prejudiced
Setting: Quidditch field, Hagrid's hut, Lockhart's office
Themes: elitism, tolerance, empathy, awareness
Symbols: camera, trophy, slugs, silver, mail, lilac, ice, venom, bone marrow
Myths/legends: the Sirens' voice and mixed heritage

Vocabulary Development:
devising: preparing and planning

exasperated: out of patience
genially: with friendliness
glowering: angry looks
kelpies: water spirits
magenta: a pinkish-purplish color
mauve: a lavender color
prattle: talk aimlessly
scalawag: worthless or betraying person
snailed: pass slowly
squelchily: to put an end to
threshold: entrance
wistful: wishful thinking

1) How does Harry react to news that Draco is the new Slytherin seeker and that his father bought high-quality brooms for the team?

2) Why does Ron respond angrily when Draco calls Hermione a Mudblood? What happens to him when his spell backfires? Is that how he intended for Draco to suffer? What do the slugs represent?

3) Why is the position of professor of Defense Against the Dark Arts difficult to fill?

4) Why does Hagrid say it is necessary for some wizards to marry Muggles?

5) What happens to Harry during his detention? What does

Ron do for his punishment? How does Harry's confusion about the voice heighten tension?

— Chapter 8: The Deathday Party —

Synopsis: Harry, Ron, and Hermione celebrate the 500th anniversary of Nearly Headless Nick's death

Setting: Hogwarts corridor, Filch's office, dungeon

Themes: contamination, disappointment, overshadowing

Symbols: cold, rain, mud, smoke, orange, black, blue, salamander, fireworks, mold, horses, blood, torches, marble, cat, writing

Myths/legends: Beowulf and Grendel

Vocabulary Development:

airy: light

aquiver: trembling

bated: inability to breath deeply during excitement

bulbous: round shape

doublet: a style of man's jacket during the Renaissance

drenched: soaked

guffaw: loud laugh

haggis: a Scottish dish

havoc: destruction

manacles: chains to imprison

pasty: a meat pie

podium: speaker's stand

scintillation: turning and reflecting light

sinew: tendon, giving strength

tangerine: a citrus fruit that has easily peeled deep orange skin and sweet, juicy pulp

tapers: thin candles

tic: an involuntary movement; twitch

torrential: downpour of rain

translucent: allowing light but not images to pass through a surface

tunic: a long shirt that sometimes reaches the knees and is belted

1) Why is Nearly Headless Nick sad?

2) What does Harry discover in Filch's office?

3) Why is the Deathday Party significant to Harry?

4) Why does Peeves antagonize Moaning Myrtle?

5) What does Harry do when he hears the voice again?

6) Why does Draco smile when he yells his threat when everyone is assembled by the scene of the first crime?

— Chapter 9: The Writing on the Wall —

Synopsis: Harry is suspected of petrifying Mrs. Norris

Setting: Lockhart's office, library

Themes: suspicion, inquiry, questioning mythical beliefs

Symbols: books, chamber, monster, heir, spiders, mirror, candles, toilet, potion

Myths/legends: Amazon assertiveness by women

Vocabulary Development:
amulets: something worn around the neck for protection, a charm
blanched: lose color
blearily: blurred
fervently: sincerely
foreboding: threatening
gullible: believes anything
ludicrous: ridiculous
persecution: harass cruelly
punctuated: to clarify
purge: rid
scuttling: hasty flight
skulking: lurking
stupor: daze
teeming: plentiful
torpor: sluggish
unleash: release

1) Why does Filch think Harry is responsible for petrifying Mrs. Norris? What is a Squib?

2) Why does Lockhart insist on offering his advice when he is merely repeating what Dumbledore says?

3) How does Lockhart provoke Snape?

4) Why does Ron believe Harry is hearing a voice that no one else can hear?

5) How does the opening of the chamber initiate the book's mystery?

6) How do students start ostracizing Harry?

7) Why does Hermione persist in learning about the Chamber? How is the history of Hogwarts revealed? How does this advance the plot?

8) Why does Harry worry that he might be Slytherin's heir?

9) What strange things do Harry, Ron, and Hermione see around Hogwarts after the Chamber is opened? How do they decide to seek answers to their questions about the heir?

— Chapter 10: The Rogue Bludger —

Synopsis: Harry is injured during a Quidditch game
Setting: classroom, library, Quidditch field, infirmary
Themes: permission, persistence, ingenuity, injury
Symbols: werewolf, monsters, book, mold, rain, green, bones, sports equipment, burnt smell, steam, grapes, camera
Myths/legends: Hecate's curses

Vocabulary Development:
cardigan: style of sweater
dregs: material remaining at the bottom of a container

ebb: fade away

forfeit: give up; surrender

git: slang for person, often used to be demeaning

grievously: hard to bear

inept: clumsy

leaden: heavy

riddled: scattered throughout

rogue: rascal

rue: regret

searing: hot

splutter: make popping sounds

thicket: trees and shrubs growing closely together

toddle: walk uncertainly

vermin: filthy insects and animals, a vile person

1) How does Hermione get a signed note to check out a restricted library book? How does this reinforce Harry's opinion of Lockhart?

2) Why does the Polyjuice Potion require the trio to steal some ingredients and break rules? How does Hermione justify this behavior? How do Harry and Ron react to her enthusiasm?

3) Why does Draco call Harry "Scarhead" at the Quidditch game? Why is the storm symbolic? How do Harry's teammates cope with the charmed Bludger?

4) What is symbolic about Harry catching the Snitch after his right arm was broken?

5) How does Lockhart de-bone Harry's arm, and what does the regrowing of bone represent? Why does Hermione defend Lockhart?

6) Why does Dobby visit Harry in the infirmary? What does he confess? Why does Dobby punish himself? What is the only way that Dobby says he can be freed?

7) Why does Dobby admire Harry? Why doesn't he tell Harry everything that he wants to know?

8) How does Colin's petrification confirm that the Chamber is open?

— Chapter 11: The Dueling Club —

Synopsis: Harry learns that he is a Parselmouth
Setting: girls' bathroom, Snape's classroom, Great Hall, Gryffindor common room, library
Themes: fear, diversion, communication
Symbols: onion, crystal, firework, wands, pairs, green, smoke, bat, snake, black, hose, snow, dark, rooster
Myths/legends: Melampus understands animals

Vocabulary Development:
aftermath: the time following an event
aghast: horrified
apoplectic: stricken
balaclava: style of hat or cap

cuffed: slapped

distraught: upset

egging: encouraging someone to take action

exasperated: frustrated, annoyed or angry

feebly: weakly

gaped: stared

gargoyle: fantastical carving

griffin: mythical animal half-lion and half-eagle

hovercraft: an aircraft that can fly in one spot

inclined: slanted, apt to go in a certain direction

malevolent: evil intent

mayhem: chaos

ominous: threatening

reproving: to express disapproval

retaliated: to take revenge

smithereens: broken into small pieces; shattered

talismans: something for good luck, a charm

waspish: sharp, unpleasant

1) How do the students react to news of Colin's attack?

2) What does Harry do to help Hermione get rare ingredients from Snape's special supplies? What happens to their classmates?

3) How does Snape express his distaste for Lockhart at the Dueling Club? What is significant about the student pairings for practice dueling? What spells do they cast on each other and why?

4) How does Lockhart's spell backfire when Draco conjures a snake? How does Harry respond?

5) Why does Harry think the snake is rendered harmless? Why does he expect to be thanked for stopping it from striking? How do the students react? Why does Snape's expression upset Harry?

6) How does Harry learn what a Parselmouth is? Why are Ron and Hermione concerned?

7) Why does Harry continue to question whether he is Slytherin's heir? How does his identity crisis affect him? Who else could be Slytherin's descendant?

8) Which students think Harry is guilty of releasing the Chamber's monster to petrify people, and why? Which students defend him and why? How does the discovery of Justin and Nearly Headless Nick reinforce opinions?

— Chapter 12: The Polyjuice Potion —

Synopsis: Harry transforms into a Slytherin to question Draco
Setting: Dumbledore's office, girls' bathroom, Slytherin common room
Themes: rebirth, transformation, ostracism, deception
Symbols: hat, phoenix, gifts, food, hair, cauldron, fire, stone wall, password, newspaper, prison, manor, cat
Myths/legends: Achilles disguises himself

Vocabulary Development:
affronted: offended
balefully: with sadness
bout: an occurrence
comeuppance: punishment
decrepit: worn-out
disembodied: voice separated from body
dollops: spoonfuls
glutinous: thick and sticky
guffaw: loud laugh
hitherto: up until now
incredulously: unbelievably
indistinguishable: cannot tell the difference
khaki: tan colored cloth
labryinthe: a maze of passages
petulantly: pouting
plummeted: plunged down from height
pompously: display of self-importance
silhouetted: outlined in light
smouldering: burning slowly
stowed: packed away in boxes or closets
stupefied: made speechless
tumblers: cups

1) What does Harry hear when he puts on the Sorting Hat in Dumbledore's office? How does this intensify his confusion?

2) Why is Harry's encounter with Fawkes significant? What does he learn that might be useful later?

3) Why doesn't Harry tell Dumbledore that he fears he is Slytherin's heir?

4) Why are the twins' jokes about Harry being Slytherin's heir funny?

5) Why is Hermione more confident than Harry and Ron about the trio's plans to transform into Slytherins and interrogate Draco? Why is her optimism ultimately ironic?

6) What is significant about the descriptions of the trio preparing and drinking the potion, then transforming into a despised enemy? How does Hermione's transformation fail? What does this symbolize?

7) Why is Harry glad to see Draco? How do Ron and Harry adjust their expressions and statements to mimic Crabbe and Goyle? What do they learn about Lucius Malfoy? Why is the Slytherin password symbolic?

8) How does Harry react to Draco's contemptuous comments about "Saint Potter" and how he wishes that he could help Slytherin's heir get rid of the Mudbloods at the school? How does his revelation that a Mudblood died when the Chamber was opened fifty years ago heighten Harry's determination to catch the heir?

9) How does Ron plan to enact revenge for Draco's nasty comments about the Weasleys and Hermione?

– Chapter 13: The Very Secret Diary –

Synopsis: Harry time travels by using Tom Riddle's diary

Setting: infirmary, girls' bathroom, Great Hall, corridor, Gryffindor dormitory

Themes: memory, affection, accusation, guilt

Symbols: Valentine's cards, water, ink, cupid, drawfs, spider, box, dungeon, dark

Myths/legends: Pandora's box

Vocabulary Development:

absentmindedly: not paying attention

bade: told, commanded

confetti: small bits of colored paper

culprit: the person responsible for an unsavory act

drenched: soaked

evaporate: disappear

extinguished: put out

furrowed: in rows

hammering: pounding

miniscule: tiny

mirth: laughter

pinchers: claws

receded: went back

surly: nasty

undaunted: not discouraged

valiantly: bravely

1) How do Harry and Ron discover the diary? For what reasons

does Ron think the book might be dangerous? Why does Harry ignore him?

2) Why does Ron recognize the name T.M. Riddle? Why does Harry think the name is familiar?

3) How does Hermione try to read the writing on the diary's blank pages? Why is Harry successful?

4) Why does Harry dislike Valentine's Day? Why is Ginny's Valentine rhyme important to the plot development?

5) Why does Harry believe what he learns when he time travels by using the diary? What does he learn about Hagrid, Dumbledore, and the monster?

— Chapter 14: Cornelius Fudge —

Synopsis: Hagrid is sent to Azkaban Prison, and Dumbledore is suspended

Setting: classrooms, Gryffindor common room and dormitory, Quidditch field, Hagrid's hut

Themes: injustice

Symbols: sunlight, double, cloak, boiling water, fruitcake, fire, cold, blackmail, dog

Myths/legends: Sheriff of Nottingham and Little John

Vocabulary Development:
irresolute: not sure how to act or respond

megaphone: flared instrument used to increase the loudness of speech

precaution: take preventive measures

raucous: loud

recount: count again or repeat

revive: bring back to consciousness

strewn: scattered

tack: direction of thought

1) Why does Harry regret being able to understand the diary? Why doesn't he ask Hagrid about what happened when he was a student at Hogwarts?

2) Why is class scheduling for the third year of Hogwarts important? What classes does Harry not want to take? Why does he select his classes?

3) Why does Harry feel betrayed by a member of Gryffindor?

4) How does Harry try to quieten the voice he hears?

5) What is Hermione's response to his dilemma?

6) Why is the Quidditch match stopped? Why is this double attack especially alarming? How does it affect school life?

7) How do Harry and Ron use the Invisibility Cloak after the attack? What private conversation do they overhear regarding Hagrid? What does this reveal about Cornelius Fudge and Lucius

Malfoy? Why does Harry think Dumbledore is speaking to him? How does Hagrid convey an important message to the boys?

— Chapter 15: Aragog —

Synopsis: Harry, Ron, and Fang escape death
Setting: Snape's dungeon, greenhouse, Forbidden Forest, Gryffindor dormitory
Themes: innocence, betrayal, revelation
Symbols: spiders, dark, light, bushes, trees, dog, car
Myths/legends: Anancy the trickster

Vocabulary Development:
buoyant: tends to float
cowering: shrinking in fear
irksome: unpleasant, irritating
lagged: fell behind
livid: furious
mullioned: divided
shepherded: guided and protected
sphere: globe, rounded

1) How does Hogwarts change while Hagrid is imprisoned at Azkaban?

2) How does Harry's mood change?

3) Why do some students change their opinion about Harry being Slytherin's heir? In what ways do others become more racist?

4) What rules do Harry and Ron accept for safety when they follow the spiders into the forest? Are these rules logical or superstitious?

5) What information about Hagrid's past does Aragog share with Harry? Why have the spiders fled the castle?

6) How do Harry, Ron, and Fang escape? How has the flying car changed?

7) How does Harry discover that Moaning Myrtle was the student killed when the Chamber was opened?

— Chapter 16: The Chamber of Secrets —

Synopsis: Ginny Weasley is abducted, and Harry enters the Chamber

Setting: classrooms, staff room

Themes: silence, protection, retreat, confrontation, daring

Symbols: mirror, pipes, faucet, engraving, serpent, red, blood, yellow, eyes, skin, rock

Myths/legends: the Gorgons turn humans to stone

Vocabulary Development:

bellowed: yelled

hubbub: commotion

inkling: first realization

mutinous: rebellious

relish: enjoy

slog: walk through wet territory
subsided: decreased, declined
teetering: balancing on edge

1) Why does Ginny leave when Percy arrives at the Gryffindor table? Why does he tell Ron that what Ginny wanted to tell Ron was not about the Chamber?

2) Why is the piece of paper in Hermione's petrified hand important? What does Harry learn about conquering a basilisk? Why haven't any of the victims been killed?

3) How does Harry conclude that the heir is a Parselmouth manipulating the basilisk?

4) What do Harry and Ron overhear when they hide in the staff room? Why do they decide to pursue immediate action?

5) Why is Lockhart reluctant to battle the basilisk? How does he justify his behavior to Harry and Ron? How does Harry disarm Lockhart's Memory Charm? Are they justified in forcing him to go with them to the Chamber?

6) Why does Moaning Myrtle enjoy narrating the story of her death? How does this information help Harry and Ron?

7) Where do the boys think the Chamber is located?

8) What do Harry and Ron discover in the tunnel? How does

Lockhart try to trick them? How does this backfire on him? Why does Harry continue alone?

— Chapter 17: The Heir of Slytherin —

Synopsis: Harry battles Tom Riddle and the basilisk
Setting: Chamber of Secrets, girls' bathroom
Themes: deception, confusion, trust, betrayal, blindness
Symbols: stone, green, shadows, pillars, red, wand, sword, phoenix, tears, fang, feathers, ruby, music, serpent, ink
Myths/legends: the Sphinx riddles travelers; Apollo and Python

Vocabulary Development:
bemused: preoccupied
contorted: twisted
daubed: dabbed, applied in spots
forsaken: abandoned
framed: set up a person as the perpetrator of a crime
goggled: stared
hoist: lift
idly: inactive
keeled: fell over
lolled: rested
placidly: calmly
retorted: replied
serpentine: snakelike, s-shaped
shrewdly: with clever thought
torrents: heavy rainfall
vaulted: curved, raised ceiling

1) How does the Chamber's architectural design offer clues to the creature that lives there?

2) What is Ginny's condition when Harry finds her?

3) How does Tom Riddle mislead Harry? How does Harry's innocence and trust betray him?

4) At what point does Harry realize that Riddle is his enemy? How does he know this?

5) Why is Riddle so bemused by Harry's confusion? Why is he so disdainful of Ginny?

6) How does Riddle's belittlement of Hagrid anger and empower Harry?

7) In what ways does Riddle's ranting provide Harry information about Hogwarts history?

8) How does Riddle reveal he is Voldemort? What does Harry learn about Voldemort's parents and his reasons for disliking Muggles?

9) Who does Harry think the greatest sorcerer is and why?

10) Why are the music, Fawkes, the Sorting Hat, and Godric Gryffindor's sword significant?

11) Why does Harry feel courageous? What is his strategy to defeat Voldemort this time?

12) What does Harry hear and believe when he thinks that he is dying? What is symbolic about his blood and the basilisk's blood pooling together? How does Harry survive?

13) What is Ginny's reaction when she awakens? How has she replaced Hermione's role in Harry's life at that moment? Why does Harry not want to explain to Ron what happened in the Chamber in front of Ginny?

14) How are Harry's sensations symbolic as he is pulled up through the pipes?

— Chapter 18: Dobby's Reward —

Synopsis: Harry is praised, and he sets Dobby free
Setting: Dumbledore's office, Hogwarts staircase, Great Hall
Themes: renewal, second chances, justice
Symbols: awards, sock, sunshine, food, pajamas, telephone
Myths/legends: Nestor's wisdom

Vocabulary Development:
abject: miserable
consorted: associated with
coursing: flowing
disheveled: untidy
faltered: hesitated, stopped

flabbergasted: very surprised
hoodwinked: fooled
incensed: enraged
meddlesome: to interfere in the affairs of others
thronging: grouping together

1) Who is waiting for Harry, Ron, and Ginny when they emerge from the Chamber?

2) Why does Harry not tell the adults how Ginny obediently carried out Riddle's commands? Why does Dumbledore encourage this lie? What does he reveal about Tom Riddle?

3) Why is Arthur Weasley upset when Ginny confides how she wrote to Tom Riddle via the diary?

4) Why does Dumbledore change his mind about enforcing expulsion for perpetual rule breaking? How are the boys rewarded?

5) What makes Lockhart finally bearable to be around?

6) How does Dumbledore reassure Harry?

7) What does Dumbledore accuse Lucius Malfoy of? How does Harry substantiate his argument?

8) How does Harry cleverly free Dobby? How does Lucius Malfoy react? Is Harry scared by his threats?

9) What happens at Hogwarts after Harry defeats Tom Riddle? What was Ginny's secret about Percy?

10) How has Harry changed when he arrives at King's Cross? How does he perceive the Dursleys?

PROJECTS AND ACTIVITIES FOR BOOK II

1) Mold clay into a model Chamber and paint it to resemble details provided in the book.

2) Use a variety of materials to make miniatures of Godric Gryffindor's sword, Fawkes, the basilisk, and other objects crucial to this book's plot.

3) Write in a journal about your activities at school. Experiment with using lemon juice as invisible ink.

4) Research how snakes have been depicted in fiction, art, and legends and write a short paper to share with classmates. Compare how snakes are portrayed as both good and evil.

5) Learn about the history of plumbing. When would it have been technologically possible for pipes to be installed inside Hogwarts? How would water have been supplied to the castle before then?

6) Study how spiders are described in literature and myths. What legends and superstitions were developed because of real spiders' behaviors?

7) Write a Valentine poem for your favorite Hogwarts character. Create another for a character you dislike.

8) Go to a park or arboretum and find a willow tree. Write a story about the tree and draw a picture of it.

DISCUSSION FOR BOOK II

1) Is being different a bad thing? When is an abnormality considered dangerous? How should unusual people be treated? Is it ever morally right to discriminate against people who are different?

2) Why is it unfair for Harry to be forbidden to use magic? How is this rule beneficial to him and others?

3) Why is it dangerous to feel superior to other people?

4) What is the real monster housed in the Chamber of Secrets?

5) Is Harry's treatment of other students, such as Colin Creevy, mean? Should Harry be punished?

6) Should Molly Weasley have punished Harry for riding in the flying car with her sons? Why does he help de-gnome the garden?

7) Why didn't Dumbledore realize that Lockhart was a fraud and dismiss him?

DEVELOPING WRITING
AND CRITICAL SKILLS

1) Analyze the theme of racism in Book II. Compare any evidence of elitism in the other Harry Potter novels.

2) Write a paper about invisibility in Book II. Cite examples of people being ignored and rendered socially invisible within the Hogwarts and Muggles societies. Expand your comments to the first and third Harry Potter novels.

3) Describe the vulnerability of characters such as Harry, Ginny, Draco, Snape, and Lockhart. Which characters seem immune to weaknesses and why? What makes them defenseless to verbal or physical attacks?

4) Compare the characters of Ginny and Dobby. How do they relate to Harry? How does he save them? What are their flaws? What are their strengths?

5) Analyze Tom Riddle's motivations to create the name "Voldemort" as his identification and how it reveals his anger at his father who abandoned his witch mother. What does it suggest about his hostilities toward other wizards?

CHAPTER 19

HARRY POTTER AND THE PRISONER OF AZKABAN

DETECTIVE QUESTIONS FOR WIZARD SLEUTHS

"Just trust yourself, then you will know how to live."
—JOHANN WOLFGANG VON GOETHE

*"It is more shameful to distrust one's friends
than to be deceived by them."*
—FRANÇOIS DE LA ROCHEFOUCAULD

*"The only ones who can forgive are dead; the living
have no right to forget."*—CHAIM HERZOG

OVERVIEW

Book III revolves around the themes of forgiveness, redemption, faith, and innocence. Now a teenager, Harry has matured since readers met him in Book I. No longer as insecure and intimidated as when he first entered Hogwarts, Harry develops resilient self confidence in this most complicated Harry Potter story so far. Harry learns to distinguish the truth from popular opinion and realizes that many people, animals, and objects are not what they initially appear to be.

Harry angrily leaves the Dursley home when Vernon's sister Marge insults his parents. Realizing that he cannot return to the Dursleys, Harry also fears expulsion from Hogwarts because he cast a vengeful spell against Marge. While Harry worries about his immediate future, he sees a dog's glowing eyes in an alley. Transported to Diagon Alley by the Knight Bus, Harry is surprised when Cornelius Fudge dismisses his inappropriate use of magic. Fudge is more concerned about Harry's safety because Sirius Black has escaped from Azkaban prison. Twelve years before, Black allegedly betrayed Harry's parents by telling Voldemort where they lived. He also was accused of killing thirteen people with one curse when he was apprehended for his complicity in the Potters' murder.

Living in the Leaky Cauldron until Hogwarts begins, Harry sees a picture of the alley dog in a book of omens which identifies it as a Grim. He also overhears the Weasleys discuss whether to tell Harry that Black is looking for him. Harry, however, is not as concerned about his safety as the adult wizards are concerned. He believes that he will be safe at Hogwarts under

Dumbledore's protection. Harry is more upset that he cannot visit the nearby village of Hogsmeade because Vernon Dursley refused to sign his permission slip. On the way to Hogwarts, Harry meets Remus Lupin, the new Defense Against the Dark Arts teacher who helps Harry when he has a severe reaction to a Dementor who is an Azkaban guard sent to apprehend Black. Harry begins to hear his parents' death cries whenever Dementors are near, and Lupin teaches him how to summon inner happiness to repel the Dementor's joylessness.

During the school year, Harry and Draco Malfoy continue their volatile rivalry. Harry sees the Grim, loses his first Quidditch match when he falls from his broom, and suffers from intense nightmares. Hired as the Care of Magical Creatures instructor, Hagrid introduces the third-year students to Hippogriffs. Draco becomes injured after he insults a Hippogriff, and he unjustly seeks punishment of both the creature and Hagrid for his resulting embarrassment. Professor Trelawney, the Divination teacher, irritates Hermione, Ron, and Harry with her imprecise behavior and predictions. Snape torments Harry but is the source of new information about James Potter.

Using his Invisibility Cloak and the Marauder's Map to visit Hogsmeade by using secret passages, Harry learns details about his parents' murder that infuriate him. His anger festers while he is busy with Quidditch practice and helping Hagrid defend the accused Hippogriff. Harry also tries to keep Ron and Hermione from ruining their friendship over squabbles concerning their pet rat and cat. The trio are together in Hogsmeade's Shrieking Shack where Harry confronts Black and chooses to listen instead of killing him. What Harry hears permanently changes him. He makes choices based on his new wisdom and sacrifices his potential happiness for others' freedom. Harry also gains a new appreciation of time and his own inner strength to protect himself and others from false accusations. He unfortunately becomes disillusioned when he realizes that Dumbledore is fallible and cannot solve every problem.

CHAPTER DEVELOPMENT: DETECTIVE QUESTIONS FOR WIZARD SLEUTHS

See Appendix B: Mythical and Legendary Characters Cited in Section III for a brief explanation of the myths and how they are reflected in the Potter novels.

— Chapter 1: Owl Post —

Synopsis: Harry receives birthday gifts from his friends
Setting: Harry's room in the Dursleys's house
Themes: self-reflection, dedication, generosity, compassion
Symbols: homework, torch, dark, owls, books, ink, presents
Myths/legends: Ilithyia (Eileithyia) and birth

Vocabulary Development:
downtrodden: beaten down
emblazoned: decorated
fez: a style of hat that is a cone and lacks a brim
gangling: awkward and lanky
luminous: shining

mutant: offspring is different from parents and others of species
ominous: threatening
souvenir: keepsake
squash: smash

1) In what three ways does Harry differ from Muggle children?

2) Why is Harry's thirteenth birthday the best one he's celebrated? How do his gifts prepare him for his third year at Hogwarts?

3) How has Harry changed since he left Hogwarts?

4) What do the three owls bring to Harry? Why are these gifts significant?

5) What has happened to Harry's friends during the summer?

— Chapter 2: Aunt Marge's Big Mistake —

Synopsis: Harry loses his temper when Marge insults his parents
Setting: Dursley home
Themes: self-defense, denial, control, derision
Symbols: fugitive, food, dogs, pig, drill, balloon, trunk, wand
Myths/legends: the Harpies

Vocabulary Development:
apoplectic: stricken
bellowed: yelled loudly
insolent: disrespectful

intently: pay close attention
jovially: pleasantly
layabout: one who does very little
matted: crushed and tangled
meringue: a baked whipped egg white dessert
namby-pamby: weak
nosh: tidbit; snack
puce: a brownish purple color
reproachful: blaming and accusing
shards: pieces of broken glass or pottery
toed: acted responsibly as expected
tweed: a kind of fabric
wastrel: a good-for-nothing person
wince: pull back in pain

1) How have the Dursleys's home and its inhabitants changed? How have they remained the same?

2) How does the family react to the news of Sirius Black's escape?

3) Why does Vernon Dursley insist on lying to his sister about Harry's school? Why does Harry agree to cooperate?

4) How does Aunt Marge insult Harry? What does he do to try to remain calm?

5) What pushes Harry over the edge? Why is he brave enough to defend himself to Vernon and leave the house? Why does Harry worry that the Ministry of Magic will punish him?

— Chapter 3: The Knight Bus —

Synopsis: Harry sees the Grim and is transported to the Leaky Cauldron

Setting: Magnolia Crescent, the Knight Bus, the Leaky Cauldron

Themes: transitions, impersonation, protection, permission, solitude

Symbols: dog, purple, three, scar, eleven, rules, silver, newspaper, candlelight, glasses

Myths/legends: Orion and Sirius

Vocabulary Development:

bowling: moving quickly

cascade: rush downward

collywobbles: creepy feelings

contemptuously: disrespectfully

crumpet: an unsweetened cake

infamous: someone who is known for their criminal actions

protruding: sticking out

tally: measure up to

testily: irritated

tottered: walked unsteadily

unfurled: unrolled; opened

1) How do Harry's emotions shift from anger to panic? What are his plans for surviving without the Dursleys and Hogwarts?

2) What does Harry see in the alley before the Knight Bus picks him up? Is he scared or curious?

3) What does Harry learn from the bus conductor Stan Shunpike and driver Ernie Prang? Why does he conceal his scar and identity? Why does he pretend to be Neville Longbottom? Why is this significant?

4) Why did Cornelius Fudge tell the Muggle Prime Minister about Sirius Black? Why did Fudge think it was safe to confide that Black is a wizard?

5) What does Harry say that upsets Stan and Ernie?

6) What does Harry worry about on the bus?

7) How does Fudge comfort Harry? Why does he defend the Dursleys? What rules must Harry follow while he lives at the Leaky Cauldron?

— Chapter 4: The Leaky Cauldron —

Synopsis: Harry resides at the Leaky Cauldron tavern and prepares for school
Setting: the Leaky Cauldron, Diagon Alley
Themes: autonomy, self-reliance, belonging, secrets, determination
Symbols: money, gold, sunshine, food, ice cream, broom, stores, books, omens, robes, cat, rat, tonic, badge, mirror
Myths/legends: Shangri-La

Vocabulary Development:
acceleration: increasing speed
aerodynamic: having to do with the forces of air
basin: wide shallow place for water
bedlam: chaos
composedly: with dignity
embossed: design cut into a surface
formidable: awesome
grappled: fought
honed: sharpened
incorporates: includes, combines various entities
laden: weighted down
ogling: staring
prototype: original model or example
raucous: loud
rent: tore
streamlined: sleek
unsurpassable: cannot be improved, the best
venerable: honorable
woebegone: sad

1) What does the Leaky Cauldron represent to Harry? What does he do while he is waiting for Hogwarts to begin?

2) Why doesn't Harry buy the Firebolt at Quality Quidditch Supplies? What does this suggest about his maturity?

3) What does Harry learn in Flourish and Blotts?

4) What is significant about the day that Harry, Ron, and Hermione shop together at Diagon Alley?

5) What does Harry learn from various members of the Weasley family while they stay at the Leaky Cauldron? How do Arthur and Molly Weasley justify their decision not to tell Harry about Sirius Black's suspected vendetta against him?

6) Why is Harry not afraid? Why is he irritated?

— Chapter 5: The Dementor —

Synopsis: Harry travels to Hogwarts and is chilled by a Dementor
Setting: King's Cross Station, Hogwarts Express, Great Hall
Themes: vulnerability, paralysis, intervention
Symbols: luggage, whistle, train, candy, chocolate, gold, feast, home, password
Myths/legends: the Furies

Vocabulary Development:
apprehensively: fearful
befuddled: confused
blandly: expressionless
cavernous: large cave-like room
clotted: coming together in bunches
dilapidated: falling apart
engulf: to cover over, surround
foreboding: ominous feeling
infuriating: makes one very angry

insolent: disrespectful
levitate: rise in air
morsels: tasty pieces of food, scraps
pallid: pale
ravenous: very hungry
shunting: directing
stowed: packed away
tumultuous: noisy and disturbing
wrought: hammered and shaped attractively

1) How does Harry travel to King's Cross station? Why does Arthur Weasley decide to warn Harry about Black? How does Harry respond?

2) Where do the children first see Remus Lupin? Who do they think he is? Why is it unusual for an adult to be on the train?

3) What do they talk about when they first board the Hogwarts Express? What details seem to foreshadow future events? Who visits them in their compartment?

4) What is symbolic about Lupin sleeping despite efforts to awaken him? What does the storm represent?

5) How does Harry react to the Dementor? Compare how the Dementor affects the other people in the compartment? How does Lupin make the Dementor leave and what might this foreshadow? What does Lupin give Harry to help restore his consciousness?

6) Why does Harry feel ashamed? How does Draco Malfoy ridicule Harry and Lupin? Why does McGonagall want to see Harry and Hermione but not Ron when they arrive at Hogwarts?

7) What new rules does Dumbledore issue during his welcoming speech? What does he say that speaks directly to Harry?

8) What is Snape's expression when Lupin is introduced to the students? How does news of Professor Kettleburn's departure suggest the dangerous aspects of the Care of Magical Creatures class?

9) Why are Harry, Ron, and Hermione surprised that Hagrid is a teacher? Why is Hagrid proud that Dumbledore chose him for the position?

— Chapter 6: Talons and Tea Leaves —

Synopsis: Harry attends new classes including Divination
Setting: Great Hall, top of North Tower, Hogwarts grounds
Themes: intuition, logic, knowledge, courtesy
Symbols: paintings, knight, ladder, red, candles, perfume, crystal balls, shawls, tea leaves, creatures, eyes, injury
Myths/legends: Cassandra the prophetess

Vocabulary Development:
aura: invisible atmosphere around a person that some people claim to be able to see and analyze
bracingly: invigorating
brandishing: waving a weapon in a threatening way

chintz: a printed and glazed brightly colored cotton fabric

contemptuous: disrespectful

crestfallen: disappointed

crinolines: stiff underskirts

disdainful: scorn

dregs: material left on the bottom of containers

gauzy: very thin and light

haughtily: with excessive pride

mundane: unexciting

poufs: puffs

resonances: intensifying sound qualities

scabbard: sheath for blade

scalding: very hot liquid; boiling

scurvy: a disease caused by lack of vitamin C;
       a term used as an insult

spectral: ghostly

stifingly: hard to breathe

swooning: fainting

tankard: container for drink

tethered: tied

undertone: underlying factor or characteristic

1) What do the twins say to make Harry feel better when Draco mocks him at breakfast? What information do they tell Harry about Dementors?

2) Why is Hermione evasive when Ron questions her about the number of classes that she is taking?

3) Who helps the students find the Divination classroom? Why does Harry think this room seems odd as compared to other Hogwarts classrooms?

4) Why have few students met Professor Trelawney? How does she discourage the students? Who does she encourage? Why does Hermione dislike the Divination class? What predictions does Trelawney make?

5) What do the patterns in the tea leaves symbolize? How might they advance the story's plot? What is a Grim?

6) What does McGonagall demonstrate in the first Transfiguration class and why might this be important to plot development? Why does she refuse to belittle her colleagues? Why does she joke about Trelawney's prediction regarding Harry?

7) Why is Hagrid surprised that the students do not know how to tame their monster book? Why is Draco contemptuous toward Hagrid? How does Draco's disdain result in his injury?

8) Why is it important not to insult a Hippogriff? Why are manners so important at Hogwarts?

9) After Draco was attacked, how does Hermione assume adult roles while Hagrid acts like a child?

— Chapter 7: The Boggart in the Wardrobe —

Synopsis: Harry watches his classmates confront their fears
Setting: Snape's dungeon, staff room
Themes: facing fear, affirmation, encouragement, self-confidence
Symbols: tadpole, toad, monsters, red, green, cold, mummy, spider, vulture, eyeball, crab, mousetrap, snake
Myths/legends: Psyche and identity

Vocabulary Development:
cowering: huddled in fear
deliberately: action on purpose
grimace: frown
offhandedly: without preparation
seething: filled with rage
spleen: malice
tatty: ragged
verge: about to begin

1) Why does Draco exaggerate the extent of his injury? How does Harry detect that Draco is faking? How does Snape respond to Draco's situation?

2) How do events and conversations that occur in Snape's Potions class advance the plot?

3) Why does Harry say that he plans to capture Black by himself? Is he serious?

4) What would Draco do if he were the person Black was hunting for? How does Draco torment Harry with his comments?

5) Why are Snape and the Slytherins disappointed when Neville's toad shrinks into a tadpole? Why does Ron say Hermione should have fibbed about helping Neville?

6) Why do the students think Lupin is the best Defense Against the Dark Arts teacher they've ever had? How does Lupin boost his students' self-confidence?

7) What does the Boggart represent to each student and Lupin? How do the Boggart and the charms to repel them advance the plot? Why does Lupin not ask Harry or Hermione to confront the Boggart? Why do the other students not notice this omission?

— Chapter 8: Flight of the Fat Lady —

Synopsis: Sirius Black breaks into the Gryffindor tower
Setting: Gryffindor dormitory and common room, Lupin's office, Hogsmeade, Great Hall
Themes: feuds, obedience, assertiveness, invasion
Symbols: rat, cat, rabbit, fox, Halloween, potion, ghosts
Myths/legends: Hestia and home

Vocabulary Development:
deciphering: decoding
listlessly: without energy

novelty: newness
squabble: fight
tactics: plan of action
tarnish: darken, to become dull
vindictive: mean

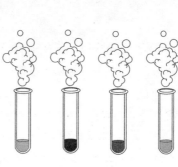

1) What creatures do the students learn to deal with in Lupin's classes? Why does Harry loathe Snape's and Trelawney's classes? How has Hagrid's class changed?

2) Why do Ron and Hermione disagree when Crookshanks attacks Scabbers? Why does Ron think Crookshanks has a vendetta against Scabbers?

3) Which of Trelawney's predictions do the students think has become true and how does Hermione explain they are wrong? How does Ron use this incident to malign Hermione?

4) Why does McGonagall refuse to give Harry permission to go to Hogsmeade with his classmates? How does he try to persuade her? How does Hermione react to Ron's criticism of McGonagall? What suggestions does Ron offer Harry for ways to sneak into Hogsmeade?

5) Why does Harry initially lie to Lupin when he asks him if he is worried about anything? Why is Harry surprised when Lupin says Voldemort's name? What does Lupin say is Harry's worst fear? Why does Harry feel relieved?

6) Why does Snape prepare Lupin's potion? How does this upset Harry? Why does Harry warn Lupin that Snape would like to teach the Defenses Against the Dark Arts class? How does Lupin respond?

7) What do Ron and Hermione bring Harry? How do they describe Hogsmeade? How does this soothe Harry?

8) What happens to the Gryffindor painting while the students are at the Halloween feast? How does Peeves assist Dumbledore?

— Chapter 9: Grim Defeat —

Synopsis: Harry is overwhelmed by Dementors and loses his
  first Quidditch game
Setting: Great Hall, Quidditch field
Themes: surveillance, substitution, vindictiveness, loss
Symbols: rumors, wind, lightning, thunder, werewolves,
  umbrellas, eyeglasses, dark, deafness, cold, voices, falling,
  injury
Myths/legends: Zeus and weather

Vocabulary Development:
abashed: embarrassed
cur: filthy dog; used as an insult
fraction: a slight amount; used to refer to
  Harry opening his eyes
inexplicably: cannot be understood
insufferable: intolerable

lunatic: madman
pensively: reflective
pompous: self-important
sodden: soaked
tirade: emotional outburst
undaunted: not discouraged
wrong-foot: cheat

1) Why do the students sleep in the Great Hall? How does this help Harry, Ron, and Hermione acquire clues about Black? How do they gain insight about the relationships between the professors?

2) How does information about the search for Black contribute to the readers' knowledge of the layout and location of Hogwarts?

3) What does Snape refer to during his conversation with Dumbledore? Why does Dumbledore defend the position that no one at Hogwarts would assist Black?

4) Why does Dumbledore dismiss Percy's suggestion and forbid the Dementors from entering the castle?

5) How does Harry's daily routine change after Black attacked the portrait? What rules are specifically issued for him?

6) How does Snape teach the Defenses Against the Dark Arts class when he substitutes for Lupin? Why does he deduct points? Why are the students so bold in their defense of Lupin? Why is Snape

so critical of Lupin and threaten to report him to Dumbledore? Why does Snape emphasize the subject of werewolves? Why does Ron defend Hermione? What is his punishment?

7) Why is the lightning storm symbolic on the day of the Quidditch game? How does Hermione help Harry's vision? How does he react when he sees the Grim? What does Harry hear when the Dementors watch the game? What cushions his fall?

8) How does his first loss affect Harry and his teammates? How did Cedric Diggory exhibit sportsmanship? How is the Whomping Willow's splintering of Harry's broom symbolic?

– Chapter 10: The Marauder's Map –

Synopsis: Harry uses a secret passage to travel to Hogsmeade
Setting: infirmary, classroom, tunnel, Honeydukes and other Hogsmeade stores
Themes: recovery, hibernation, rebellion, revelations, betrayal
Symbols: creatures, prisoners, fortress, frost, quiet, tunnel, hot, cold, dark, dust, secrets, charm, crater
Myths/legends: the duality of Dionysus; Hades

Vocabulary Development:
bonbons: a type of chocolate candy
demurred: declined
fitfully: unevenly
indignation: righteous anger
nougat: a type of candy with creamy, chewy, and nutty centers

opaline: white and luminous
scoff: deride
smithereens: shattered into tiny pieces
squelching: put an end to
succulent: full of flavor
unhinged: make crazy

1) Why does Harry not tell his friends about seeing the Grim and hearing his mother's voice?

2) Why does Ron lose 50 points before Lupin's return? How does Lupin react to the students' complaints about Snape?

3) Why does Harry confide in Lupin? What does Lupin tell him about Dementors? Why does he say Harry is more sensitive to Dementors than the other students? Why are the Dementors getting restless? How does this information intensify the plot?

4) How does Harry convince Lupin to teach him anti-Dementor techniques?

5) What do the Weasley twins give Harry before Christmas? Why do they no longer need it? Why does Harry decide to use it?

6) How do Ron and Hermione react to Harry's sudden appearance in Hogsmeade? What does Harry learn about his parents' murder while he is there? How does this knowledge increase tension?

7) What is a Secret-Keeper?

8) How do the professors describe Peter Pettigrew? Why do they feel empathy for him?

9) What did Cornelius Fudge give Black at Azkaban?

10) What revelations are included in this chapter that explain details about Harry's past and wizard history? How does this advance the plot?

— Chapter 11: The Firebolt —

Synopsis: Harry receives a new broomstick from an anonymous donor

Setting: Gryffindor common room, Hagrid's hut, library

Themes: hate, vengeance, inner conflict, judgement, joy, comfort

Symbols: photographs, poison, creatures, tea, books, food, cake, broom

Myths/legends: Laocoon and the Trojan Horse

Vocabulary Development:

beadily: small, round, glittering

berating: scolding; belittle

brood: dwell

casting: searching

devoid: empty

flagon: a container for liquids

laden: filled

tripe: digestive organs; slang for nonsense or worthless

1) How is Harry affected by the conversation he overheard in Hogsmeade? How does this influence how he perceives his friendships?

2) Why is Harry upset that Ron and Hermione cannot understand his pain and need for vengeance? Why does Harry say that Draco comprehends the situation better than Ron and Hermione? How does this make them feel? How do they try to remind Harry that the Malfoys are allied with Voldemort and do not care for Harry?

3) What distracts Harry from confronting Hagrid about withholding information concerning his parents? How do the children try to comfort Hagrid? What three horrible things does Hagrid say he keeps thinking of and how do these events relate to the plot? Why does Hagrid worry about being sent to Azkaban again?

4) Why is the Firebolt significant? Who do the boys think the anonymous gift giver is? Why does Hermione think the broom is cursed? What sets off the Pocket Sneakoscope?

5) Why does Trelawney warn the diners not to be the first person to leave the Christmas feast? How do people respond to her prediction?

6) How does McGonagall learn about Harry's new broom? Why does she confiscate it? Why does Ron get angry at Hermione, and how does she defend her actions?

— Chapter 12: The Patronus —

Synopsis: Harry learns to defend himself against his fears

Setting: Gryffindor common room, History of Magic classroom

Themes: disagreement, memory, happiness, anguish, dilemmas, vanishing

Symbols: wand, shrieks, chocolate, homework, kiss, passwords, blood

Myths/legends: Sisyphus's struggle

Vocabulary Development:

astounded: amazed

averted: avoided

clamp: securely attach

confiscated: taken

detour: alternate path

imperceptibly: not detectable

rekindled: lit again

shirty: uptight

utterly: completely

yeomen: an assistant or military officer

1) How does Harry react to the loss of his new broom? How does this affect the trio's friendship?

2) What is the difference between a Patronus and the charm the other students used to counter the Boggart? Why is it easier for Harry to master this difficult charm than to attempt the basic spell? Why is it necessary for him to master such powerful

magic? What memories does Harry select? What information does he learn during this exercise?

3) Why does Lupin apologize to Harry?

4) Why does Harry trust Lupin enough to ask him if he had known Black when they were attending Hogwarts? How does Lupin react to this question? How does Harry know not to push Lupin for more information?

5) Why does Harry want to hear his parents' voices despite how awful it makes him feel?

6) Why is Hermione stressed? What strange details have friends told Ron about Hermione's classes?

7) Why doesn't Harry want to order a Nimbus Two Thousand and One?

8) What does Lupin tell Harry about the Dementor's Kiss? Why does Harry think Black deserves this punishment? Why does Lupin question his logic? Why can't Harry explain what he overheard in Hogsmeade?

9) Why can't Neville enter Gryffindor House?

10) What is Hermione's favorite subject? Why does Harry think she should take fewer classes?

11) What clues does Ron find in the turret when Scabbers disappears?

— Chapter 13: Gryffindor versus Ravenclaw —

Synopsis: Harry wards off threatening spectators to win a
  Quidditch match
Setting: Quidditch field, Gryffindor common room and
  dormitory
Themes: self-confidence, admiration, sabotage, carelessness
Symbols: cat, eyes, wand, t-shirt, penalties, party, dream, stag,
  knife
Myths/legends: Mordred and Arthur

Vocabulary Development:
abysmally: dreary, the worst
basking: enjoying
consequences: results
disarray: not organized
engulfed: covered, surrounded
extricate: remove, to pull out
phenomenal: amazing
precision: exactness
quarry: something being hunted
sabotage: intentional damage
thunderstruck: shocked
tumultuous: noisy and violent

1) How does each character react to Scabbers' vanishing? How

does this worsen the relationship between Hermione and Ron? How does Harry distract Ron?

2) Why does Harry notice Cho Chang? Why is Wood upset that she recovered after being injured?

3) How does Harry's broom improve the Gryffindors' moods?

4) What does Harry see in a tree? How does this interrupt the chapter's tone?

5) How does Harry cope when he thinks he sees a Dementor? How are Draco, Crabbe, and Goyle punished for pretending to be a Dementor? How does this add comic relief to the story?

6) Why is Hermione aloof during the celebration? How does Harry try to encourage her to interact?

7) What is significant about the dream Harry is having when Black breaks into the turret?

8) Why is Sir Cadogan proud? Why is Neville ashamed?

— Chapter 14: Snape's Grudge —

Synopsis: Henry scares Draco in Hogsmeade and is interrogated by Snape
Setting: Great Hall, Hagrid's Hut, Hogsmeade, Snape's Office
Themes: heroics, forgiveness, resourcefulness, revenge, disapproval

Symbols: map, owls, mud, ghost, cloak, trolls
Myths/legends: Pentheus's rage

Vocabulary Development:
astonishment: disbelief
disquiet: anxious
hallucinations: imaginary sights and sounds
immense: great
impassive: not showing reaction
malice: hate
miniscule: tiny
pang: sudden pain
pirouette: spinning ballet movement
plummeted: dropped
sludge: thick dirty waste

1) What safety measures are taken after Black's intrusion? Why does Harry decide not to tell any professors about the secret passage?

2) Why is Ron more interesting to the Hogwarts students than Harry after the break-in? How does he embellish his account in response to his sudden fame?

3) How is Neville punished?

4) How does Hagrid defend Hermione to Harry and Ron and what does he suggest they do to mend the friendship?

5) Why does Harry agree to meet Ron in Hogsmeade? How does Hermione react to their decision?

6) How does the encounter with Draco, Crabbe, and Goyle at the Shrieking Shack change Harry's life? What is symbolic about Harry's enemies only seeing his floating head?

7) Why does Harry not admit his guilt to Snape despite being pressured? What does Snape reveal about Harry's father during his jealous tirade? Does his information seem true? Why does Harry yell at Snape to be quiet? How does Snape belittle Harry's father? Why does Snape enjoy tormenting Harry like this?

8) What happens when Snape tries to use the Marauder's Map? How does Harry know not to speak when Lupin arrives? How does Lupin protect the map? Why do his comments hurt Harry's feelings?

9) Why doesn't Harry retrieve the Invisibility Cloak from the secret passage?

10) Why is Hermione upset when Harry and Ron return to the Gryffindor corridor?

– Chapter 15: The Quidditch Final –

Synopsis: Harry helps Gryffindor win the Quidditch Cup
Setting: classrooms, Quidditch field
Themes: sorrow, apology, departures, antagonism, triumph

Symbols: tears, crystal ball, visions, cat, dog, penalties
Myths/legends: Aeneas's victories

Vocabulary Development:
clairvoyant: can see the future
contentment: happiness
doddery: vulnerable
enmity: hostility
exuberant: wildly happy
haring: chasing
pathetic: pitiful
reprovingly: scolding
rosettes: a satin decoration pleated or gathered to resemble a rose
verdict: judgment
writhing: moving in pain

1) How does Hagrid's letter help heal Ron's and Hermione's relationship?

2) Why does Hermione hit Draco? How is this a turning point in her character development?

3) Why does Ron decide to find information to exonerate Buckbeak?

4) Why does Hermione miss Charms class? How does Ron comfort her?

5) Why does Trelawney skip ahead of schedule to reading crystal

balls? What are the different student reactions to this activity? Why does Hermione dismiss what Trelawney says she sees in Harry's crystal ball before she finishes her comments? Why does Hermione quit the class? Does this fulfill a prediction?

6) What nightmares does Harry have the night before the Quidditch match versus the Slytherins? What does he see outside his window? How do these unconscious and conscious visions advance the plot?

7) What is Harry's strategy to outsmart Draco to win the game? How do the Slytherins interfere with Gryffindor players? How is cheating punished? How does the play-by-play description heighten tension?

8) How is the final race of Harry and Draco toward the Snitch symbolic of Harry's rush to vanquish Voldemort and his followers before they destroy him? How might his victory flight foreshadow future celebrations when Harry finally banishes Voldemort?

9) Why is it symbolic that Harry is "Thrust into the light"? How does this victory shift the plot toward resolution?

— Chapter 16: Professor Trelawney's Prediction —

Synopsis: During Harry's Divination examination, Professor Trelawney goes into a trance and predicts the return of Voldemort

Setting: Divination tower; Hagrid's hut

Themes: tests, appeals, restraint

Symbols: heat, examinations, tortoise, creatures, plants, axe, crystal ball, sunset, pumpkins, jug, rat, purple, red

Myths/legends: Demeter's sorrow for Persephone; Sibyl

Vocabulary Development:

averted: prevented

bemoaning: complaining

euphoria: joy

flourished: living very well

offhand: not planned

resounding: echoing

rummaging: looking through contents

quagmire: swampy

subdued: quiet

sultry: hot and humid

wafts: floats

1) Near the end of the school year, what tests are the students taking and how does this influence their moods and activities?

2) Why does Ron not insist that Hermione explain how she can take two exams at the same time?

3) Why does Ron speak so assertively to Cornelius Fudge? Why does Hermione criticize Ron for this action? Why does she think the appeal will not be fair?

4) What happens during Harry's Divination examination? Why

doesn't Trelawney believe Harry when he tells her about what she said in her trance?

5) Why doesn't Harry tell his friends about Trelawney's prediction?

6) Why does Hermione retrieve the Invisibility Cloak from the hunchbacked witch statue? Why is Ron surprised by her boldness?

7) What do the trio discover in Hagrid's hut?

8) Why do the students leave Hagrid's hut before the execution? What noises do they hear? What slows them down?

9) Why was Hermione surprised that the execution occurred?

— Chapter 17: Cat, Rat and Dog —

Synopsis: Crookshanks disables the Whomping Willow, and Harry and Hermione travel through the tunnel
Setting: Hogwarts grounds, secret passage, Shrieking Shack
Themes: friendship, confusion, contrasting points of view
Symbols: dusk, tree, eyes, squeals, trap, broken leg, wands
Myths/legends: Perseus slays Medusa

Vocabulary Development:
deftly: skillfully
fray: struggle
hurtled: to move forward with great force

1) How do Harry, Ron, and Hermione express their shock that the execution happened?

2) Why is the setting sun symbolic? How does this represent the passing of time?

3) How does the conflict between Crookshanks and Scabbers and the black dog and Harry intensify action? What happens to Harry during his first physical contact with the dog? Why does Ron intervene between the dog and Harry?

4) What prevents Harry and Hermione from pursuing the dog who is dragging Ron? Why doesn't Harry want to get help as Hermione suggests?

5) What stops the Whomping Willow's attack? Why do Harry and Hermione follow Crookshanks? What do they discover at the end of the tunnel? How does the setting enhance the plot?

6) How do they know to go upstairs in the Shrieking Shack? How does the room remind them of their dormitories and why is this important?

7) Who do they discover in the room? How are they disarmed?

8) What comment enrages Harry? Why does he feel compelled to react by using magic to hurt someone instead of using it for defense? Why is he so loud?

9) Why does Ron stand on his broken leg? Why does Hermione shush Harry?

10) How does Harry recover the wands? Why is Harry's voice shaky but his hand steady?

11) How does Crookshanks protect Black? Why doesn't Harry kill Black?

12) How does Lupin disarm Harry? How does Harry react when Lupin helps Black stand up and hug him?

13) Which of Hermione's three accusations about Lupin is correct? How logical is her reasoning? Why does Harry say Dumbledore was wrong to hire Lupin?

14) Why does Lupin give the wands back to the children? How does the stunning information he tells them about the map and Scabbers accelerate the plot's momentum?

— Chapter 18: Moony, Wormtail, Padfoot and Prongs —

Synopsis: Harry learns about his father's life at Hogwarts
Setting: Shrieking Shack
Themes: disbelief, sanctuary, self acceptance, rescue, redemption
Symbols: werewolf, moon, joke, knot, haunted house
Myths/legends: Proteus shapeshifts and predicts the future

Vocabulary Development:
convulsively: fitfully
derisive: critical
marvel: wonder
prod: push
wane: grow weaker

1) Why do the students not believe Lupin?

2) Why does Lupin stop Black from killing Peter Pettigrew? Why does he say the students deserve an explanation of why Black hates Pettigrew? Why is Harry especially entitled to the truth?

3) How does Black know that the Marauder's Map never lies?

4) In what ways does Hermione try to reason with Lupin? How does she know who all of the Animagi are?

5) What is Ron's explanation for the creaking door opening? Why is Lupin familiar with the Shrieking Shack and its legend? What does he reveal about the Whomping Willow? What does Harry learn about his father's school years at Hogwarts?

6) Who are Padfoot, Wormtail, Prongs, and Moony? What roles did they play at different times at Hogwarts? How responsible were they with their magic? Why did they break rules?

7) Why does Snape dislike Lupin and his friends? Why does

he hold a grudge years later? Why is Black not empathetic toward Snape?

8) How does Snape reveal himself?

— Chapter 19: The Servant of Lord Voldemort —

Synopsis: Harry decides to spare Peter Pettigrew's life
Setting: Shrieking Shack
Themes: mercy, dignity, respect, daring
Symbols: cords, kiss, silk, newspaper, toe, finger, secret, bully, manacles, pulse, wands
Myths/legends: Merope plots to kill her son Aepytus

Vocabulary Development:
deranged: crazed
fathom: understand
groveling: begging
grudge: deep-seeded feeling of resentment
imploringly: pleaded
jauntily: with spirit
mirthless: without humor
overrode: alternate decision made despite previous agreements
recoiled: drew back
revulsion: disgust
staggered: shocked

1) How does everybody in the shack react to Snape's appearance? How does he explain how he located them? Why does Snape

praise Harry for his carelessness with the Invisibility Cloak?

2) How does Lupin try to convince Snape to listen to him and why does he call Snape a fool?

3) How does Snape seize control of Lupin, Black, and the students?

4) How does Black try to bargain with Snape? How does Snape act irrationally?

5) What does Harry do to stop Snape from delivering the men to the Dementors? Why does Harry resort to the extreme of knocking Snape out?

6) What proof does Black show Harry that indicates Scabbers is really Peter Pettigrew? What does he claim really happened the day so many Muggles were killed? What other mysterious things about Scabbers are clarified?

7) Why does Harry still not believe Black's story?

8) Why does Black blame himself for the Potters' deaths?

9) What happens when Black and Lupin try to transform Scabbers?

10) How does Lupin restrain Black from attacking Pettigrew?

11) How does Pettigrew react to Blacks' use of Voldemort's

name? Why does Black say Pettigrew's life is in jeopardy from Voldemort's followers? What does Pettigrew claim is the truth?

12) How does Hermione's use of the title "mister" affect Black?

13) What strengthened Black in prison and how did he escape from Azkaban? What does he reveal about Dementors?

14) What convinces Harry that Black is telling the truth about Pettigrew betraying the Potters and hoping to deliver Harry to Voldemort someday? How do Ron and Hermione react to Pettigrew's pleas for mercy? How does Pettigrew appeal to Harry's humanity and sense of justice? How does he justify his service to Voldemort?

15) Why does Harry stop Lupin and Black from killing Pettigrew? Why is his decision crucial for resolution of the plot?

— Chapter 20: The Dementors' Kiss —

Synopsis: Harry repels the Dementors from seizing Black
Setting: secret tunnel, Hogwarts grounds, lake
Themes: hope, relief, escape, innocence, rescue
Symbols: godfather, werewolf, moon, lake, stag, fog, screams, sockets, mouth, scabs, rattle, brightness, unconsciousness
Myths/legends: Theseus saves Pirithoüs's life

Vocabulary Development:
ebbing: going back, lessened

lolling: lacking support, relaxed
putrid: spoiled

1) What does Black promise Harry in the tunnel? How does Harry respond to his offer of a home? How does this unconditional acceptance transform Black? How will this free both Harry and Black?

2) Why does Harry think it will be funny to tell the Dursleys that he plans to live with the convict they saw on the news? How does this flashback help move the plot forward?

3) Why doesn't Harry run when Black tells him to as Lupin starts transforming into a werewolf? How does the fight between Lupin and Black as Animagi affect Harry?

4) How does Pettigrew escape? Why does he hurt Ron and Crookshanks?

5) Why do Harry and Hermione run to the lake instead of getting help for Ron and Snape?

6) How does Harry conjure a Patronus to protect Black, Hermione, and himself from the Dementors? Why does he feel alone?

7) What does Harry see when the Dementor raises its hood? How does this confirm or disagree with previous information provided by characters? What does Harry hear and feel as the Dementor tries to seize his soul?

8) What does Harry think he sees that forces the Dementors to leave? What is symbolic about Harry fainting?

— Chapter 21: Hermione's Secret —

Synopsis: Harry and Hermione manipulate time to change history

Setting: Hogwarts infirmary, corridors, towers, and grounds, Hagrid's hut, Forbidden Forest, lake

Themes: timeliness, truth, false interpretations, innocence, justice, courage

Symbols: hourglass, closets, trees, shadows, flying, garden, tower, rope, window, moonlight, bush, dark, stretchers, cloud

Myths/legends: Bellerophon and Pegasus

Vocabulary Development:
battlements: top part of a castle
confounded: confused
gilded: gold covered
meander: wander
obscuring: hiding
reedy: raspy sound
stem: stop

1) Where does Harry wake up? What conversation does he overhear?

2) Why is Snape being praised? How does he explain the children's behavior to Cornelius Fudge? In what ways does he sug-

gest Harry should be treated? Does Fudge agree? How is Snape hypocritical when he says he does not practice favoritism?

3) What news makes Harry and Hermione anxious to see Dumbledore? Why doesn't Fudge believe their statements that Black is innocent and Pettigrew is guilty? How does Madam Pomfrey quieten Harry?

4) Why does Dumbledore say that Black's story is not credible? How is Dumbledore powerless to convince people of the truth? How does this awareness of Dumbledore's vulnerability affect Harry?

5) What does Dumbledore mean when he says they need "more time"? What does Hermione know that will help Harry save Black? What rule does Dumbledore emphasize is essential for their success? Why does he tell them where Black is being kept? What does he mean when he says Harry and Hermione could "save more than one innocent life tonight?"

6) What time is it when Dumbledore leaves the infirmary?

7) Where does the Time-Turner transport Harry and Hermione? How much time do they have to rescue Black?

8) How do Harry and Hermione repeat their previous actions of that night? In what ways is the story altered on their second trip to Hagrid's hut?

9) Why is changing time occasionally permitted if it is in violation of one of the most vital wizard laws? What does Hermione warn might happen if Harry encounters his earlier self in the hut?

10) How does Buckbeak's contrariness intensify the suspense?

11) How is Harry and Hermione watching their previous adventures crucial for resolving all of the subplots? What new information and insights do they acquire from their observations?

12) Why does Hermione discourage Harry from believing that he saw his father?

13) Where do Harry and Hermione hide from Lupin?

14) Why does Harry ignore Hermione's warnings about not being seen and risk going to the lake? What does he realize about his earlier vision and what is his reaction? What form does his Patronus take? Why was Harry's disobedience crucial for his survival? Why is Hermione impressed with him instead of being angered?

15) What types of magic do Harry and Hermione use to rescue Black? How does Black express his gratitude to them? What does Black's departure symbolize for himself and Harry?

– Chapter 22: Owl Post Again –

Synopsis: Harry victoriously returns to his Muggle home

Setting: Hogwarts corridors, infirmary, Great Hall, grounds, Hogwarts Express and King's Cross Station

Themes: euphoria, disappointment, hiding, unity

Symbols: chocolate, dragons, squid, eyes, family, friends, owl, sun, letter, permission slip, fugitive

Myths/legends: Hector's nobility

Vocabulary Development:

boisterous: loud

gloating: bragging

impenetrable: cannot enter

jangling: clinking sound

reproving: scolding

sanctuary: a safe place

slipstream: the still air behind a moving object

sweltering: very hot and humid

wryly: with a twisted expression

1) How do the close calls Harry and Hermione encounter during their final ten minutes of repeated time contribute to Black's escape?

2) How does Dumbledore react when he sees them rushing toward the infirmary? How is the time cycle completed?

3) What do they hear when Black's disappearance is discovered? Why does Snape immediately blame Harry? What

do Fudge and Dumbledore think of his accusations? Why does Dumbledore say that Snape is merely disappointed and not mentally unbalanced?

4) What creatures does Fudge suggest should guard Hogwarts instead of Dementors?

5) Why do the trio stay at Hogwarts instead of going to Hogsmeade with their classmates? Why don't they confide in Hagrid about what happened to Buckbeak?

6) Who tells the students that Lupin is a werewolf and why? Why does Lupin resign his position? Why is Lupin proud of Harry? What does he confirm about Harry's father? What does he give Harry?

7) Why is Dumbledore skeptical of predictions? How will Pettigrew be indebted to Harry according to Dumbledore? How will this annoy Voldemort? Why does Dumbledore think Harry is noble? Why does he suggest that Harry may be grateful in the future that he saved Pettigrew? What wisdom does Dumbledore share with Harry about love and self confidence?

8) Why is Harry saddened after the initial excitement of Black's escape? What improves his mood at school and on the train? How have all the major characters changed since the beginning of school? How is Vernon Dursley predictably the same? Why does Harry speak to him so boldly?

9) Does the final chapter resolve all the plot twists satisfactorily? How are unanswered questions such as the location of Black and Pettigrew characteristic of serial novels?

PROJECTS AND ACTIVITIES FOR BOOK III

1) Make a list of each of Harry's birthday gifts and explain their meaning. What would you give Harry? Hermione? Ron? Hagrid? Write a thank you letter from Harry to his friends.

2) Draw a map of your school, house, or a local mall, sketching in secret passages you would like to use.

3) Make an outline of the significant clues that are provided in the plot. How many of these clues did you notice when you first read the book?

4) Write a journal entry about any nightmares you've had. Did you react the same way Harry did? What would you advise him to do to help stop his nightmares?

5) Prepare a paper discussing what the words "hate" and "evil" mean to you and why they should not be used carelessly. Mention how you feel about the characters' use of those words.

6) Black convinces Harry that he is telling the truth. Write a persuasive speech about a topic that interests you or something about yourself that people misunderstand.

7) If you have a garden, plant a pumpkin like those Hagrid grows. Or buy a pumpkin when they are in season and decorate it the way you think a pumpkin at Hogwarts would appear.

8) Write an essay about an experience you had when something or someone was not like you thought it was at first. How did you react?

9) If you were an Animagus, what kind of animal would you be? Write a paragraph explaining why.

10) Write a report about stags, especially about their depiction in history and mythology.

11) What type of dog do you think the Grim was? Write a paragraph describing the breed you selected and include the characteristics of that breed. Support your opinion.

DISCUSSION FOR BOOK III

1) Why did Harry decide not to kill Black or Pettigrew? What do you think he should have done?

2) Why are appearances often deceptive? Are rumors usually not factual?

3) Discuss the irony of being indebted to someone you dislike, or have him or her indebted to you.

4) What inconsistencies did you detect in the story, such as how Black accessed his Gringotts's vault to pay for the Firebolt while he was a fugitive?

5) Describe aspects of Ron's and Hermione's friendship that might indicate they will later form a romantic relationship.

6) If Crookshanks is an Animagus, who might he possibly be?

7) What clues in the story suggested that Lupin is a werewolf?

8) How does the permission slip symbolize Harry being caught in limbo between childhood and adulthood? When do the children switch roles with adults?

9) Why does the Minister of Magic talk to Harry like an equal?

10) Discuss Harry's worst fear. Do you think he should fear something else?

11) Analyze the relationship between Lupin and Snape. How are the men similar and different? Why does Lupin tolerate Snape's derision?

12) How does the slashed painting and action by ghosts remind readers that there is another world operating within Hogwarts?

13) Discuss Lupin's role as a father figure.

14) How does Hermione change in this novel? What changes do you think will be permanent? How will she be the same when she returns to Hogwarts? Why is she so serious about her schoolwork?

15) Why can't Harry's friends understand his anxiety about his parents?

16) Discuss the ethical and moral issues of Dumbledore's decision to assist Harry and Hermione to free Black and Buckbeak.

17) What revelations about students help to develop their characters and suggest possible future plot developments?

18) What does the Dementor's Kiss parallel in popular culture and in literature?

19) Reread the section where Harry and Hermione return to Hagrid's shack. Write an essay about whether you think Dumbledore's statements reveal that he knew Harry and Hermione had changed time? If so, what do you think this suggests about Dumbledore? If not, what do you think his comments meant?

DEVELOPING WRITING AND CRITICAL SKILLS

1) Write an essay describing how effective the new settings introduced in this book were at developing the future plot.

2) Prepare a similar paper discussing new characters and their role in advancing the book's and series' plots.

3) Analyze the dog imagery in Book III. Compare the Grim with Fluffy in Book I.

4) Write a paper describing how the Quidditch defeat affected Harry and whether or not it was an effective literary twist.

5) Rowling continues to use petrified imagery in Book III. Prepare an essay comparing paralysis in all three books, noting to whom it happens, when, and why.

6) Discuss the role of voices in the series, especially the voices Harry hears.

7) Analyze how the Animagi paradoxically represent ambiguity and freedom, then compare this transformation to the maturing of a child into an adult.

8) Describe how the Dementors emphasize unseen emotional scars that Harry bears. Expand your discussion to the psychological stresses that affect various characters in this book.

9) Book III differs from the previous books in the series because Harry does not confront Voldemort directly. Write a critical

essay about whether this was a satisfactory conclusion or if you would have preferred for Voldemort to have been included.

10) Explain how the Dursleys are gradually losing power over Harry and how he is becoming more empowered to be self-sufficient.

11) Write about Neville's carelessness with the password and his resulting punishment. Compare this situation with previous infractions. What does this suggest about his character?

12) Discuss time as a metaphor in the novels. What do you think the manipulation of time represents?

HARRY POTTER TIMELINE

WITH SIGNIFICANT DATES IN SCOTTISH AND WORLD HISTORY FOR RESEARCH ASSIGNMENTS

"The best thing about the future is that it comes only one day at a time." —ABRAHAM LINCOLN

INTRODUCTION

This timeline is intended to highlight fictional events in Harry Potter's life as well as significant dates concerning his author, J.K. Rowling, and associated releases of publications and activities concerning the series. The historical references are meant to provide readers with a recognizable context to understand the books' settings, both geographical and historical, and as material to consult for the history chapter's activities (Chapter 12).

Readers can research the historical background of people and events included in the timeline to learn more about England and Scotland, and especially to discover who the people were, such as astronomers Galileo Galilei and Nicolaus Copernicus, and how they contributed to the evolution of western civilization. Entries also suggest ideas for further research and elaboration: the seventeenth-century siege of Londonderry might encourage readers to learn more about the ongoing political turmoil between Catholics and Protestants in Ireland and consider how that conflict could be compared to the ideas and situations presented by the Harry Potter novels.

Many more factual events occurred during the time outlined of which the residents of Hogsmeade and Hogwarts, as well as Muggles, might have been aware and possibly influenced by. An excellent resource is the extensive Scottish timeline at **http://scottishculture.about.com** site as well as both print and internet historical resources for prehistory as well as ancient and modern history events, such as when animals were domesticated, megaliths were built in Europe, and various civilizations developed agricultural, architectural, and technological advances. Almanacs and encyclopedias include historical time-lines, and Ellen Jackson's, *Turn of the Century,* (1900) explains how the lives of children changed in Great Britain and North America from the years 1000 to 2000 (unfortunately, the book entitled *Sites of Historical Sorcery* which Hermione referred to is not available to Muggles).

Because the Potter novels are set in Great Britain and enjoy a large North American readership, most timeline events are European or American related. Readers are encouraged to explore what was happening simultaneously in Asia, Africa, South America, and the Middle East. Also, students could study major occurrences such as the Great Depression and the Civil Rights Movement by applying the themes, motifs, and human reactions to strife shared by the Potter series.

TIMELINE

*denotes events related to the Harry Potter novels,
J.K. Rowling's life and career, and publication events

2700 B.C. Dedi, an Egyptian conjurer, performed magical illusions with animals

1792-1750 B.C. Time of Babylonian King Hammurabi's reign during which the Code of Hammurabi forbade witchcraft

*382 B.C. Ollivanders, who created Harry Potter's wand, began to make "Fine Wands" for wizards and witches

8-4 B.C. scholars estimate that this was the period when Jesus Christ was born

100s A.D. Roman General Gnaeus Julius Agricola commanded

the invasion of Britain, which
was called "Caledonia" after
the Romans secured control

122 Roman Emperor Hadrian
directed that a structure,
named Hadrian's Wall, be built from Solway
Firth to the Tyne River's mouth to separate Scotland
from England and hinder invasion by the Picts' movement.

367 The Roman emperor Valerian initiated the first recorded
witch hunt

409 Romans withdrew from Britain, and the native tribes called
the Picts, Saxons, and Angles dominated the region; missionaries began converting people to Christianity

circa 406-453 Attila the Hun seized territory from the Roman
and Byzantine Empires

800s-1100s Viking raiders usurped English territory and property

***circa 990** Hogwarts was established by Godric Gryffindor,
Salazar Slytherin, Helga Hufflepuff, and Rowena Ravenclaw

circa 1000 Beginning of the Middle Ages

1066 Norman Invasion of Britain

1095 Crusades began

April 9, 1139 England's King Stephen recognized David I as
king of an independent Scotland in the Second Treaty of
Durham

late 1200s Roger Bacon, a Franciscan monk and alchemist,
was accused of using black magic

1211 China invaded by Genghis Khan

1215 Magna Carta signed by King John under pressure from
English nobles to reduce royal power

1231 Pope Gregory IX's "Excommunicamus" started the medieval Inquisition

*1289 International Warlock Convention held

*1296 the year of a case Hermione found while preparing Buckbeak's defense in which a Manticore "savaged someone" and was not punished because people were too scared to approach it

August 28, 1296 England's Edward I held a parliament at Berwick and demanded that all Scottish landholders sign the "Ragman Roll" sparking the Wars of Independence

September 11, 1297 Scotland's William Wallace, known as Braveheart, defeated England's Edward I at the Battle of Stirling Bridge

June 12, 1298 Wallace won against English foes at the Battle of Black Ironside

July 22, 1298 Edward I defeated Wallace at the Battle of Falkirk

August 5-23, 1305 English captured Wallace after he was betrayed by perceived allies, and he was executed

March 27, 1306 Robert I ("The Bruce") was crowned king of Scotland at Scone

July 7, 1307 King Edward I died and was succeeded by Edward II

June 24, 1314 Robert the Bruce defeated Edward II at the Battle of Bannockburn

April 6, 1320 The Declaration of Arbroath stated "For we fight not for glory nor for riches nor for honour, but only and alone for freedom, which no good man surrenders but with his life"

1324 Lady Alice Kyteler's witchcraft trial was the recorded in England

September 21, 1327 Edward II died, and Edward III was crowned king

March 17, 1328 Robert I and Edward III signed the Treaty of Edinburgh, recognizing that Scotland was independent and concluding the 30-years-long Wars of Independence

June 7, 1329 Robert the Bruce died at Cardross Castle, and his son David II began to rule Scotland

1337-1453 Hundred Years' War between England and France that ended in the expulsion of France from the British Isles

1347 the Black Death, an epidemic plague spread by flea-infested rats, infected Europeans, killing one third of the population

1371 David II died, and his nephew Robert II became king

October 28, 1371 the Treaty of Vincennes established a Franco-Scottish alliance

April 25, 1382 the real-life Nicholas Flamel allegedly made gold from mercury

1390 King Robert II died, and his son Robert III began to rule

March 30, 1406 English troops captured King Robert III's son James I near Flamborough Head; five days later King Robert III died, and James I was named king in absentia; after 18 years of captivity, James I was freed on December 4, 1423, and was crowned on May 2, 1424

1414 Nicholas Flamel died at the age of 116

1431 Joan of Arc was burned at the stake

February 21, 1437 King James I was murdered, and his son James II was crowned one month later

November 29, 1440 King James II, ten years old, witnessed the murder of the 6th Earl of Douglas and his brother David during the "Black Dinner" at Edinburgh Castle

1450-1451 St Andrew's University and Glasgow University were founded

1452 artist and inventor Leonardo da Vinci was born

1453 Ottoman Turks captured Constantinople

1455 Johann Gutenberg's printing press revolutionized people's access to books and enhanced literacy

August 3, 1460 an exploding cannon killed King James II during the siege of Roxburgh Castle, and his young son, James III was crowned king

*****1473** World Cup Quidditch match in which all 700 fouls occurred

1478 the Spanish Inquisition began

June 1488 King James III was killed at the Battle of Sauchieburn, and son James IV was crowned king

1486 *Malleus Maleficarum* (*Hammer of Witches*) was published and was the catalyst for witch hunts and trials throughout Europe

1492 Christopher Columbus discovered North America

*****October 31, 1492** Sir Nicholas de Mimsy-Porpington (Nearly Headless Nick) died

1500s Dr Johann Faustus became well-known for his magical talents and fortune telling, inspiring legends and literary works about his life

Circa 1500 beginning of Renaissance; Ottoman Empire peaked in power

September 1513 James IV killed at the Battle of Flodden Field, and his son James V was named king

1517 Protestant Reformation began when Martin Luther displayed his Ninety-five Theses

February 29, 1528 the Protestant martyr, Patrick Hamilton, was burned at the stake at St. Andrews, Scotland

1541 Witchcraft became a felonious offense by English common law

1543 Nicolaus Copernicus's book *De Revolutionibus Orbium Coelestium (On the Revolutions of the Celestial Spheres)* was published in which he described his heliocentric theories (the sun, not the Earth, is the center of our solar system); in 1616 this book was censored

September 9, 1543 Mary Queen of Scots, daughter of James V, was crowned at Stirling Castle after her father's death

July 3, 1544 Clan Fraser fought Clans Ranald, Cameron and Donald at the Battle of the Shirts, and 988 of 1,000 fighters died

1550-1650 Religious Wars engulfed Europe

1552 calendar changed from Julian system to Gregorian method

May 3, 1557 the Reformation was started in Scotland by John Knox

July 10, 1559 Mary Queen of Scots' husband, Francis, crowned King of France when his father Henri died

1566 Agnes Waterhouse, the first English woman executed as a witch, was hung at Chelmsford

June 19, 1566 James VI, future king of Scotland and England, was born to Mary Queen of Scots and her second husband Lord Darnley

June-July 1567 Mary Queen of Scots imprisoned, and one-year-old James VI was crowned king

July 10, 1576 Bassandyne printed the first Bible (New Testament) in Scotland

1584 *The Discoverie of Witchcraft* written by Reginald Scot was published

February 8, 1587 Mary Queen of Scots was executed at Fotheringay Castle

1588 the Spanish Armada was defeated in the English Channel

September 15, 1595 Edinburgh High School pupils rioted because they were denied a holiday

1600s Scientific Revolution

January 1, 1600 the first time the New Year in Scotland was observed on this date—previously celebrated on March 25

March 24, 1603 after Queen Elizabeth I died, the crowns of England and Scotland were combined with the coronation of King James VI (Mary's son) who was also referred to as James I

1603 The MacGregors massacred the Colquhouns at the Battle of Glenfruin, resulting in the name MacGregor being banned in many places in Scotland

1603 *Daemonologie in Forme of a Dialogue* published by King James VI/I in response to Scot's book *The Discoverie of Witchcraft,* which he demanded be burned

November 4, 1605 beneath the Houses of Parliament, Guy Fawkes was arrested with 20 barrels of gunpowder that he planned to use to spark an explosion to kill the king and parliament members; Parliament stated that the public should celebrate the fifth day of November annually to express thankfulness that disaster was averted

*1612 the Hogsmeade inn served as headquarters of a goblin rebellion

1618-1648 Thirty Years' War fought chiefly on German soil between Protestants and Catholics

1633 Galileo Galilei refused to denounce his Copernican beliefs that the Earth revolved around the sun and was placed under house arrest; copies of his book, *Dialogue on the Two Chief World Systems,* published the year before, were burned

*1637 Werewolf Code of Conduct was issued

1642-1648 English Civil War—Oliver Cromwell, known as Ironsides, capably led Parliamentary forces, winning victories at Marston Moor against Royalist troops; he defeated the Scots at Preston.

1648 Margaret Jones was the first person found guilty and executed as a witch in the Massachusetts Bay Colony

August 1648 Scottish Covenanters, who believed Presbyterianism should be the sole Scottish religion, allied first with Parliamentary forces then with Royalist troops in exchange for religious promises to remove the Anglican church from Scotland

January 30, 1649 Great Britain's King Charles I, son of James VI of Scotland (and also called James I of Great Britain), was executed by order of Cromwell

1649-1651 Cromwell established the British Commonwealth and sought to subdue Ireland and Scotland, defeating the Scots at Dunbar and Worcester and permitting massacres at Drogheda and Wexford

June 17, 1652 almost a third of Glasgow was destroyed by fire

December 16, 1653 Cromwell was named Lord Protector of England, Scotland and Ireland

September 3, 1658 Cromwell died

*January 12, 1659 Reports were made of a "frisky" camel cavorting through Edinburgh—was it possibly connected to Hogwarts?

May 29, 1660 Royal Oak Day was declared when King Charles II returned to England

June 19, 1660 the Restoration of Charles II as king; he permitted the Anglican church to resume activity; Covenanters were persecuted, and they sought to overthrow the monarchy

September 2, 1666 Great London Fire began

1682 Peter the Great became czar of Russia and modernized the Russian Empire

February 6, 1685 King Charles II died, and James II was crowned king two months later

1687 Sir Isaac Newton published *Philosophiae Naturalis Principia Mathematica,* which discussed his three laws of motion

May 29, 1687 James II established the Order of the Thistle

June 10, 1688 James Francis Stuart was born, and the Jacobites (opponents of William and Mary—see next entry) later called this "White Rose Day" for the "Old Pretender" (see 1745-1746)

November 1688-January 1689 William of Orange and his wife Mary arrived in southwest England, and James II was deposed, releasing the Great Seal in the Thames River; William and Mary were acknowledged as rulers of the United Kingdom in what is called the Glorious Revolution; Presbyterianism became Scotland's state religion again

1688-1689 siege of Londonderry, Ireland

1692 Salem, Massachusetts, witchcraft trials

November 1, 1695 the Scottish Parliament created the Bank of Scotland

1700s the Enlightenment

March and May 1707 the final meeting of the Scottish Parliament at Edinburgh was held (until resumed in 1999), and the Act of Union of English and Scottish parliaments was issued on May 1, 1707

*1709 Warlocks' Convention outlawed dragon breeding

1718 the "leeries," or lamplighters, began illuminating Scotland by tending oil lamps in public areas

*1722 a case occurred in which a Hippogriff was convicted and executed

May 25, 1726 the first circulating library was established at Edinburgh

1735 The British Witchcraft Act declared that people could no longer be prosecuted for witchcraft unless they pretended to practice magic

1737 Charles Perrault's *Histories or Tales of Olden Times* was published in London

1745-1746 Jacobite uprising by Charles Edward Stuart, known as Bonnie Prince Charlie, who occupied Edinburgh but was defeated at the Battle of Culloden

August 1, 1747 the Proscription Act banned Scots from wearing tartans and carrying weapons because of the 1745 uprising

November 1, 1753 Scots felt tremors from a Lisbon earthquake

June 20, 1756 146 people were imprisoned in the Black Hole of Calcutta, a 14 foot by 18 foot dungeon in the British East India Company's Fort William when it was captured by Indian attackers after a four-day battle

1769 Baron Kempelen created a magical chess set

1769 Industrial Revolution began when James Watt invented and patented a steam engine

1775-1783 American Revolution

July 1, 1782 Proscription Act repealed

1789-1799 French Revolution

1791 the first issue of *The Conjuror's Magazine* was published

*1796 Edward Jenner developed a smallpox vaccine; he had a
home in Yate near where Joanne Rowling lived as a child

1800-1815 Napoleonic Wars

1804 Napoleon Bonaparte crowned emperor

1811 London became the first city in the world with a population of one million people

1812 the Grimm Brothers' fairy tales were published in Germany

1815 Napoleon defeated at Waterloo

1823 Jacob and Wilhelm Grimm's folktales were first published
in English with the title *German Popular Stories* as translated
by Edgar Taylor

September 20, 1835 Magician Richard Potter died

1835 Halley's Comet appeared

June 28, 1838 Victoria was crowned Queen of Great Britain;
her reign until her death in 1901 was a period of aggressive
British imperialism in which people commented that the sun
never set on the British Empire

1839 inventors developed technology for successful photography

February 21, 1842 a railway between Glasgow and Edinburgh
was established

1848 revolutions swept Europe

January 29, 1848 Scotland began using Greenwich Mean Time

1851 the Great Exhibition was held at London

1853 George Cruikshank's book *Cinderella and the Glass Slipper*
was published in London; his periodical *The Fairy Library*

was issued from 1853 to 1864

1861-1865 American Civil War

September 13, 1862 Union troops found Confederate General Robert E Lee's "lost order" which alerted them to the location of enemy forces

1863 John Nevil Maskelyne built a wooden cabinet with mirrors for magical performances

April 14, 1865 United States President Abraham Lincoln assassinated

1865 Lewis Carroll's *Alice's Adventures in Wonderland* and *Through the Looking Glass* were published

July 9, 1867 Scotland's first senior soccer association, the Queen's Park Football Club, was organized

July 13, 1868 Scottish Reform Act permitted all male heads of household to vote

1871 Germany unified

March 27, 1871 Scotland was the champion of the first Scotland/England rugby match played

November 30, 1872 a tie game of 0-0 occurred when the first international football (soccer) match was played by Scotland versus England

March 1873 the Scottish Football Union and the Scottish Football Association were established

1874 magician Harry Houdini was born

*1875 Decree for the Reasonable Restriction of Under-Age Sorcery was issued

1890s Andrew Lang's fairy books were published in London

1900 L. Frank Baum's *The Wizard of Oz* was published

April 5, 1902 25 people were killed and 500 injured during an

English/Scottish football game when portions of Ibrox Stadium collapsed

December 17, 1903 Wilbur and Orville Wright flew the first airplane

April 17, 1909 Fans rioted during the Scottish Cup Final at Hampden Park

1910 Halley's Comet appeared

1914-1918 World War I; the Ottoman Empire disintegrated

May 22, 1915 three trains crashed at Quintinshill, killing 227 people

1917 the March and October Revolutions overthrew the Russian czar and established the Union of Soviet Socialist Republics (USSR)

February 24, 1923 the "Flying Scotsman," a steam train, began traveling between London (the King's Cross station) to Edinburgh

*1926 probably the year that Tom Marvolo Riddle was born

*1929 probably the year that Hagrid was born; also the year that the American stock market crashed, starting the Great Depression

1937 J.R.R. Tolkien's *The Hobbit* was published

November 1938 Synagogues throughout Germany were burned, and this act of violence is known as Kristallnacht

May-June 1940 350,000 Allied troops valiantly held Dunkirk, France, against German attack before ultimately evacuating

1939-1945 World War II

*1942-1943 Tom Riddle's sixth year at Hogwarts; the Chamber of Secrets was opened by Slytherin's heir; Moaning Myrtle was killed

*June 13, 1943 The date in Tom Riddle's diary which became a window that Harry Potter used to time travel to the year 1943, when he sees Hagrid and Riddle as teenaged boys; accused of opening the Chamber, Hagrid, a third year student, was expelled, and his wand was snapped in two. In 1943 Albus Dumbledore was a transfiguration professor.

June 6, 1944 The D-Day Invasion occurred during which Allied troops landed on the beaches at Normandy, France

*1945 Albus Dumbledore defeated Grindelwald, a dark wizard

August 1945 atomic bombs were detonated over Japan; the Cold War began

1950 C.S. Lewis's *The Lion, the Witch, and the Wardrobe* was published

December 25, 1950 the Stone of Destiny was taken out of Westminster Abbey

1950-1953 Korean War

1950-1954 United States Senator Joseph McCarthy's communist "witch hunt" occurred

*1950s period during which James and Lily Potter were probably born

December 1952 a heavy, deadly fog covered London

1957 the Sputnik satellite orbited Earth

1959-1975 Vietnam War era

November 22, 1963 United States President John F. Kennedy, Jr., was assassinated

*July 31, 1965 Joanne Kathleen Rowling was born

May 25, 1967 the Celtic Football Club won the European Cup

January 15, 1968 Western Scotland struck by 100 mile per hour winds from a hurricane which caused destruction in Glasgow, killing 20 people, damaging 250,000 homes, and causing 1,700 people to become homeless

April 4, 1968 Martin Luther King, Jr. assassinated

July 20, 1969 Neil Armstrong was the first human to walk on the moon

*1970s period during which James and Lily Potter probably attended Hogwarts and were married with Sirius Black serving as best man. Other students during this time included Remus Lupin, Severus Snape, Peter Pettigrew, and Davey Gudgeon. James and Lily were Head Boy and Head Girl. The Whomping Willow was planted to conceal the secret passage.

*circa 1971 Voldemort begins seeking followers

February 15, 1971 new decimal currency standards were issued in Britain, replacing the previous system of 12 pennies per shilling and 20 shillings per pound

September 1, 1971 the last gas street lamps were extinguished

*April 1978 the Weasley twins were born

*1980 Rowling's mother develops multiple sclerosis

May 18, 1980 Mount St. Helens volcano in America's Washington State violently exploded

Summer 1980 the United States boycotted the Olympics held at Moscow to protest the Soviet Union's invasion of Afghanistan

*July 31, 1980 Harry Potter was born to James and Lily Potter; Sirius Black was named Harry's godfather

*September, 1980 (perhaps on the 10th) Hermione was born

*October 31, 1981 James and Lily Potter were murdered at their home in Godric's Hollow, and Harry vanquished Lord Voldemort; strange events were reported in the Muggle news; Hagrid delivered Harry to the Dursleys's house where Dumbledore and McGonagall monitored Harry's transfer from the wizard to the Muggle world

*1981-1991 Harry dreamed about flying motorcycles and green flashes of lights; strange things happened when he was scared or angry, especially when Dudley and his friends bullied Harry; Harry's hair grew fast, and clothes that he detested mysteriously shrunk; the Dursley home contained no photographs of Harry's parents

December 21, 1988 the explosion of a Pan Am 747 above Lockerbie, Dumfries, Scotland, killed 243 passengers and 16 crew members aboard the airplane and 11 Lockerbie residents on the ground

Fall 1989 the Berlin Wall was torn down, and the Soviet Union began to collapse

*1990 J.K. Rowling's mother Anne died

*Summer 1990 Rowling had an epiphany about Harry Potter while riding on a London-bound train and she began outlining and writing details for future books

January-February 1991 Gulf War

*1991 J.K. Rowling moved to Oporto, Portugal, and met her future husband

*1991-1992 years in which *Harry Potter and the Philosopher's/ Sorcerer's Stone* is set; Harry was eleven years old in this book

*Late Spring/Early Summer 1991 Harry went to the zoo with the Dursleys, unintentionally freed the Brazilian boa constrictor, and was confined to his cupboard

*July 1991 Harry received his first letter; more mysterious letters were delivered after Vernon Dursley confiscated the envelopes; the Dursleys took Harry away and temporarily abandoned their home to avoid the letters

*July 31, 1991 on his eleventh birthday, Harry met Hagrid (who magically gave Dudley a pig tail to express his anger at the Dursleys); Harry learned that the Dursleys had lied to him about his parents being in a car accident and that he is a famous wizard; he visited Diagon Alley, was introduced to Professor Quirrell, and had an encounter with Draco Malfoy; the Gringotts bank was robbed

*September 1, 1991 Harry met the Weasleys and Hermione Granger, boarded the Hogwarts Express, ate wizard candy and collected wizard cards with Dumbledore's and Nicolas Flamel's names on them, saw Hogwarts for the first time, was sorted into Gryffindor House, and first was aware of seeing ghosts and professors, including Dumbledore and Snape (whom he probably had seen as a child but could not recall those memories); Hogwarts students were warned to stay away from the third floor corridor on the right side; the Dursleys took Dudley to London to have his pig tail surgically excised prior to attending Smeltings

*Fall 1991 Harry learned to fly on a broomstick and was elected Seeker of his Quidditch team; he saw the giant dog in the forbidden corridor when he wandered around Hogwarts at night because Draco Malfoy challenged him to a duel; Harry realized the stolen Stone was hidden at Hogwarts; he received a Nimbus Two Thousand broom and practiced with his house Quidditch team

*October 31, 1991 Harry's first Halloween at Hogwarts; Harry and Ron knock out a mountain troll

*November 1991 Harry played in his first Quidditch match, and his broom moved erratically because of an enemy's jinx; Harry caught the Snitch in his mouth

*December 25, 1991 Harry's first Christmas at Hogwarts; his gifts included the Invisibility Cloak which he used to explore the castle that night and discover the Mirror of Erised in which he saw his parents

1991 the Soviet Union ceased to exist and that geographical region became known as Russia again

1992 Men and women suspected of being witches were burned to death in Kenya

*Spring 1992 Harry caught the Snitch in a Quidditch match against Slytherin House refereed by Snape; Harry, Ron, and Hermione searched for information about Nicolas Flamel; Harry helped send Norbert away from Hogwarts and met centaurs when he was punished with detention in the Forbidden Forest

*June 1992 Harry, Ron, and Hermione took exams; they solved puzzles to search for the Stone; Harry confronted and exposed Quirrell as the culprit; the Stone was destroyed and the Flamels prepared to die; Gryffindor won the House Cup

*1992-1993 years in which *Harry Potter and the Chamber of Secrets* is set; Harry was twelve-years-old during this book

*July 31, 1992 Harry's twelfth birthday; he met Dobby; the Dursleys hosted the Masons for dinner;

Harry was punished for the ruined evening by being confined to his room for three days and told that he could not return to Hogwarts

*August 1992 The Weasley brothers rescued Harry; he lived at the Burrow and went to Diagon Alley (after being misdirected to Knockturn Alley and overhearing a sinister conversation between the Malfoys) with the Weasleys where he met Gilderoy Lockhart, and Arthur Weasley; Lucius Malfoy fought while Ginny Weasley selected her schoolbooks

*September 1, 1992 Harry's second term at Hogwarts began after he and Ron crashed the Weasleys' flying car into the Whomping Willow because Dobby prevented them from accessing the barrier at King's Cross station

*September-October 1992 Ron received a Howler; students began classes, learning how to re-pot Mandrakes, prepare potions, and ignore Lockhart's egotistical boasts; Harry began Quidditch practice and endured the adoration of first year students; Draco Malfoy announced that he was the Slytherin's new Seeker and that his father had equipped team members with newly released Nimbus Two Thousand and One models; Malfoy called Hermione a Mudblood, and Ron reacted angrily, his spell backfiring and causing him to cough up slugs; Harry and Ron performed their detentions for using the flying car, and Harry heard a strange voice in Lockhart's office while Ron polished a plaque engraved with T.M. Riddle's name

*October 1992 J.K. Rowling married Jorge Arantes

*October 31, 1992 Harry's second Halloween at Hogwarts; he attended the Deathday Party recognizing the 500th anniversary of Nearly Headless Nick's semi-beheading and heard the strange voice for the second time; Mrs. Norris was petrified, and the Chamber was opened

*November 1992 Harry, Ron, and Hermione searched for clues about the Chamber; students at Hogwarts suspected that Harry was Slytherin's heir; a Bludger broke Harry's arm during a Quidditch match with Slytherin, but he caught the Snitch; Lockhart cast a spell which removed the arm bone, and Harry was taken for recuperation to the infirmary where Dobby visited him with new warnings; Colin Creevey was petrified; Harry heard and spoke Parseltongue during the Dueling Club meeting

*December 1992 Justin Finch-Fletchley and Nearly Headless Nick were petrified while Harry was nearby, increasing others' belief that he was guilty; Harry was taken to Dumbledore's office where he saw Fawkes and tried the Sorting Hat on again; Harry, Ron, and Hermione completed the Polyjuice Potion to transform into Slytherins in order to seek information from Draco Malfoy about the heir of Slytherin; Hermione became a cat instead and was hospitalized

*January 1993 Harry and Ron discovered T.M. Riddle's diary

*February 14, 1993 Ginny sent Harry a Valentine; he discovered how to read the diary that night and time traveled to when Riddle and Hagrid were Hogwarts students and was misled to believe that Hagrid opened the Chamber in the 1940s

*Spring 1993 Harry, Ron, and Hermione selected third year classes to plan for future careers; Riddle's diary was stolen from Harry's trunk; Harry prepared to begin a Quidditch match versus Hufflepuff House when Professor McGonagall

canceled the game because Hermione and Penelope Clearwater were found petrified; Hogwarts students were placed under strict rules to protect them; Harry and Ron used the Invisibility Cloak to visit Hagrid and overheard a conversation with Dumbledore, Lucius Malfoy, and Cornelius Fudge; Hagrid was taken to Azkaban prison

***Summer 1993** Harry, Ron, and Fang encountered Aragog, who told them that Hagrid was innocent, and they were saved by the Weasley's car; Harry and Ron realized that Moaning Myrtle had been murdered by Slytherin's heir in the 1940s; they read the paper clutched in Hermione's hand; Ginny Weasley was seized by Slytherin's heir

***June 13, 1993** Harry skirmished with Tom Riddle in the Chamber, rescued Ginny, cleared Hagrid's name, freed Dobby, and celebrated Gryffindor's second consecutive win of the House Cup; after an antidote was administered, Hermione recovered; exams were canceled; Gilderoy Lockhart left to regain his memory; and Hagrid gave Harry an album filled with photographs of his parents

***1993-1994** years in which *Harry Potter and the Prisoner of Azkaban* is set; Harry was thirteen-years-old during this novel

***July 31, 1993** Harry's thirteenth birthday; he received presents from Hagrid, Ron, and Hermione

***July 1993** Rowling's daughter Jessica was born; Harry watched Sirius Black on news reports that covered his escape; Harry left the Dursleys after a confrontation with Marge Dursley; he saw the black dog, traveled on the Knight Bus, boarded at the Leaky Cauldron, and admired the new Firebolt racing broom model

*August 31, 1993 Hermione bought Crookshanks, and Ron fretted about Scabbers' health; Harry overheard Arthur and Molly Weasley discuss how Sirius Black posed a threat to Harry

*September 1, 1993 Harry's third term at Hogwarts began; he was driven to King's Cross Station in a Ministry of Magic car, met Professor Lupin, and saw a Dementor on the Hogwarts Express

*September-October 1993 Professor Trelawney predicted Harry's fate and told him that the dog he had seen was a bad omen known as a Grim, that he would argue with Hermione, and that one student would leave her class by Easter; Professor McGonagall demonstrated how she could become a cat while discussing Animagi in Transfiguration class; the third-year students encountered the Hippogriffs in Hagrid's Care of Magical Creatures class, and Draco Malfoy was injured; Harry watched his classmates learn how to subdue the Boggart with humor; Crookshanks attacked Scabbers

October 16, 1993 Lavender Brown receives a letter telling her that her pet rabbit Binky was killed by a fox. This fulfills Professor Trelawney's prediction that something Lavender dreaded would happen on that date.

*October 31, 1993 Harry's third Halloween at Hogwarts; Ron and Hermione visited Hogsmeade, and Harry talked to Lupin; Snape brought Lupin a mysterious potion to drink; Sirius Black slashed the Fat Lady, and students spent the night in the Great Hall

*November 1993 Gryffindor played Quidditch against Hufflepuff instead of

Slytherin because Draco Malfoy still claimed to be injured; Harry fell off his broomstick after he saw the Grim again and because the Dementors attended the match; Gryffindor lost the game, the first since Harry started playing at Hogwarts; he was briefly hospitalized

*December 1993 Rowling and baby Jessica moved to Edinburgh; the Weasley twins gave Harry the Marauder's Map, and he secretly visited Hogsmeade where he overheard a conversation about Black betraying his parents; the notice for Buckbeak's hearing was delivered to Hagrid

*December 25, 1993 Harry received a Firebolt as a Christmas present from an anonymous gift giver

1994 100 people were accused of witchcraft and executed in South Africa

*1994 Although she had written part of her novel in Portugal, Rowling wrote most of Book I during this year, drafting much of the book at Nicolson's, a neighborhood cafe

*January 1994 Professor McGonagall confiscated Harry's new Firebolt to test it for jinxes; Harry began anti-Dementor lessons with Lupin; Harry confronted a Boggart and learned to conjure a Patronus; Scabbers disappeared; Ron and Hermione ceased speaking to each other

*Spring 1994 Malfoy, Crabbe, and Goyle disguised themselves as Dementors during the Gryffindor/Ravenclaw Quidditch match, and a confused Harry conjured a Patronus; he also caught the Snitch for a Gryffindor victory; the Gryffindors celebrated late that night; Ron woke up to see Sirius Black by his bed; Hagrid told Harry and Ron to be kinder to Hermione; Harry used the Invisibility Cloak to visit

Hogsmeade again with Ron, scared Draco, and was revealed;
Snape confiscated the Marauders' Map

*April 20, 1994 Buckbeak's hearing before the Committee for the
Disposal of Dangerous Creatures was held at London; Hagrid
wrote Hermione that Buckbeak had been condemned to die

*April-June 1994 Hermione hit Draco when he belittled Hagrid;
Hermione quit the Divination class as Professor Trelawney had
predicted; Harry saw Crookshanks with the black dog by the
forest one night; Gryffindor defeated Slytherin for the
Quidditch Cup (the first win by Gryffindor since Charlie
Weasley was Seeker), and Harry became a hero; students prepared for the examinations O.W.L.s and N.E.W.T.s

*June 6, 1994 date for Buckbeak's execution; Professor Trelawney
went into a trance during Harry's Divination test and warned
that the Dark Lord would reappear; Harry, Ron, and
Hermione visited Hagrid to comfort him and found Scabbers
in his hut; as the trio walked toward the castle, the black dog
attacked them and dragged Ron with Scabbers in his pocket
into the tunnel by the Whomping Willow; Crookshanks
helped Hermione and Harry enter the tunnel safely; they forgot to bring the dropped Invisibility Cloak; Harry encountered Sirius Black and Peter Pettigrew at the Shrieking Shack;
when Snape and Lupin arrived, Harry learned about his
father's and his friends' Animagi secrets when they were students and the truth about Sirius Black and the villain who
actually committed the crime for which Black was accused;
Ron was hospitalized with a broken leg; using the Time-
Turner, Harry repeated the previous hours' events, saw the stag
by the lake, which he believed was his father, and with

Hermione rescued Sirius Black and Buckbeak; Lupin returned the Invisibility Cloak and the Marauder's Map to Harry

*June 1994 Sirius Black gave Harry permission to visit Hogsmeade and sent an owl to replace Ron's rat

*Summer 1994 the Quidditch World Cup was held

*1994-1995 years in which Book IV is set; Harry was fourteen-years-old during this book

*July 31, 1994 Harry's fourteenth birthday

*September 1, 1994 Harry's fourth term at Hogwarts began

*1995 Rowling finished writing the first Harry Potter novel

June 3, 1995 Lightning killed spectators at a soccer match near Puerto Lempira, Honduras The lightning was blamed on witchcraft

*July 31, 1995 Harry Potter's fifteenth birthday

*September 1, 1995 Harry's fifth term at Hogwarts began

*1996 Rowling receives an offer from Bloomsbury Publishing to publish the first Harry Potter novel

*1996 Rowling received a grant from the Scottish Arts Council to complete her second Harry Potter novel

March 13, 1996 a deranged shooter killed a teacher and sixteen children at a Dunblane, Scotland school

*July 31, 1996 Harry's sixteenth birthday

*September 1, 1996 Harry's sixth term at Hogwarts began

November 27, 1996 deaths caused by E-coli were reported in Lanarkshire, Scotland

*July 1997 *Harry Potter and the Philosopher's Stone* was released in Great Britain by Bloomsbury Publishing

*1997 twelve children listen to Rowling read at the Edinburgh book festival; Scholastic Press bid highest at an auction, win-

ning North American publishing rights to the Harry Potter novels; *Harry Potter and the Philosopher's Stone* received the Smarties Book Prize, was shortlisted for the Carnegie Medal and Guardian Fiction Prize, and was the overall winner of the 1997 Children's Book of the Year; Hale-Bopp comet appeared

*July 31 1997 Harry's seventeenth birthday

*September 1, 1997 Harry's seventh term at Hogwarts began

*1998 800 tickets sell out within five hours for listeners to attend Rowling's readings at the Edinburgh book festival compared to twelve attendees the previous year

*June 1998 Harry graduated from Hogwarts and began his career

*July 1998 *Harry Potter and the Chamber of Secrets* was released in Great Britain and became the number one bestseller for both children's and adult books within one week

*July 31, 1998 Harry's eighteenth birthday

*September 1998 an edition of *Harry Potter and the Philosopher's Stone* designed for adult readers was released in Great Britain; Scholastic published *Harry Potter and the Sorcerer's Stone* in the United States

October 25, 1998 An entire soccer team was killed by lightning near Kinshasha in the Democratic Republic of Congo Fans believed that the tragedy was caused by sorcery

*1998 *Harry Potter and the Philosopher's Stone* won Britain's National Book Award

*1998 *Harry Potter and the Chamber of Secrets* won the Smarties Award (the first author to win twice consecutively) and was shortlisted for the Whitbread Book Award

*January 1999 *Harry Potter and the Chamber of Secrets* was released in paperback in Great Britain

May 12, 1999 the Scottish Parliament met after 282 years of being inactive

*****June 2, 1999** originally scheduled for release in September, *Harry Potter and the Chamber of Secrets* was published in the United States by Scholastic because of customer demand causing people to make internet purchases from British stores

*****July 8, 1999** At 3:45 p.m. *Harry Potter and the Prisoner of Azkaban* was released in Great Britain by Bloomsbury Publishing

*****September 8, 1999** *Harry Potter and the Prisoner of Azkaban* was released in the United States by Scholastic Press, which also released *Harry Potter and the Sorcerer's Stone* in paperback

*****September 26, 1999** *Harry Potter and the Sorcerer's Stone, Harry Potter and the Chamber of Secrets,* and *Harry Potter and the Prisoner of Azkaban* secured the top three spots of the *New York Times* fiction bestseller list

*****October 5, 1999** the Listening Library audiobook, *Harry Potter and the Sorcerer's Stone,* was released

January 1, 2000 the date many people consider the start of a new millennium

*****January 2000** *Harry Potter and the Prisoner of Azkaban* was involved in the controversial Whitbread Book Award decision and won the Children's Book Award category

*****February 2000** Rowling was named author of the year at the British Book Awards

*****July 8, 2000** English language editions of Book IV published in Great Britain and the United States

January 1, 2001 another date many people consider the start of a new millennium

*November/December 2001 Book #5 probably will be published; Warner Brothers scheduled to release the first Harry Potter movie to coincide with the holidays

*Fall 2002 Book #6 probably will be published

*Fall 2003 Book #7 probably will be published

SECTION IV

~

WHILE YOU'RE WAITING
FOR THE NEXT
HARRY POTTER NOVEL

CHAPTER 20

RELATED TITLES

". . . if there was anything I was going to scream
about, it would be a book." —J.K. ROWLING

"Even now, if I was in a room with one of the Narnia
books I would pick it up like a shot and re-read it."
—J.K. ROWLING

INTRODUCTION

The following chapter discusses books that share some characteristics of the Potter legacy and will provide readers who have enjoyed Harry Potter with hours full of enjoyment. The reading level of these novels varies and will require parental/teacher/librarian assistance in choosing which ones are appropriate for individual students.

Related Titles

Rowling's novels reflect characters, situations, and settings that resemble counterparts in literary classics such as the Bible, William Shakespeare's plays, Charles Dickens' novels, and the Grimm brothers' fairy tales, as well as traditional British children's school stories. The Potter novels also share archetypes and plots with the children's literature genres of science fiction and fantasy. Rowling's works are most frequently compared to novels written by Roald Dahl, C.S. Lewis, and J.R.R. Tolkien.

Dahl's *Matilda* (1988) portrays a neglected child genius who develops extraordinary powers, and his other books *The Witches* (1983) *Charlie and the Chocolate Factory* (1964) and *James and the Giant Peach* (1961) also are reminiscent of the Harry Potter novels. Lewis' seven-volume *The Chronicles of Narnia* series and Tolkien's *Lord of the Rings* trilogy focus on imaginary worlds with fantastical characters pursuing quests like Harry's in his wizard environment.

Lewis Carroll's *Alice's Adventures in Wonderland* and *Through the Looking Glass* (1865) and L. Frank Baum's *The Wizard of Oz* (1900) feature supernatural creatures, magical plants, and a magical setting somewhat like Hogwarts. Rowling incorporates chess themes in her stories as did Carroll. Alice and Harry are both pawns being manipulated by more powerful forces. Baum uses number and color imagery reminiscent of Hogwarts. His protagonist Dorothy undergoes a series of tests and puzzles to reach her objective like Harry, Ron, and Hermione face in each novel. Dorothy, like Harry, is an orphan living with her aunt and uncle.

James M. Barrie's *Peter Pan* (1928) and P.L. Travers' *Mary Poppins* (1934) also transport ordinary children to worlds where enchantment thrives. Wart, the future King Arthur and protagonist of T.H. White's *The Once and Future King* (1958), is similar to Harry, learning about his powers from the wise wizard Merlyn. Similarly, Ged studies with mages, masters of magic, at a sorcery school in Ursula K. LeGuin's *A Wizard of Earthsea* (1968), endures a malicious classmate similar to Draco Malfoy, and defeats an evil shadow that he realizes is himself.

Many of Stephen King's books investigate themes, suggest symbolism, create settings, and introduce dualistic heroes and villains like those portrayed in the Potter series. King's vivid plot and character developments, intense conflicts, dark and emotional tones, appealing literary style, and inclusion of the supernatural in seemingly normal situations might remind readers of Rowling's imaginary world. King often casts children as his main characters, and they act independent of adults, participating in mental and physical battles pitting good versus evil, much like Harry and his friends. In *The Girl Who Loved Tom Gordon* (1999), nine-year-old Trisha McFarland becomes lost and is stalked in the Maine woods, which are sinister and reminiscent of the Forbidden Forest which Harry, Ron Weasley, and

Hermione Granger explore, confronting their fears and finding self-knowledge much like Trisha. The protagonist of *Carrie* (1974) endures ostracism at school and has unusual powers like many of the Hogwarts students. *Christine* (1983) features an independently acting car like the Weasleys' flying car, although much more malevolent. The dog in *Cujo* (1981) is malicious like Fluffy. *Salem's Lot* (1975) and *The Shining* (1977) depict contained environments, much like Hogwarts is isolated from external authorities. *Silver Bullet* (1985), *Eyes of the Dragon* (1987) and the *Dark Tower* series (1982-) offer wizardry, magic, shapeshifting, and fairy tale imagery resembling Harry's world.

Thomas Hughes' *Tom Brown's Schooldays* (1857) describes nineteenth-century English boarding school experiences at a centuries-old institution that still exists and parallels Harry's life at Hogwarts. The students play vicious games of rugby, just as the Hogwarts students assertively compete at Quidditch. Ian Fleming's *Chitty Chitty Bang Bang: The Magical Car* (1964) narrates the adventures of a British family named Pott with a flying car, like the Weasleys', that helps rescue others, and much of the book is filled with puns and clever names like Rowling's. Mary Norton's *Bed-knob and Broomstick* (1957) tells about British children traveling with a witch to comprehend the wonder of the world and themselves.

Jane Yolen's *Wizard's Hall* (1991) parallels the Harry Potter stories the most in that an apprentice wizard, Henry Thornmallow, a farm boy who lives with his mother, is sent to a training hall where he learns the benefits of perseverance and to believe and trust in himself in order to vanquish an evil presence which is never named because that would empower the dangerous being to be magically transported to the school. Yolen includes strong female characters like Hermione as classmates, and the courses are similar to those Harry and his friends take. The protagonist, like Harry, uses his newly realized powers to save his school, friends, and the world. Yolen's *The Pit Dragon* trilogy and *The Tartan Magic* series share settings and situations with the Potter series, and her *The Mary Celeste: A History Mystery* (1999) inspires readers to research history and could be paired with study of Homer's *Odyssey*.

Diane Duane's wizard series, including *So You Want to Be a Wizard* (1983), *Deep Wizardry* (1985), *High Wizardry* (1990), and *A Wizard Abroad* (1993), features the adventures of eighth-grader Nita Callahan who discovers that she has magical abilities while escaping from bullies who resemble the Dursleys. Nita, like Harry, has been leading an ordinary life and learns that magic can also be problematic. Duane's characters also are careful to not name potentially powerful items and people, and many wizard motifs are reminiscent of Harry's tales.

Elizabeth Winthrop's *The Castle in the Attic* (1985) describes the adventures of an American boy who goes on a quest to save his toy soldier's kingdom from a wicked wizard who also must not be named because he turns people into lead. He is warned not to stray from the path through the Enchanted Forest and calls himself Muggins, a circus clown's name, when he auditions as a court fool.

Julie Edwards' *The Last of the Really Great Whangdoodles* (1974) shares many aspects of the Potter books. Edwards' story tells how the children with the surname Potter learn about rare magical creatures known as Whangdoodles from a wise professor. He teaches them how magical beings live in separate worlds where they have been forgotten by mortals. The professor urges the children to exercise their imagination to find and help a lonely Whangdoodle. The theme that an open mind is powerful supplements symbolism about outsiders, memory, and identity which resonate in the Potter stories.

Many children's books rely on the plot device of a child discovering they have previously unknown qualities that change their lives. Stanley Yelnats, in Louis Sachar's *Holes* (1998), is removed from his home to live at a juvenile detention center as punishment for a crime he is falsely accused of. Like Harry, Stanley is surrounded by diverse personalities, myth-based beliefs and traditions, and puzzles to solve, including a family secret, in order to understand who he truly is. Joan Carris' *Witch-Cat* (1984) tells how twelve-year-old Gwen Markham learns that she is descended from a famous Welsh witch and gains self-confidence through her discovery of magic. S.P. Somtow's *The Vampire's Beautiful Daughter* (1997) depicts the duality of the protagonist who must decide whether to be a mortal or vampire, much like Harry struggles with his Muggle and wizard identities.

The relationship between Hermione and Harry can be compared to the main characters of Robin McKinley's *Beauty* (1978) which also stresses the importance of names having precise meanings. Patrice Kindl's *Owl in Love* (1993) presents similar clever wordplay and owl and medieval imagery through the adventures of Owl Tycho, a teenage shapeshifter who is the daughter of witches. Harper Lee's *To Kill a Mockingbird* (1960) features a trio of characters that could be compared to the three major Harry Potter characters: Harry is Jem, Hermione is Jem's sister Scout, and Ron is the neighbor's cousin Dill. Jem, Scout, and Dill bravely confront injustice while befriending the mysterious Boo. In the process, Jem's arm is broken much like Harry suffers a fractured limb. The Potter characters also resemble the protagonists in Alexandria LaFaye's *The Year of the Sawdust Man* (1998) and *Edith Shay* (1998) who discover their inner strengths to withstand obstacles and learn about themselves in the process.

The *Dark Materials* trilogy written by Philip Pullman chronicles the life of a young British girl in a fantastical British setting. She has a daemon, or familiar, who attends to her somewhat like Hedwig comforts Harry. Authors writing books that are either predecessors or contemporaries of the Harry Potter stories and that also feature themes of good versus evil with magical characters and dark lords include Lloyd Alexander (the *Prydain* chronicles which portrays Taran versus the Horn King), Diana Wynne Jones (*Dark Lord of Derkholm Wizards' University*), Tamora Pierce (*Circle of Magic* series), Susan Cooper (the *Dark is Rising* series featuring Harry Potter's counterpart, eleven-year-old Will Stanton who battles evil), Patricia C. Wrede (*The Enchanted Forest* chronicles, in which wizards are more often enemies than guides to the protagonist, the princess Cimorene), T.A. Barron (*Lost Years of Merlin Saga*), Meredith Ann Pierce (*Darkangel Trilogy*), Edith Pattou (*Songs of Eirren*), and Edward Eager's magically-themed books.

In Brian Jacques' *Redwall* series, Martin the mouse hero also experiences the loss of his family to an evil enemy. Magic and fairy tale imagery can be found in Edith Nesbit's *The Enchanted Castle* (1907), Marian Cockrell's *Shadow Castle* (1945), and Jon Scieszka's *Time Warp* series about a trio of young boys being transported to different eras by a magic book. Alan Dean Foster's *Dinotopia* is set in dualistic territory like Hogwarts which is simultaneously nurturing and treacherous. Ellen Raskin's clever *The Westing Game* (1978) features puzzles like those in the Potter series. In the medieval mystery, Vivian Vande Velde's *Never Trust a Dead Man* (1999), the teenaged protagonist Selwyn Roweson is falsely accused of murder and is assisted by the witch Elsywth to prove his innocence. She transforms his victim into a bat and provides Selwyn magical disguises to search for the killer. Avi's *Midnight Magic* (1999) is set at a castle almost as convoluted as Hogwarts and home to intrigue, magic, puzzles, and a ghost. Mangus the Magician and his twelve-year-old servant Fabrizio solve a mystery in the year 1491.

Other children's books that are set in the medieval period and depict strong-willed characters like Harry, Ron, and Hermione and similar settings and tone as Hogwarts include Marguerite de Angeli, *The Door in the Wall* (1949), Karen Cushman's *Catherine, Called Birdy* (1994) and *The Midwife's Apprentice* (1996), Gail Carson Levine's *Ella Enchanted* (1997), Mercedes Lackey's *Firebird* (1996), Dodie Smith's *I Capture the Castle* (1948), Eloise McGraw's *The Moorchild* (1996), and Gregory Maguire's *The Dream Stealer* (1983). The fictional world of Fantastica in Michael Ende's *The Neverending Story* (1984) is reminiscent of Harry Potter's magical environment. The teachers at Hogwarts, especially Lupin, are similar to the main character in Felice Holman's more modern fictional setting *Professor Diggins' Dragons* (1966). Sarah Sargent's Weird *Henry Berg* (1980) and *Watermusic* (1986), and Jenny Seed's *The Strange Large Egg* (1996) tell about dragons hatching from eggs like Norbert and how music charms supernatural creatures like Fluffy.

History and time travel are frequent themes in children's literature. Margaret J. Anderson's *Searching for Shona* (1978) describes the experiences of children evacuated from London during World War II. Several of her other books are time travel stories set in ancient Britain: In *The Circle of Time* (1980), *The Journey of the Shadow Bairns* (1980), and *The Druid's Gift* (1989). Anderson's *The Ghost Inside the Monitor* (1990) is similar to Susan Cooper's *The Boggart* (1993) and the poltergeists at Hogwarts. Other time travel books that can be compared to the Harry Potter series include Nancy Bond, *String in the Harp* (1976); Philippa Pearce, *Tom's Midnight Garden* (1958) and *Way to Sattin Shore* (1983); Pamela Service, *The Reluctant God* (1988); Margaret Greaves, *Cat's Magic* (1980); Mary Downing Hahn, *Time for Andrew* (1994); and Sonia Levitin, *The Cure* (1999).

Witches are represented both in historical fiction and contemporary tales. The Salem witchcraft trials are featured in Anne Rinaldi's *A Break With Charity* (1992) and Kathryn Lasky's *Beyond the Burning Time* (1994). Colonial witches in New England are the topic of Elizabeth George Speare's *The Witch of Blackbird Pond* (1958). Modern witches are either alluded to or are characters in Lois Duncan *Gallow's Hill* (1997) and Eva Ibbotson's *Which Witch?* (1999) and *The Secret of Platform 13* (1998), which reminds readers of the special King's Cross station platform in the Harry Potter series.

Word play and school life are imaginatively showcased in Kate Klise's *Regarding the Fountain: A Tale, in Letters, of Liars and Leaks* (1998). Lois Lowry's *The Giver* (1993) describes a closed community that is isolated like Hogwarts, and her *Number the Stars* (1989) portrays the development of a child's personal courage to confront evil like Harry achieves in his transitional first year at Hogwarts. Katherine Paterson's *Bridge to Terabithia* (1977) revolves around a fantasy world based on children's magical creativity. S.E. Hinton's *The Outsiders* (1967) reveals social antagonisms among young adults much like the strife between groups at Hogwarts, especially the Slytherins and Gryffindors. Robert Cormier's *The Chocolate War* (1974) also offers insights about school culture and verbal and physical violence. Sharon Creech's *Bloomability* (1998) features a protagonist who attends a boarding school where her uncle is headmaster.

In many children's books, magic supplements fictional characters' internal strength by offering them reliance on an external facade of strength until they realize the extent of their abilities. Prolific authors whose books explore the role of magic in character development and probably will appeal to Harry Potter readers include Joan Aiken, David Almond, Lynne Reid Banks, John Bellairs, Marion Zimmer Bradley, Angela Brazil, Terry Brooks, Angela Carter, Bruce Coville, Alan Garner, Margaret Mahy, Anne McCaffrey, Daniel Pinkwater, and Terry Pratchett. Picture books with themes related to the Harry Potter series include Mark Shannon's *The Acrobat and the Angel* (1999),

Ruth Sanderson's retelling of *Twelve Dancing Princesses* (1990), Robert Munsch's *The Paper Bag Princess* (1993), Colin McNaughton's *Captain Abdul's Pirate School* (1994), and Donald Carrick's *Harald and the Giant Knight* (1982).

Many literary classics share themes, plots, motifs, and characterizations with the Harry Potter series. Jane Austen's *Jane Eyre* (1847) depicts an English orphan's struggle for autonomy. Edgar Allan Poe's *The Fall of the House of Usher* (1839) might remind readers of the chaotic condition of Hogwarts. H. G. Wells' *The Time Machine* (1895) and *The Invisible Man* (1897) suggest Harry's use of the Time-Turner and Invisibility Cloak. Jules Verne's *Journey to the Center of the Earth* (1864) can be compared to the subterranean exploration and activity at Hogwarts. Frances Hodgson Burnett's *The Secret Garden* (1911) describes a place where the characters feel safe and can restore their physical and emotional health like Harry does at Hogwarts. The puzzles in Agatha Christie's mysteries and Sir Arthur Conan Doyle's Sherlock Holmes stories offer twists much like Rowling's novels. George Orwell's *Animal Farm* (1945) and *1984* (1949) portray the absurdity of modern society that can be associated with Muggles. Shirley Jackson's terrifying, subtle psychological thriller, *The Haunting of Hill House* (1959), foreshadows the Shrieking Shack.

Many of the authors mentioned in the preceding paragraphs have written numerous books with themes about magic and sorcery, and readers should ask librarians and booksellers to help them find other titles that would interest them. In addition to novels, many popular series feature magic, wizardry, and witches, including the *Sabrina the Teenage Witch* series and

Salem's Tails; the *Magic Attic Club* series in which characters time travel using a mirror; the *Magic Tree House* series by Mary Pope Osborne; R.L. Stine's *Goosebumps*; K.A. Applegate's *Animorphs*; *The Unicorns of Balenor* series by Mary Stanton; Alvin Schwartz's *Scary Stories* series; *The Magic School Bus* series by Joanna Cole and Bruce Degen; *Dragon Slayers Academy* by K.H. McMullan; Jill Murphy's *The Worst Witch* series about magic at a boarding school; Tony Abbott's *The Secrets of Droon* series; *A Series Of Unfortunate Events* by Lemony Snicket (pseudonym of Daniel Handler); and *The Magic Elements Quartet* by Mallory Loehr. Magic and sorcery have also served as important themes in numerous movies, including *Star Wars* and *Raiders of the Lost Ark*.

EPILOGUE:
HARRY'S FUTURE

"He [Harry] has quite a full agenda coming up."
—J.K. ROWLING

*"There will be no Harry Potter's midlife crisis or
Harry Potter as an old wizard."*—J.K. ROWLING

WHAT'S IN STORE FOR HARRY

The first three Potter novels have provided a wealth of thought provoking wisdom, concepts, and information, enticing Potterites to speculate on possible developments in the evolving saga. Fans post possible story lines on internet sites and hope that Rowling will reveal details that readers can use to decipher well-guarded secrets regarding future books in the series.

During interviews, Rowling drops hints about Harry Potter's forthcoming adventures, but she refuses to divulge major twists and specifications about her vague references. Rowling stresses that Harry will be busy during his remaining years at Hogwarts, but she does not reveal what will occupy his time. Although she has outlined the remaining three books, she says that she may change storylines as she writes. Her comments that she will not write about Harry enduring a middle age crisis or maturing to be an elderly wizard suggest that Harry may die young like his parents, become a Muggle, or disappear into secluded obscurity after defeating Lord Voldemort decisively in Book VII. Rowling's propensity for happy endings in the first three Potter novels plus her protective feelings toward Harry suggest that the latter conclusion is probably the most plausible. It is also the scenario that fits most closely with the pattern of the archetypal hero, which Harry closely resembles.

In an interview, she stated that wizards have longer lifespans than Muggles, and this might also affect how she is perceiving Harry's post-Hogwarts' life. She acknowledges that after she completes the seven books in the Harry Potter epic that she will probably experience feelings of grief after devoting thirteen years of her life to telling Harry's saga. She even compared her future emotions as the bereavement felt when a close friend dies, but Rowling also concedes that she might consider writing another Harry Potter book years after she has finished the seven books that she initially planned. However, she insists that there is no wizard university to continue Harry's education. Of course, a potential Book VIII might be a prequel to Harry's adult life rather than another sequel in his Hogwarts life.

Rowling confirms that Lord Voldemort's powers are strengthening and that more characters will die to emphasize the dastardly nature of evil. She says that only after careful consideration did she decide to include so many deaths to accentuate the deepening conflict between good and evil forces and the resulting victimization of innocents. She wants to demonstrate the finality of death because so many fans ask her when Harry's parents will return, as if magic can make the impossible possible. Loss and grief will be themes in all of the remaining books as Harry deals with the demise of people he cherishes and reveres. As the books' dark tones intensify, there will probably be more anti-Potter attempts to ban the books.

Rowling has announced that Hermione will become less insufferable. Other story developments in future books include enhanced information about the Sorting Hat and introductions to other wizard schools and pupils. New creatures will enter Harry's life. The Dursleys may no longer enjoy prosperity, and Dudley may have to adjust and cope with less luxurious circumstances. Rowling will not confirm whether Harry stops living with the Dursleys. She does say that Scabbers will return, and, in a rare accomplishment, an older character will learn to perform magic without benefit of childhood training or the Hogwarts curriculum. Harry and Sirius Black will communicate somewhat sporadically because Black is still a fugitive.

Professor Trelawney's first valid prediction will be disclosed, and Sirius Black, Remus Lupin, Crookshanks, Aragog, the Marauders' Map, and the flying car will make encore appearances. The new Defense Against the Dark Arts teacher has a magical eye but he may not stay long so that Lupin, whom Rowling has said would be the one Hogwarts teacher she would like to instruct her daughter Jessica, may return. Ron's discomfort from being impoverished will be evident when Harry provides him needed items or money. Ron's female cousin will also make her debut. More information will be provided about the Malfoy family. Rumors suggested that Neville Longbottom is Peter Pettigrew's son but Book IV confirms he is not. During an online chat session, Rowling clarified that she will explain how a magical quill at Hogwarts knows when a magical child is born and records the name in a book which Professor McGonagall consults to deliver invitations by owl when those children are age eleven. And throughout all his adventures, Harry will grow up and not be suspended in some unnatural, perpetual adolescence.

By Book VII Harry will fulfill his destiny of avenging his parents' murder and become an adult wizard. Freed from most Ministry of Magic restrictions designed to protect underage wizards and people near them, Harry can autonomously perform magic wherever he chooses. The Dursleys, particularly Dudley, will no longer be protected by Hogwarts' rules prohibiting magic off campus, and Rowling warns that Dudley should expect some sort of magical retribution from Harry to avenge the years he endured Dudley's tormenting assaults. Revelations about Lily Potter's and Petunia Dursley's family will probably be part of future plots. Readers may also learn about friendships and vendettas between ancestors of current Hogwarts students.

Perhaps the Dursleys were somehow involved financially or socially with Voldemort and his followers, and might have even been involved somehow in the Potters' murder, and this is why they react with such terror at the mention of magic, and why they torment Harry out of guilt. Or maybe no such allegiances existed, and they are just non-empathetic, clueless, self-absorbed Muggles. Startling disclosures about Harry might entail news of a long-lost sibling, even a twin (male or female), or other familial relation who has served as his humanly Patronus since Book I. Rowling told a fan that Book VII explains why only some wizards and witches become ghosts, suggesting that happy people do not haunt the living, perhaps providing a clue to the emotional status of Harry's parents when they were alive. She also said that the Potters' careers were essential to a future plot and will explain why Harry inherited so much gold.

The final Potter novels will probably thrill most readers as what appeared to be slight occurrences and the introduction of seemingly inconsequential characters in earlier books prove to be crucial factors for plot development. Readers may feel compelled to chide themselves for not recognizing culprits and turning points as they raced through the text to find out what happened next. A master craftsman, Rowling has carefully constructed her series like a resilient centuries-old castle, building a solid foundation then deliberately placing each stone to balance other stones and buttress the entire structure.

Decades from now, tales of Harry Potter may be passed around old-fashioned campfires and state-of-the-art digital communication systems. Robots may read the books to children in their habitat units on space stations. "I'd be delighted if I thought in 50 years time someone would say, you know the Potter novels, who wrote them?" Rowling stated during a televised segment about her career. "I would want the books to be as widely read as possible," she asserted but humbly confided in a manner reminiscent of Harry Potter's response to his fame, "I don't have any particular desire personally to be as well known as possible at all. In fact, I have no desire for that at all." Rowling believes in the magical power of stories, and someday all of her works will be available for readers to devour voraciously from Book I to VII, and literary critics to interpret characters, themes, and symbolism with a comprehensive awareness of the complete Harry Potter cycle from beginning to end. Until that time, Potterites worldwide will squirm in anticipation of each treasured new Harry Potter release.

ACTIVITIES

1) Write a review of the seventh Harry Potter book, speculating what will happen to the main characters.

2) Prepare a eulogy for one of the main characters, telling about

his/her life, family, accomplishments, and legacy. Share your completed eulogies with others to compare ideas. This could be developed into a classroom readers' theater activity.

DISCUSSION

1) With the clues Rowling has provided in her books and interviews, what do you think will happen in each of the remaining books?

2) What do you think Harry's future will be like? Ron's? Hermione's? What do you think will happen to the Dursleys and Aunt Marge? The professors, Hagrid, and Hogsmeade residents? The Malfoys and other antagonists?

DEVELOPING CRITICAL SKILLS

1) How effective has Rowling's plotting been to provide supporting evidence for the ultimate conclusion of the series?

2) Do heroic sagas usually have happy endings? Cite examples to support your hypothesis.

SECTION V

BIBLIOGRAPHY
AND
APPENDICES

CHILDREN'S LITERATURE BIBLIOGRAPHY

These children's literature sources are recommended to supplement understanding of the Harry Potter series and to initiate research about other children's literature authors and works. Readers should consult bibliographies in these sources as well as those in books listed in each section's recommended reading for additional citations of articles and books about more specific topics within the field of children's literature.

JOURNALS

ALAN Review (Assembly on Literature for Adolescents of the National Council of Teachers of English)
Bookbird: World of Children's Books
The Bulletin of the Center for Children's Books
The Bulletin of Children's Literature
Canadian Children's Literature
Children's Literature
Children's Literature Association Quarterly
Children's Literature in Education: An International Quarterly Children's Folklore Review
The Horn Book Magazine
The Lion and the Unicorn
Once Upon a Time
Phaedrus: An International Annual of Children's Literature Research
Publisher's Weekly

The Reading Teacher
School Library Journal
Signal: Approaches to Children's Books

REFERENCE SOURCES

Most of these are multi-volumes, appearing several times each year, and sometimes are published with varying titles and editors.

Authors & Artists for Young Adults (Gale)
Beacham's Desktop Guide to Literature for Intermediate Students
Beacham's Guide to Literature for Young Adults (Gale)
Beacham's Encyclopedia of Popular Fiction (Gale)
Research Guide to Biography and Criticism: Literature (Beacham)
Cambridge Guide to Children's Books
Children's Book Review Index (Gale)
Children's Literature Abstracts (The International Federation of
   Library Associations)
Children's Literature Review (Gale)
Contemporary Authors (Gale)
Dictionary of Literary Biography (Gale)
Library Literature (H.W. Wilson Co.)
Masterplots (Salem Press)
Masterplots II, Juvenile and Young Adult Fiction Series and three-
   volume supplement (Salem Press)
Something About the Author (Gale)
Something About the Author, Autobiography Series (Gale)
St. James Guide to Children's Writers (Gale)
St. James Guide to Young Adult Writers (Gale)

MONOGRAPHS

Aries, Philippe. *Centuries of Childhood: A Social History of Family Life*. Translated by Robert Baldick. New York: Vintage Books, 1962. A scholarly history of children with an emphasis on France.

Attebery, Brian. *The Fantasy Tradition in American Literature from Irving to Le Guin*. Bloomington: Indiana University Press, 1980. Comprehensive analysis defining the term fantasy, examining specific books, and exploring their cultural roots.

Attebery, Brian. *Strategies of Fantasy*. Bloomington: Indiana University Press, 1992. Critiques fantasies more recent than those addressed in his 1980 book and presents new theoretical insights. Suggests ways for readers to read fantasy and pose questions for further exploration. Notes the importance of gender in fantasy literature.

Bel Geddes, Joan. *Childhood and Children: A Compendium of Customs, Superstitions, Theories, Profiles, and Facts*. Phoenix, AZ: Oryx Press, 1997. Interesting compilation of information about specific individuals as well as children as a group.

Bussing, Sabine. *Aliens in the Home: The Child in Horror Fiction*. New York: Greenwood Press, 1987. Study of young characters in horror literature and film and what these children symbolize.

Carpenter, Angelica Shirley, and Jean Shirley. L. *Frank Baum: Royal Historian of Oz*. Minneapolis, MN: Lerner Publications Company, 1992. An intriguing biographical account of Baum that includes information about efforts to ban the Oz books.

Carpenter, Humphrey, and Mari Prichard. *The Oxford Companion to Children's Literature.* New York and Oxford: Oxford University Press, 1984. Although dated, this is a useful reference to study children's literature.

Chase, Carole F. *Suncatcher: A Study of Madeleine L'Engle and Her Writing.* 2nd ed. Foreword by Madeleine L'Engle. Philadelphia, PA: Innisfree Press, Inc., 1998. Literary criticism of L'Engle's work, focusing on the religious elements incorporated in her literature.

Clark, Beverly Lyon, and Margaret R. Higonnet, eds. *Girls, Boys, Books, Toys: Gender in Children's Literature and Culture.* Baltimore, MD: Johns Hopkins University Press, 1999. A collection of articles about how gender is portrayed in children's books.

Demers, Patricia, and Gordon Moyles, eds. *From Instruction to Delight: An Anthology of Children's Literature to 1850.* Toronto: Oxford University Press, 1982. Provides historical information about early children's literature and the transition from didactic stories to entertaining works.

Harvey-Darton, F.J. *Children's Books in England: Five Centuries of Social Life.* Rev. ed. by Brian Alderson. Cambridge: Cambridge University Press, 1982. In-depth coverage of the history of British publishers, writers, and books since the Middle Ages.

Hearne, Betsy, and Roger Sutton, eds. *Evaluating Children's Books: A Critical Look: Aesthetic, Social, and Political Aspects of Analyzing and Using Children's Books.* Urbana-Champaign, IL: University of Illinois, Graduate School of Library and Information Science, 1993. Explains what readers should be aware of to read a book critically, understand its stylistics, and apply it to lessons.

Hettinga, Donald R. *Presenting Madeleine L'Engle.* New York: Twayne Publishers, 1993. A thorough biographical and critical examination of L'Engle's literary work.

Hobbs, Sandy, Jim McKechnie, and Michael Lavalette. *Child Labor: A World History Companion.* Santa Barbara, CA: ABC-CLIO, 1999. Comments about the role of children in industry and other forms of employment in various historical eras and addresses literary child characters who work.

Hunt, Peter, ed. *Children's Literature: The Development of Criticism.* London and New York: Routledge, 1990. Valuable source outlining the primary concepts of literary criticism of children's books.

Hunt, Peter, ed. *Children's Literature: An Illustrated History.* New York and Oxford: Oxford University Press, 1995. A beautifully illustrated volume that discusses the development of children's literature.

Hunt, Peter. *An Introduction to Children's Literature.* New York and Oxford: Oxford University Press, 1994. Basic resource for readers beginning to study children's literature.

Jacobsen, Marcia. *Being a Boy Again: Autobiography and the American Boy Book.* Tuscaloosa and London: The University of Alabama Press, 1994. Although this book focuses on American boys, it also discusses the role of British boys in children's literature.

Lurie, Alison. *Don't Tell the Grown-Ups: The Subversive Power of Children's Literature.* Boston: Little, Brown and Company, 1990. Explains that children's literature challenges adult and societal values, offering children fictional examples of characters who are imaginative and enjoy less rigid lifestyles than many adults.

McGillis, Roderick. *The Nimble Reader: Literary Theory and Children's Literature*. New York: Twayne Publishers and London: Prentice Hall International, 1996. Interesting insights about readers' response to children's literature and other ways to interpret young adult books.

Nodelman, Perry, ed. *Touchstones: Reflections on the Best in Children's Literature*. 3 vols. West Lafayette, IN: Children's Literature Association, 1985-1989. Volumes of outstanding children's literature criticism about selected books.

Nodelman, Perry. *The Pleasures of Children's Literature*. 2nd ed. White Plains, NY: Longman, 1996. More recent literary criticism from the author who concentrates on recommended books.

Pinchbeck, Ivy and Margaret Hewitt. *Children in English Society*. 2 vols. London: Routledge and Kegan Paul, 1969-1973. Historical account of British children.

Pipher, Mary. *Reviving Ophelia: Saving the Selves of Adolescent Girls*. (New York: Ballantine, 1995). Analyzes the psychological development of children, specifically the self-esteem of teenage girls.

Pipher, Mary. *The Shelter of Each Other: Rebuilding our Families*. New York: G.P. Putnam's Sons, 1996. Examines the deterioration of families and social values in the United States, recommending solutions for social problems and psychological healing.

Pollack, William S. *Real Boys: Rescuing Our*

Sons from the Myths of Boyhood. New York: Henry Holt & Company, 1999. Discusses boys' perceptions of masculinity and social expectations for males and how these attitudes influence their behavior.

Rogers, Pat, ed. *The Oxford Illustrated History of English Literature.* Oxford: Oxford University Press, 1987. A comprehensive presentation and context of books with literary merit published in England.

Rowe Townsend, John. *Written for Children: An Outline of English Language Children's Literature.* London: Lippincott, 1990. Studies British and American writing specifically for children.

Schakel, Peter J., ed. *The Longing for a Form: Essays on the Fiction of C.S. Lewis.* Kent, OH: Kent State University Press, 1977. Anthology of essays written by Lewis scholars, presenting theories and criticism regarding different aspects and symbolism of the Narnia series.

Schakel, Peter J. *Reading with the Heart: The Way into Narnia* Grand Rapids, MI: William B. Eerdmans Publishing Co., 1979. Investigation of how Lewis' spirituality influenced his literary creativeness.

Schakel, Peter J., and Charles A. Huttar, eds. *Word and Story in C.S. Lewis* Columbia: University of Missouri Press, 1991. Collection of analytical essays exploring motifs, characterizations, themes, and other literary stylistics in Lewis' books.

Shannon, George. *Folk Literature and Children : An Annotated Bibliography of Secondary Materials.* Westport, CT: Greenwood Publishing Group, 1982. Useful guide to locate sources to supplement the study of folklore in children's literature.

Streatfeild, Noel. *Magic and the Magician: E. Nesbit and Her*

Children's Books. London: Abelard Schuman, 1958. Entertaining biography of Nesbit's work and discussion of British reaction to children's books.

Sullivan, C.W., III, ed. *The Dark Fantastic: Selected Essays from the Ninth International Conference on the Fantastic in the Arts*. Westport, CT: Greenwood Press, 1997. Anthology of selected papers presented at the 1988 conference, and topics include literature, film, and illustration.

Sullivan, C.W., III, ed. *Science Fiction for Young Readers*. Westport CT: Greenwood Press, 1993. Collection of scholars' views about specific topics related to science fiction works written for children.

Sullivan, C.W., III, ed. *Young Adult Science Fiction*. Westport, CT: Greenwood Press, 1999. This anthology includes an extensive bibliography and recommends sources for further study in the field.

Sutherland, Zena. *Children & Books*. 9th ed. New York: Longman, 1997. A classic reference book for researchers of children's literature.

Sutherland, Zena. *History in Children's Books: An Annotated Bibliography for Schools and Libraries*. Brooklawn, NJ: McKinley Publishing Co., 1967. Despite being dated, this resource is valuable for its thorough coverage of world history as presented in children's books.

Sutherland, Zena, Betsy Hearne, and Roger Sutton, eds. *The Best in Children's Books: The University of Chicago Guide to Children's Literature, 1985-1990*. Chicago: University of Chicago Press, 1991. An annotated bibliography that provides crucial information about a five-year period of children's literature.

Takanishi, Ruby, and David A. Hamburg, eds. *Preparing Adolescents for the Twenty-first Century: Challenges Facing Europe and the United States.* New York: Cambridge University Press, 1997. Discusses such issues as the development of life skills and the transition from school to work which helps readers understand similar experiences of fictional characters such as Harry Potter.

Zipes, Jack, ed. *Spells of Enchantment: The Wondrous Fairy Tales of Western Culture.* New York: Viking, 1991. A classic text that includes a variety of essays analyzing European fairy tales which have been disseminated to North America and other parts of the world.

INTERNET SOURCES

Children's Literature Sites:

Children's Literature Association
  http://ebbs.english.vt.edu/chla/

Children's Literature Webring
  http://nav.webring.org/cgi-bin/navcgi?ring=kidlit;list

Children's Literature Web Guide
  http://www.acs.ucalgary.ca/~dkbrown/index.html

Kay Vandergrift's Children's Literature Page
  http://www.scils.rutgers.edu/special/kay/childlit.html

Fairrosa Cyber Library of Children's Literature
http://www.dalton.org/libraries/fairrosa

The Horn Book Magazine
http://www.hbook.com

International Reading Association
http://www.reading.org

Canadian Children's Book Centre
http://www3.sympatico.ca/ccbc

Children's Bestsellers—Publishers Weekly
http://www.publishersweekly.com/bsl/currentChildrens.asp

Children's Book Committee (Bank Street)
http://www.bnkst.edu/bookcom/

Children's Book Council
http://www.cbcbooks.org

Children's Book Guild
http://www.childrensbookguild.org/index.html

Children's Literature Newsletter
http://www.childrenslit.com

Children's Literature: A Guide to the Criticism
http://www.unm.edu/~lhendr/

Database of Award-Winning Children's Literature
http://www2.wcoil.com/~ellerbee/childlit.html

Carol Hurst's Children's Literature Site
http://www.carolhurst.com

Achuka Children's Books UK
http://www.achuka.co.uk

The de Grummonds Children's Literature Collection
http://avatar.lib.usm.edu/~degrum/

ALAN Review
http://www.lib.vt.edu/ejournals/ALAN/alan-review.html

American Children's Literature (Yale-New Haven Teachers Institute)
http://130.132.143.21/ynhti/curriculum/units/1997/2/

Bulletin of the Center for Children's Books
http://www.lis.uiuc.edu/puboff/bccb/

Caldecott Medal Home Page
http://www.ala.org/alsc/caldecott.html

Newbery Medal Home Page
http://www.ala.org/alsc/newbery.html

A Rhyme and a Reason
http://www.geocities.com/Athens/Forum/3041/

School Library Journal Online
  http://www.slj.com/

Science Fiction and Fantasy for Children
  http://libnt1.lib.uoguelph.ca/SFBib/index.htm

Stories from the Web
  http://hosted.ukoln.ac.uk/stories/index.htm

KidsClick: Web Guide and Search Tool for Kids by Librarians
  http://sunsite.berkeley.edu/kidsclick!/

Kerlan Collection
  http://www.lib.umn.edu/special/kerlan/

Society of Children's Book Writers and Illustrators
  http://www.scbwi.org

Library Sites:

Digital Librarian
  http://www.servtech.com/~mvail/home.html

Internet Public Library
  http://www.ipl.org/

American Library Association (links to pages about children's
literature and awards)
  http://www.ala.org

Library of Congress
http://www.loc.gov

Educational Resources Information Center (ERIC)
http://www.accesseric.org:81/

Internet School Library Media Center
http://falcon.jmu.edu/~ramseyil/index.html

Thinking Critically About World Wide Web Resources
http://www.library.ucla.edu/libraries/college/instruct/
web/critical.htm

Practical Steps in Evaluating Internet Resources
http://milton.mse.jhu.edu/research/education/practical.html

Literature Sites:

Cambridge History of English and American Literature
http://www.bartleby.com/cambridge/

Project Gutenberg Home Page
http://www.promo.net/pg/

Online Literary Criticism Collection
www.ipl.org/ref/litcrit

National Council of Teachers of English
http://www.ncte.org

Book Lovers' Site
   http://www.cclslib.org/prendergast/booklo.html

Celebration of Women Writers
   http://digital.library.upenn.edu/women/

About.com Literary Sites
   http://authors.about.com
   http://kidsbooks.about.com
   http://yabooks.about.com
   http://classiclit.about.com
   http://contemporarylit.about.com
   http://kidslangarts.about.com
   http://fantasy.about.com
   http://mysterybooks.about.com

Online Book Sources:

Cherry Valley Books
   http://www.cherryvalleybooks.com
Bibliofind Search for Out-of-Print Books
   http://www.bibliofind.com

Advanced Book Exchange
   http://www.abebooks.com

Beacham Publishing
   http://www.beachampublishing.com

Authors:

Learning About the Author and Illustrator Pages
    http://www.scils.rutgers.edu/special/kay/author.html

Surfing with the Bard
    http://www.ulen.com/shakespeare

Lewis Carroll Society of North America
    http://www.lewiscarroll.org/

Into the Wardrobe: The C. S. Lewis Web Site
    http://cslewis.drzeus.net/

Roald Dahl Home Page
    http://www.roalddahl.org/index2.htm

Redwall Abbey (Brian Jacques)
    http://www.redwall.org

Tolkien Society
    http://www.tolkiensociety.org/

Peter Rabbit Web Site
    http://peterrabbit.co.uk/templates/index.cfm

APPENDIX A:
CHARACTERS

— Major Characters —

Harry Potter
Lily Potter
Vernon Dursley
Dudley Dursley

James Potter
Lord Voldemort
Petunia Dursley

— Hogwarts Faculty and Staff —

Albus Dumbledore
Severus Snape
Remus J. Lupin
Professor Binns
Madam Poppy Pomfrey
Teaches Arithmancy.

Rubeus Hagrid
Professor Quirrell
Professor Flitwick
Sibyll Trelawney
Madam Pince
Professor Sinistra

Minerva McGonagall
Gilderoy Lockhart
Professor Sprout
Madam Hooch
Professor Vector
Argus Filch

— Prominent Wizards —

Godric Gryffindor
Rowena Ravenclaw
Cornelius Fudge
Peter Pettigrew
Lucius Malfoy

Helga Hufflepuff
Salazar Slytherin
Sirius Black
Professor Armando Dippet

— Hogwarts Students —

Ronald Weasley	Hermione Granger
Percy Weasley	Fred Weasley
George Weasley	Ginny Weasley
Draco Malfoy	Vincent Crabbe
Gregory Goyle	Dean Thomas
Seamus Finnigan	Neville Longbottom
Oliver Wood	Lee Jordan
Colin Creevey	Parvati Patil
Unnamed Patil twin	Lavender Brown
Angelina Johnson	Alicia Spinnet
Katie Bell	Tom Marvalo Riddle
Olive Hornby	Davey Gudgeon
Penelope Clearwater	Davies
Cho Chang	Terry Boot
Lisa Turpin	Mandy Brocklehurst
Cedric Diggory	Justin Finch-Fletchley
Ernie Macmillan	Hannah Abbott
Susan Bones	Millicent Bulstrode
Blaise Zabini	Pansy Parkinson
Marcus Flint	Adrian Pucey
Bletchley	Terence Higgs
Warrington	Montague
Derrick	Bole
Derek	Morag MacDougal
Moon	Nott
Sally-Anne Perks	Miss Fawcett

— Hogwarts Ghosts and Characters —

Peeves

The Fat Friar

Sir Nicholas de Mimsy-Porpington (*"Nearly Headless Nick"*)

Sir Patrick Delaney-Podmore

Bloody Baron

Moaning Myrtle

Fat Lady

Sir Cadogan

Gregory the Swarmy

Dementors

Boggart

Patronus

Wailing Widow

Witch statue

— Relatives —

Harry's magical family in the Mirror of Erised

Harry's muggle maternal grandparents

Marvalo

Arthur Weasley

Molly Weasley

Bill Weasley

Charlie Weasley

Ron's grandfather

Ron's Uncle Bilius

Mrs. Weasley's second cousin
Mr. Granger
Mrs. Granger
Neville's grandmother
Neville's Great Uncle Algie
Neville's Auntie Enid
Marjorie Dursley
Peter Pettigrew's mother

— Minor Characters —

Mafalda Hopkirk

Perenelle Flamel

Doris Crockford

Madam Malkin

Mr. Borgin

Ernie Prang

Celestina Warbeck

Walden Macnair

Cassandra Vablatsky

Bathilda Bagshot

Emeric Switch

Arsenius Jigger

Quentin Trimble

Mundungus Fletcher

Wendelin the Weird

Veronica Smethley

D.J. Prod

Nicolas Flamel

Dedalus Diggle

Florean Fortescue

Mr. Ollivander

Stan Shunpike

Madam Marsh

Madam Rosmerta

Perkins

Miranda Goshawk

Adalbert Waffling

Phyllida Spore

Newt Scamander

Vindictus Viridian

Mortlake

Gladys Gudgeon

Madam Z. Nettles

Mrs. D.J. Prod

The McKinnons

The Prewetts

Chudley Cannons

Agrippa

Morgana

Alberic Grunnion

Paracelsus

Cliodna

Emeric the Evil

Elfric the Eager

Bandon Banshee

The Bones

Greek chappie

Wizard Baruffio

Ptolemy

Hengist of Woodcroft

Circe

Merlin

Grindelwald

Uric the Oddball

Griphook

— Muggles —

Muggle Prime Minister

Mrs. Next Door

Mr. and Mrs. Mason

Yvonne

Dennis

Gordon

Vernon's secretary

Mrs. Hetty Bayliss

Martin Miggs

Muggle teacher

Woman at zoo entrance

Zoo director

Barbers

Muggle woman

Mrs. Figg

Jim McGuffin

Colonel Fubster

Piers Polkiss

Malcolm

Mrs. Polkiss

St. Brutus

Angus Fleet

Headmistress

Two London Muggles

Keeper of the reptile house

Newscaster

King's Cross guards

Muggle man

— Animals and Creatures —

Hedwig	Fawkes	Scabbers
Trevor	Errol	Hermes
Mrs. Norris	Basilisk	Fang
Fluffy	Norbert	Hippogriffs
Buckbeak	Crookshanks	Grim Aragog
Mosag	Binky	Gorilla
Ripper	Tortoise	Dobby
Mountain troll	Ronan	Bane
Firenze	Dead unicorn	Wagga
Wagga werewolf	Chameleon Ghouls	Weasley ghoul
Gnomes	Manticore	Red Caps
Kappas	Grindylow	Hinkypunks
Flobberworms	Blood-Suckin' Bugbear	Cornish pixies
Yeti	Vampire	

Tibbles, Snowy, Mr. Paws, and Tufty
Brazilian boa constrictor

— Plants —

The Whomping Willow
Devil's Snare
The Mandrakes
Venemous Tentacula

– Objects –

Flying car
Harry's wand
Sorting Hat
Mirror of Erised
Marauder's Map
Time-Turner
Remembrall
Pocket Sneakoscope
The Knight Bus
Nimbus Two Thousand
Nimbus Two Thousand And One
Firebolt
Cleansweep Seven
Cleansweep Five
Comet Two Sixty
Shooting Star
Silver Arrow

– Unnamed Characters –

Cloaked wizards and witches
Unkempt old women in green clothing
Bald man wearing purple coat
Goblins
Clerk at Apothecary
Flourish and Blotts manager

Quality Quidditch Supplies store owner
Witch at Magical Menagerie
Conductor
Driver
Hogwarts Express candy cart woman
Hit Wizards
Representative of the Committee for the Disposal of
Dangerous Creatures
Two employees of Accidental Magic Reversal Department
Lockhart's assistant
Photographer
Armenian warlock
Witch with a harelip
Bath witch
Townspeople of Ouagadagou
Transylvanian villager
Charlie's friends
Magic of Ministry car drivers
Small wizard wearing a nightcap
Elderly witch
Vampires
Hag

APPENDIX B:
MYTHICAL AND LEGENDARY
CHARACTERS CITED IN SECTION III,
CHAPTER DEVELOPMENT

Some of the following myths have direct parallels in the Potter novels while others simply suggest mythic proportions to the story. Even when the parallels are only suggestive, they illustrate the influence of myth and legends on the undercurrents of literary imagination.

Good assignments are for students to research fully the meanings of these myths and discuss or write about how they relate to the Potter novels or other works of literature.

Achilles: The Greek warrior whose mother held him by his heel to dip him into the River Styx to protect him from harm. Achilles' mother also disguised him in an unsuccessful attempt to prevent him from fighting in the Trojan War. He died when he was injured in his heel. The mountain troll's vulnerable nostril is like Achilles' heel, and Harry's and Ron's transformation into Crabbe and Goyle and their thwarted efforts to learn who the Slytherin heir is resembles Achilles assuming another identity.

Aeneas: The son of Anchises and Aphrodite, he was a famous Trojan War hero, as described in Virgil's *Aeneid,* who won many victories on the battlefield. He proves himself a worthy warrior and wins the respect of his peers and commanders, just as Harry becomes famous for his winning skills on the Quidditch field.

Aepytus: The third son of Merope. She hid her son in Arcadia during a rebellion in which his father and two brothers were slain and falsely reported that her son had been murdered when and the leader, Polyphontes, forced her to marry him. When he was older, Aepytus returned, disguised himself, and pretended that he had murdered Aepytus. Merope, believing that this man, who was really her son, plotted to kill him until she discovered his true identity. Together they caused Polyphontes' death. Her confusion was like that which Harry experienced in the Shrieking Shack.

Amazon: Strong female warriors living in the Caucasus who battled the Greeks. Their assertiveness resembles Hermione's determination to find answers to puzzling questions to rescue her friends.

Anancy: A Caribbean folklore character who appears as a spider and enjoys tricking people. The giant spider Aragog initially seems helpful but then turns threatening when he tries to kill Harry, Ron, and Fang.

Androcles: A Roman slave who removed a thorn from a lion's paw. Years later, the lion remembered Androcles' act of kindness and refused to kill him when they were thrown in an arena together. Despite his evil master's commands, Dobby's concern for Harry intensifies because of Harry's considerate treatment toward the house elf.

Apollo: One of the best-known Greek gods, he was known as the God of Truth because he never lied, like Hagrid insisting that the Dursleys tell Harry the truth about his parents. Apollo also killed the enormous snake, Python, just as Harry slays the basilisk.

Argus: Having a hundred eyes, this monster could be subdued only when it heard music. Fluffy fell asleep when Hermione played Harry's flute.

Atlas: A Titan son of Iapetus, he carried the weight of the world on his shoulders as punishment for revolting against Zeus. His brother Prometheus was also punished. Harry and Hermione physically bear the weight of Norbert to carry him up the tower, as Atlas bore the wight of the world, and they symbolically endure the burdensome load of peer disapproval when they are severely punished for breaking rules.

Bellerophon: A Greek hero who killed the Chimera, a creature that was one-third third goat, serpent, and lion, by riding on the magical horse Pegasus to safely fly close enough to shoot arrows. He resembles Sirius Black using Buckbeak to escape.

Beowulf and Grendel: As described in a medieval poem, the heroic Beowulf pursued the monstrous Grendel after that beast killed Beowulf's kinsmen and friends in their castle in a scene as macabre as the setting of the Deathday party.

Boetians: Residents of an ancient Greek district who were known for their wealth and cultural backwardness somewhat like the Dursleys and Malfoys.

Camelot: The location of King Arthur's castle and court which was considered an ideal place of happiness and cooperation, somewhat like the Weasleys' home, the Burrow.

Cassandra: Daughter of Priam, she was given the power of prophecy by Apollo who loved her. She especially could foresee trouble and warned the Trojans that the Greeks would attack. However, when she later rejected Apollo's love, he retaliated by causing people not to believe her. Cassandra was tormented knowing about forthcoming disasters without being able to prevent them. Professor Trelawney's predictions are also not taken seriously, and she may well predict a catastrophic event in future novels.

Cerberus: The multi-headed dog who guarded the underworld, keeping anyone who was alive from going there, much like Fluffy prevented people from passing through the trapdoor.

Chiron: A centaur who was half man and horse. He was respected for being wise and good like Firenze in the Forbidden Forest.

Demeter (*Ceres in Latin*): The daughter of Cronus and Rhea, she was the Goddess of the Corn. When her daughter Persephone was abducted by Hades and taken to the underworld, Demeter's grief caused the world to freeze. Professor Trelawney's trance causes the surroundings to come to a cool standstill during those minutes.

Dionysus (*also known as Bacchus*): The son of Zeus and Semele, the God of Wine had a dual nature in which he was sad and withdrawn during winter and joyous and sociable during summer, resembling Harry's duality of being an obedient, cautious student then a rebellious, impulsive boy when he receives the Marauder's Map. Harry is also sad and withdrawn in his Muggle life and happy at Hogwarts.

Echo: A nymph whose voice Hera removed, preventing her from speaking to Narcissus, whom she loved. Echo gazed at Narcissus with adoration much like Harry stares at his family in the Mirror of Erised but is unable to converse with them.

Ericthonius (*also called Erechtheus*): The half-man, half-snake who was the son of Hephaestus and raised by Athena. He was King of Athens. He foreshadows Harry's ability to empathize and communicate with the boa constrictor at the zoo and anticipates a royal future for Harry.

The Furies (*also named the Erinyes*): A trio of justice seekers named Alecto, Megaera, and Tisiphone, they were depicted by Virgil as living in the underworld or by Greek poets as dwelling above ground. Like the Dementors, they were vicious in seeking wrongdoers to punish.

The Gorgons: Resembling dragons, these three creatures turned humans to stone with their stare, like the basilisk which Harry confronted in the Chamber of Secrets. Medusa was a Gorgon whose hair was live snakes

Hades: The name of the underworld and its ruler. The secret passages between Hogwarts and Hogsmeade resemble the dark, scary underworld.

The Harpies: Hideous beasts with beaks, claws, and wings who were known as "the hounds of Zeus" because of their predatory nature. A foul smell lingered wherever they had been. Aunt Marge and her bulldog have characteristics similar to these creatures.

Hecate: The Goddess of Night who dwells in the underworld during the day and on Earth when it is dark. She is also known as the Goddess of the Dark of the Moon and the Goddess of the Crossways because of moonless nights and haunted places, particularly where three roads intersect. Baying hounds were said to announce her arrival, and people feared her evil curses much like the Slytherins' threats and antagonistic actions before and during the Quidditch game against Gryffindor.

Hector: The Prince of Troy, son of Priam and Hecuba, and a warrior during the Trojan War. He was killed by Achilles, and his nobility and death inspired a hero-cult somewhat reminiscent of Harry's status in the wizard world by the conclusion of Book III.

Hestia: The sister of Zeus, she was the Goddess of the Hearth and protector of newborns who were walked in a circle around the hearth as a ritual to be included in the family. She oversaw home life much like the Fat Lady in the portrait guards the entrance to Gryffindor tower and protects the children who live there. When Hestia was not respected, homes were vulnerable to attacks such as the assault on the Gryffindor portrait.

Icarus and Daedalus: A Greek craftsman and his son who flew with waxen wings that Daedalus made. Icarus flew too near the sun, and his wings melted. Their attempts to fly are like Harry and his classmates learning to soar on broomsticks.

Ilithyia (*also spelled as Eileithyia*): The daughter of Hera, she watched over women giving birth and is remembered on birthdays. By sending Harry gifts on his birthday, Hagrid, Hermione, and Ron are honoring his birth much like people paid tribute to Ilithyia to celebrate the birth of children.

Janus: A Roman god with two faces like Professor Quirrell.

Lachesis: One of the three Fates who is known as the Disposer of Lots and decides others' destinies somewhat like the Sorting Hat determines which house each Hogwarts student will join and be identified with throughout their life, influencing their careers, relationships, and legacies.

Laocoön: A priest who lived in Troy and warned the residents that they should beware of Greeks bearing gifts. He was killed by two serpents that emerged from the sea, and the Trojans saw this as a sign that they should accept the Trojan Horse. Hermione and Professor McGonagall act like Laocoön and warn Harry that the Firebolt might be jinxed.

Lares: Roman gods that represent the spirits of specific ancestors. Every family had its own Lares and Penates to protect the household. Towns had public Lares shared by residents who offered them food both at home and in the city. The Hogwarts ghosts watch over the castle and their former houses like the Roman Lares.

Little John: A member of Robin Hood's gang of rogues in medieval English legends, he is a gigantic man like Hagrid, whose name is comical because of how it contrasts with his physical stature. In Book II, Hagrid is like Little John being apprehended by the Sheriff of Nottingham in the form of Cornelius Fudge.

Medussa: A Gorgon whose gaze turned people to stone. Snakes furiously writhed on her head like the Whomping Willow's branches twisted to hurt anyone or anything who came near the tree.

Melampus: He rescued two snakes after their parents were killed. They gratefully licked his ears so that he understood animals' languages. He used this knowledge to make prophecies based on animal communications. His abilities parallel Harry's awareness that he is a Parselmouth.

Mercury (*also known as Hermes*): The son of Zeus and Maia, he swiftly delivers news and is a messenger like Hedwig and the other owls who bring wizards and witches letters and packages.

Merlin's imprisonment by Vortigen: According to legend, Vortigen was a cruel British fifth century king who trapped the young Merlin before he became King Arthur's trusted friend. Vortigen wanted to use Merlin's blood to reinforce the mortar in a tower. During the summer, Harry is similarly trapped at the Dursleys' house, being expected to obediently perform strenuous and neverending chores despite health risks.

Merope: Her husband Cresphontes, the king of Messenia, and two sons were killed by followers of Polyphontes who forced her to marry him. Merope saved one of her sons, Aepytus, by sending him to Arcadia. As an adult, he disguised himself, claiming to have killed Aepytus, and Merope sought revenge. When she realized that he was her son, she asked him to help her punish Polyphontes. The dilemma of distinguishing between murderers and victims a problem the Harry Potter characters contemplate in Book III.

Midas: King of Phrygia. Bacchus promised that all his wishes would come true and he wished that everything he touched would turn to gold. Unfortunately, because everything he touched did turn to gold, he was unable to drink and eat, so he bathed in the River Pactolus' source to reverse his fortune. He was himself a personification of the philosopher's stone, and a moral lesson in using power incorrectly.

Minos: One of three judges in the underworld, he also ruled Crete. Poseidon gave him a bull which he intended for Minos to sacrifice in his honor. Instead, Minos kept the bull. Poseidon caused Minos' wife to fall in love with the bull, and they gave birth to the Minotaur, which Minos confined in a maze. Officials sacrificed children to the Minotaur to prevent it from becoming angry. Just as Theseus entered the maze to confront the Minotaur, Harry sacrifices his safety to confront the monstrous Voldemort in the maze-like chambers of Book I. Ironically, Harry as a child is intended to be sacrificed but instead of becoming the victim is able to confront and subdue evil.

Mordred: King Arthur's son or nephew according to various sources. King Arthur dreamed that Mordred was a serpent who would destroy him and his court. Mordred believed that he was King Lot's son until he met a priest who told him the truth and prophesied that he would cause great destruction. Mordred first befriended and then betrayed Arthur through various disguises. Their relationship resembles the hatred between Harry and Draco that results in Draco's disguise as a Dementor to scare Harry during the Quidditch game.

Narcissus: A self-absorbed young man who fell in love with himself when he saw his reflection. He died because he could not stop looking at his image. Gilderoy Lockhart is also obsessed with his appearance and superficial matters and is unable to appreciate other people's inner strengths and resources nor understand their motivations and behavior.

Nemesis: A goddess who pursues justice. She righteously uses her anger to punish wrongdoers. Harry is the Nemesis of Quidditch opponents who cheat.

Nestor: An elderly Greek chieftain during the Trojan War, he was considered to be wiser than Odysseus. He suggested that Agamemnon seek reconciliation with Achilles whom he had wronged. Achilles initially refused the offer but ultimately realized the need for unity over an individual's concerns. Harry is wise like Nestor when he cleverly wins a devoted ally by freeing Dobby from Lucius Malfoy's control.

Odysseus: After being away from home for a decade during the Trojan War, he yearned to return to his wife Penelope. Instead, seven years passed when his ship was blown off course and he traveled through unknown areas of the globe. Harry, whose valor in the face of uncertainty closely resembles Odysseus', ventures into uncharted territory to attend Hogwarts for seven years. Harry's adventures can be marked by progressive stops along his path just as Homer related Odysseus' adventures in *The Odyssey.*

Orion: A huntsman who was a large, handsome man. He killed all of the wild animals on the island of Chios to secure the king's permission to marry his daughter. After being insulted, the vengeful king blinded Orion and fled. Other versions say that Orion was injured by angry gods. A constellation was named for Orion, and Sirius, the dog star, follows its path in the universe. Either Peter Pettigrew or Harry could be considered the Orion that Sirius Black, in the form of a dog, pursues to resolve past incidents.

Orpheus: The son of a Thracian prince and one of the Muses, he was a gifted musician whose talented performance on a lyre soothed the beast Cereberus (see above). Ancient magicians developed talking heads, such as Orpheus, which listeners thought spoke to them but were really voiced by speakers using tubing. Such deceptions, which appear to be magical but are only tricks, are used throughout the Potter novels.

Pandora: The world's first mortal woman who was given gifts from the gods. Angry at Prometheus for stealing fire from him, Zeus gave Pandora a box filled with evil because he thought she would marry Prometheus and he would suffer. She married another man who opened Zeus' box and let evil loose, much like Ginny frees Tom Riddle to unleash horror at Hogwarts by opening the diary.

Penates: Roman gods that protected the hearth and storehouses. Each family had its own Penates, as well as Lares (see above), to defend the house. The spirits that patrol the corridors at Hogwarts watch over students in the Great Hall, classrooms, and houses as well as monitoring the buildings on the grounds.

Pentheus: The King of Thebes and Dionysus' cousin, he raged about Dionysus' extreme behavior, which prevented him from realizing that Dionysus was a divine god. In retaliation, Dionysus caused his mother, Agave, to believe Pentheus was a lion and she killed him. Pentheus' blinding anger resembles Snape's inability to forget his grudge about James Potter and his friends when they played a joke on Snape while students at Hogwarts.

Perseus: The son of Zeus and Danaë, he killed Medusa (see Gorgons above) with the help of Hermes and Athena. Similarly, Crookshanks assisted Harry and Hermione by immobilizing the Whomping Willow, a Medusa-like organism, so that they could enter the secret tunnel's entrance by its roots.

Pirithous: The King of the Lapithae and a reckless, adventurous friend of Theseus. Like Sirius Black attempted with Harry in the Shrieking Shack, Pirithous bravely risked

Theseus' wrath to form their friendship. Theseus saved Pirithous' life much like Harry prevented the Dementors from sucking out Black's soul.

Ponce de Leon, Juan (1460-1521): A factual Spanish explorer who sailed with Christopher Columbus on his second trip to North America in 1493. He captured Boriquen (modern Puerto Rico) where natives told him of an island named Bimini which contained the legendary Fountain of Youth. Its waters kept people young, somewhat like the Philosopher's/Sorcerer's Stone acts as an elixir granting eternal life. During his search for the Fountain of Youth, Ponce de Leon discovered Florida.

Poseidon: Zeus' brother and the next most powerful god, he controlled the seas and underwater regions and produced storms. He gave King Minos (see above) the bull which fathered the Minotaur that dwelled in the maze. Poseidon parallels Voldemort causing chaos at Hogwarts and positioning Quirrell in the underground labyrinth to seize power.

Procrustes: A giant from Eleusis, he insisted on conformity. He placed his victims on an iron bed, and cut off parts of limbs that were longer than the bed or stretching people who were shorter than the bed. Theseus punished Procrustes with his own method. Like Procrustes, Lucius Malfoy ruthlessly has strict expectations for wizards to conform to his ideals and does not tolerate individualism.

Prometheus: A Titan son of Iapetus and brother to Atlas, he stole fire from heaven to give to humans and was punished by Zeus. His empathy for humans is like Harry's desire to help everyone who is worthy of his wizardly powers.

Proteus: Described as either Poseidon's son or attendant, he could shapeshift like the Animagi. Proteus could also predict the future, somewhat like the foreknowledge that Remus Lupin and Sirius Black seem to have about Peter Pettigrew's possible actions after he is exposed as a villain.

Psyche: The youngest daughter of a king, she was extraordinarily beautiful. Men traveled from around the world to see her and neglected the goddess Venus, who asked her son Cupid to cause Psyche to fall in love with the world's worst creature. Instead, Cupid fell in love with Psyche but would only talk to her and refused to reveal himself. Like the Boggart, he assumed different shapes in her mind, representing her fears. Cupid made Psyche promise not to try to learn his identity. He left after she broke her promise. They later were married. Psyche symbolizes humans' souls.

Shangri-La: Described in James Hilton's novel *Lost Horizon,* this is where people enjoy never-ending peace and youthfulness. Harrys savors his freedom and adventures during the weeks he spends at the Leaky Cauldron and blissfully explores Diagon Alley in Book III.

Sheriff of Nottingham: The law enforcer in medieval Nottinghamshire, England, who searches the woods for the legendary Robin Hood and his band of thieves who rob the rich to give to the poor. Cornelius Fudge acts like the Sheriff of Nottingham pursuing Hagrid (the parallel to Little John in Robin Hood) in Book II.

Sileni and Satyrs: The Sileni were horse men that walked on two legs, and the Satyrs were goat men who walked on four legs and were sometimes depicted with horse features. They are like the centaurs that Harry encounters in the Forbidden Forest.

The Sirens: Living on an island, these half-women half-birds have beautiful voices that bewitched sailors. They lured the men to the Sirens' home in the sea with promises of knowledge and wisdom, but the sailors were never seen again except as skeletons on the island's beach. Their voices are like the voices Harry hears that lure him in the wrong direction.

Sirius: The brightest star in the Canis Major constellation, which is also known as the dog star that pursues Orion, the hunter who sometimes is depicted as a bad person who was punished by the gods for his behavior. Sirius Black is the mythical Sirius following either Harry, as the good Orion, or Pettigrew, as the bad Orion.

Sisyphus: Former King of Corinth who lives in Hades. He is condemned to eternal failure for betraying Zeus's trust by the impossible task of rolling a huge rock up a hill. Sisyphus' struggle resembles Harry's repeated frustration to summon an effective Patronus.

Sphinx: A monster in Greek mythology that has a lion's body and a woman's head. She riddles mortals, killing everyone who answers incorrectly and vowing to commit suicide if anyone guessed correctly. Her mockingly, evasive manner resembles Tom Riddle's threatening taunts in the Chamber of Secrets.

Theseus: Featured in many myths, he became King of Athens, promising that everyone would be equal. His adventures included searching for the Golden Fleece (from a ram whose wool was made of gold). He often saved the life of his impulsive friend Pirithoüs, similar to how Harry saves Sirius Black's and Ron's lives.

The Titans: Enormous gods known as the Elder Gods who were exceptionally strong and powerful. Zeus was the grandson of Cronus (Saturn in Latin) and seized his grandfather's throne, initiating the Golden Age of harmony and joy in mythology. Prominent Titans included Atlas and Prometheus. (See those definitions above for chapter development parallels).

The Trojan Horse: A large, beautiful wooden horse the Greeks left outside the walls of Troy, saying that it was an offering to Athena. The Trojans moved the horse into the walled city, and during the night the Greek soldiers who were concealed inside the horse, exited to open the gates for the Greek Army's assault. The Firebolt is similar to the Trojan Horse in that it was presented in the form of a gift but is possibly meant to cause harm.

Zeus: The most powerful god, he controlled the sky, throwing thunderbolts when he was angry and causing great storms. The stormy weather when Hagrid confronted the Dursleys in the island hut and during the Quidditch match in Book III represent anger and fear like that Zeus expressed and caused. There is also a reference here to Poseidon, who created sea storms to control the events of mortals.

SECTION VI

ONLINE RESOURCES

The following topics are available on Beacham Publishing's website: **www.beachampublishing.com**

Harry Abroad: Harry's Success in Foreign Countries

Projects and Activities, Discussion Questions, Writing and Research Questions, Websites, Reading for Research

Bibliography Grouped by Subject Areas: By or About J.K. Rowling; Readers' Response; The Censorship Controversy; Commercial Aspects of Harry; Legal Proceedings; Reviews of the novels; Literary Criticism/Teaching; Translations; Media/Recordings; Prizes

Continuing analyses and study/research questions and resources for future novels in the Potter series.

INDEX

ABOUT ELIZABETH D. SCHAFER

Elizabeth D. Schafer earned a Ph.D. in the History of Science and Technology from Auburn University and completed graduate courses in children's literature and creative writing at Hollins University where she received the Shirley Henn Memorial Award for Critical Scholarship of Children's Literature in 1998. She is the co-author of *Women Who Made A Difference in Alabama* (1995). Schafer is a writer for the History News Service and has contributed articles, book reviews, and lesson plans to encyclopedias, journals, and magazines, including *Cobblestone: American History for Kids; Calliope: World History for Young People; Footsteps: African American History for Young People; Faces: People, Places, and Cultures; Odyssey: Adventures in Science; Organization of American Historians Magazine of History; African American Review; Women in World History; The American Revolution, 1775-1783: An Encyclopedia, History in Dispute; American National Biography; St. James Encyclopedia of Popular Culture; Cambridge Guide to Children's Books; St. James Guide to Children's Writers,* 5th edition; *St. James Guide to Young Adult Writers,* 2nd edition; and *Beacham's Guide to Literature for Young Adults.* Schafer has won awards in the *Writers' Digest* national writing competition: non-rhyming poetry (1994), children's non-fiction (1997), and children's non-fiction and fiction (1998), and her adult fiction has been appeared in the magazine *The Mythic Circle.* She is a member of the Society of Children's Book Writers and Illustrators and the Children's Literature Association.

Dr. Schafer can be contacted by e-mail at
novelprof@yahoo.com.